This book opens the door to the best day-care option
your child may ever have.
That door is the door to your own home.

Photography by
NATALIE J. PELAFOS
Saint Louis, Missouri

Dr. Debra K. Shatoff

Psychologist and
Marital and Family Therapist,
St. Louis, Missouri

In-Home
Child Care

A Step-by-Step Guide to
Quality, Affordable Care

Family CareWare, Inc.
St. Louis, Missouri

Published by Family CareWare, Inc., P.O. Box 50257, St. Louis, MO 63105-5257.

Printed in the United States of America

To order additional copies of this book or the optional computer diskette, see Appendix A. Call toll-free (888) 601-CARE (2273), or fax order form to (314) 725-6350. St. Louis, MO area residents may call 314-862-6636.

ATTENTION HOSPITALS, CORPORATIONS, PRESCHOOLS, AND ORGANIZATIONS:
Quantity discounts are available on bulk purchases of this book for gift or educational purposes or fund raising. For information, please contact Family CareWare, Inc., at 314-862-6636.

Edited by Eberly Milles, Ph.D

Project Coordination by Barbara Merritt

Book Design by Ellen B. Zanolle

Photography by Natalie J. Pelafos, St Louis, MO, 314-962-5003

Photographs on the dedication page were provided by the author

Library of Congress Catalog Card Number: 97-60853

Publisher's Cataloging-in-Publications

Shatoff, Debra K.
    In-home child care : a step-by-step guide to quality, affordable care / Debra K. Shatoff — 1st ed.
    p. cm.
    Includes bibliographical references and index.
    ISBN 0-9659215-0-6

    1. Child care workers—Employment—United States.   2. Child care—United States.   I. Title.

HQ778.7.U6S43 1998   649'.1'0973
                                            QBI97-40928

10 9 8 7 6 5 4 3 2 1

In Memory of

ARIELLA ROSE SHATOFF
6/2/92-7/21/92

MARY NELL SCHIRBER SORENSON
12/2/54-9/28/92

ELIZABETH ROSE HENRY
1/28/86-12/26/95

*There were gifts deeply embedded in the pain of their loss,
the most precious being a new openness to life and death.*

· · · · · · · · · · · · · · · ·

In Celebration of

*Jerry and Elan, my husband and my son,
whom I forever feel blessed and honored to have as my family.*

About the Author

Debra K. Shatoff, Ed.D., received her doctorate in Counseling Psychology from Boston University and her master's degree in Clinical Psychology from Southern Illinois University at Edwardsville. She is licensed both as a psychologist and as a marital and family therapist and has been in private practice for over 15 years working with individuals, couples, and families. She has served on the faculty of the Menninger Marriage and Family Therapy Training Program in St. Louis since 1984 and is a Clinical Member and Approved Supervisor of the American Association of Marriage and Family Therapy.

Dr. Shatoff discovered firsthand the joys and challenges of parenting after the age of 40 when she and her husband of 17 years had their son, Elan. In finding and hiring excellent caregivers for their son, she found herself becoming a resource for many of her friends, family, and neighbors, sharing with them the materials and expertise she developed. This book came into being when her friends encouraged her to share her successful ideas and practical materials with a broader audience.

Acknowledgments

Writing this book has been a wonderful journey for me. I've loved the solitude of writing, the challenge and thrill of a first draft, and the sense of accomplishment that comes many drafts later. To carve out space in one's life to write a book requires a strong supporting cast. Some of my happiest moments in writing this book have involved reflecting on the generous support I've received and working collaboratively with this great team of people.

Two people were instrumental in helping me get started: Leslie Martyn-Gennari, M.S.W. and Scott Gordon, M.B.A. Thanks Scott and Leslie for believing in me. I did it!

The Foreword was written by people I respect and admire: Jean M. Thomas, M.D., M.S.W. and Kevin P. O'Connell, M.S.W. Thank you for your contribution and endorsement of my work.

I would like to extend special thanks to Col. Ronald A. Battelle, Lt. Jack Webb, and Mary Wickenhauser at the St. Louis County Police Department for sharing their information and expertise on hiring and conducting background record checks on job applicants. Their expertise was invaluable and is reflected in Chapters 8 and 12.

My accountant, Miriam G. Wilhelm, C.P.A., generously served as a reader for Chapter 18. Mark Sableman, J.D., and Harry (Hal) W. Wellford, Jr., J.D., reviewed the manuscript and offered advice on legal matters. Eduardo Gomez-Maqueo, M.S., and Eric Lazarian, with support from James Milles, J.D., did a fine job with the computer diskette. Waleed Al-Eisa, M.S., M.S., my friend with computer expertise, always graciously helped me. Without him, God knows, the computer might have ended up

in the garden two stories below my window. And, very importantly, Zachary A. Pryor, M.Div., my office manager, worked hard to clear my desk of other work so that I could sit down and write on a clean space with an uncluttered mind.

Three very special people worked hard throughout this project, bringing their personal and professional expertise, wisdom, and fresh outlooks to the book. They were my readers, all working parents: Sandra A. Hendin, Ph.D., a counseling psychologist, James J. Deckert, M.D., a family physician, and Karen Barker, a successful business owner. These wonderful friends were very generous and deserve a great deal of credit.

The real inspiration behind this book came from my son's caregivers. Their genuine love and devotion to Elan kept me writing. I just had to tell other parents about in-home child care. When someone loves your child and provides excellent care, you begin to love them back and they become like family. Like many love relationships, it is a love that evolves. One day you discover yourself looking at that person, your eyes brimming with tears of love. Junshan Hou, Kevin P. O'Connell, Feng-Fa Huang, Betty J. Rich, Feixia Zhang, and Karen E. Kruse, my eyes are brimming.

I also want to thank Elan's teen caregivers: Anne Mooney, Seth Berkowitz, and Kristina Watkins. If Elan grows up to be like you, I will be very proud.

I have had many supportive friends and family throughout this project. Thank you to all of you, including Jim Barker, Alan Boime, Celine Gordon, Sandy and Al Gordon, Ann Green, Antony Hebblethwaite, Jule Henry, Jay L. Hoecker, M.D. and the entire Hoecker family, I.W. Klein, Maureen Latham, Kathy McVoy, M.S.W., Wendi Schirvar, Nan Shoaff, and all the moms in my son's neighborhood play group. My parents and my 15 siblings and their families, the Schirbers, and my husband's family, the Gordons, generously offered support, interest, and enthusiasm along the way. A special thanks to everyone who contributed in this way.

I also want to give special thanks to my friends and family who have understood when my phone chats have been brief and our visits infrequent over the past 2 years. Many of you have helped in countless ways along the way. I wish space would allow me to mention each person who helped me with this project: Your names are inscribed on my heart. Thank you, and I love you.

Everyone involved in the publication of this book was top notch, and I believe a band of angels served on their selection committee. I was very fortunate to have Barbara Merritt as the publishing project coordinator; she is very experienced, creative, and wonderful to work with. Working with Ellen B. Zanolle, the book designer, was more than great. I was very pleased with the design and her pleasant, collaborative spirit. Tim Leach did a superb job writing and working with me on the cover copy. Thank

you, Tim. Natalie J. Pelafos, a photographer whom children welcome into their world, was a pleasure to work with and a true professional, in every sense of the word.

And, my editor, Eberly Milles, Ph.D., is absolutely the best editor one could have. I loved working with her; she is excellent, hard-working, and a delight. Eberly, thank you so much.

And, finally, I want to thank Jerry and Elan. These two guys mean the world to me. Thank you for understanding "it's Mom's time to work" and for going off and having a great time together. Jerry, you are passing on your warmth, humor, and caring to Elan. What a fine legacy.

Debra K. Shatoff

Foreword

In-Home Child Care: A Step-By-Step Guide to Quality, Affordable Care guides the quest for responsible, responsive, and personalized child care and invites the reader to enter the heart and life of the author, Debra K. Shatoff, Ed.D., a psychologist, a marital and family therapist, and a parent.

An inspired, practical, methodically detailed, and user-friendly text, *In-Home Child Care* also offers an optional computer diskette (available by special order) and encourages parents to copy or quickly tailor the book's many incredibly insightful resources, including forms, schedules, and checklists. A few of these resources are the Personalized List of Important Caregiver Qualities; the Job Application Form; the Childhood Emergencies, Health, and Safety Resource List; A Report on Our Child's Day; and the Employer's Checklist for Keeping Track of the Caregiver's Schedule and Payment of Salary and Taxes.

Well-researched, up-to-date, clear, and readable, *In-Home Child Care* is also personal. Dr. Shatoff shares her hopes, fears, and delights in her own process of finding care for her long-awaited son:

> *When I think of in-home caregivers, I think of my son's shining eyes and excitement when they arrive each day ... I think of the laughter, the delight and concern for our son that we share together ... the nicknames they have given him. ... the songs they have taught ... I think of the peace of mind both my husband and I feel when we leave for work.*

In-Home Child Care highlights physical care and emotional security; nurturing of relationships between caregiver and child, parent and caregiver; and "creating a village" because "it takes a whole village to raise a child."

JEAN M. THOMAS, M.D., M.S.W.
Director, Department of Child and Adolescent Psychiatry; Director, Early Development Program, Cardinal Glennon Children's Hospital; Associate Professor, Psychiatry and Pediatrics, Saint Louis University School of Medicine, St. Louis, Missouri

In early January 1995, I saw the Shatoff's child-care ad on the university bulletin board. The number to call was printed on tear-away tabs at the foot of the page. As yet, none had been taken, and as I pulled one off, I could have sworn that the paper was still warm from the copier! As things would later turn out, this was one of those moments in life when I was in the right place at the right time.

Debra and Jerry, Elan's parents, are great people. Their attitude towards me has been one of unfailing warmth, support, respect and consideration. They've made me feel like a valued partner in the work of raising Elan.

This sense of partnership, of shared mission and vision, is something the Shatoffs have done masterfully with all of Elan's caregivers. In my case, the lion's share of cultivating this partnership was accomplished in their careful application procedure. The rest has been done along the way. As Elan moved from one stage to another in early childhood and as his parents' expectations of childcare evolved with him, they were able to bring me along, thanks to the atmosphere of open communication that has permeated our relationship.

This book is born of Debra's experience, professional training, talent and a desire to share her insights and ideas with others. It is a practical guide that can help families create similarly positive, peaceful, and productive arrangements for in-home child-care. I believe that Debra's book offers something very special to families who may be struggling to care for the ones who are most important to them in a world of conflicting demands. Certainly what the Shatoffs have designed, others can tap into for their good and, above all, for the good of their children.

KEVIN P. O'CONNELL, M.S.W.
The author's son's child caregiver
while attending graduate school

Contents

Foreword   **xi**

Preface   **xix**

1   Introduction: Why In-Home Child Care is the Best Alternative   **1**

2   Identifying Pools of Potential Applicants in Your Community   **15**

3   Advertising Your Child-Care Position   **35**

4   How to Make In-Home Child Care Affordable for Your Family   **49**

5   Making Your Child-Care Position Appealing to Applicants   **59**

6   Qualities to Look for in a Caregiver   **63**

7   Your First Phone Contact with an Applicant   **71**

8   The Job Application Form   **79**

9   The Child-Care Agreement Form   **91**

10   Screening Completed Job Applications   **111**

11   Conducting the Job Interview   **115**

Contents

12 Investigating an Applicant's Background   127

13 Calling the Applicant's References   153

14 Orienting the Caregiver to Your Child and Your Home   163

15 Maintaining a Positive Working Relationship
    with Your Caregiver   177

16 Ensuring That Proper Procedures are Followed in
    Handling Illness and Medical and Household Emergencies   185

17 Ensuring That Your Child Receives Consistently Excellent
    Care in Your Absence   197

18 An Easy System for Keeping Track of the Hours Worked
    by the Caregiver and for Paying the Salary and Taxes   207

    Appendix A   Ordering Form for the Computer Diskette
    and Additional Copies of This Book   229

    Appendix B   Instructions for the Computer Diskette   232

    Index   235

xiv

Boxes

Box 1.1: Advantages of In-Home Child Care   **11**

Box 2.1: Employment Eligibility Verification Requirements   **30**

Box 2.2: Au Pair Agencies   **33**

Box 3.1: Sample Job Announcement for Non–Live-In Child Caregiver   **37**

Box 3.2: Sample Job Announcement for Live-In Child Caregiver on Salary   **38**

Box 3.3: Sample Job Announcement for Live-In Child Caregiver (Barter Arrangement)   **39**

Box 3.4: Sample Job Ads for Caregiver   **41**

Box 3.5: Sample Letter for Family, Friends, and Work Associates   **42**

Box 3.6: Sample Letter to Send to a Church or Synagogue   **44**

Box 3.7: Sample Letter for an Organization or English Language School   **45**

Box 3.8: *Sample Letter for a Department Chairperson at a University or College*   **46**

Box 3.9: *Sample Letter to a University, College, or Seminary Office of Student Affairs, Job Placement, or Career Development*   **47**

Box 6.1: *Required Qualifications for Child Caregivers*   **65**

Box 6.2: *Child Caregiver Qualities Questionnaire*   **66**

Box 6.3: *Personalized List of Important Caregiver Qualities*   **68**

Box 7.1: *Initial Phone Call Form for In-Home Child-Care Applicants*   **73**

Box 8.1: *Job Application Form for an In-Home Child Caregiver*   **82**

Box 9.1: *Child-Care Agreement Form*   **95**

Box 10.1: *Checklist for Evaluating Job Applications*   **113**

Box 11.1: *Child Care in the Home Job Interview Form*   **120**

Box 12.1: *Instructions for Caregiver Applicants on How to Request a Criminal Record Check*   **133**

Box 12.2: *Criminal Record Request Form for a Child Caregiver Job Applicant*   **135**

Box 12.3: *Instructions for Caregiver Applicants on How to Request a Child Abuse and Neglect Record Check*   **139**

Box 12.4: *Request Form for a Child Abuse and Neglect Background Investigation on a Child Caregiver Job Applicant*   **141**

Box 12.5: *Instructions for Caregiver Applicant for Requesting the Driving Record Check*   **144**

Box 12.6: *Instructions for Caregiver Applicant for Requesting Academic Transcript*   **147**

Box 12.7: *Academic Transcript Request Form*   **148**

Box 12.8: Instructions for Providing Verification of Training in Emergency Medical Procedures for Children   **149**

Box 12.9: Instructions for Undergoing the Infectious and Communicable Diseases Medical Examination   **151**

Box 12.10: Infectious and Communicable Diseases Medical Examination Form for Child Caregiver   **151**

Box 13.1: Form for Calling a Job Reference Provided by the Child-Care Applicant   **159**

Box 14.1: Orientation Checklist   **171**

Box 14.2: Information About Our Child Form   **172**

Box 16.1: Childhood Emergencies, Health, and Safety Resource List   **189**

Box 16.2: Consent Form for Emergency Medical Care   **191**

Box 16.3: List of Important Phone Numbers   **194**

Box 16.4: Emergency Information Sheet   **195**

Box 17.1: A Report on Our Child's Day   **203**

Box 18.1: Employer's Checklist for Keeping Track of the Caregiver's Schedule and Payment of Salary and Taxes   **209**

Box 18.2: Monthly Time Sheet and Pay Form   **216**

Box 18.3: Weekly Hours for Child-Care Barter Arrangement   **218**

Preface

As a parent, one of my major concerns has been that my child receive excellent care, especially during his early formative years. I am convinced, both professionally and personally, that young children receive the highest quality of care when they receive one-on-one care from an attentive, loving, emotionally available caregiver. One-on-one care is especially important before the age of 3 when nurturing and personal attention are critical. This personalized care can be provided by a parent, a relative, or a caregiver employed by the family in the home. *The term in-home child care refers to personalized care provided in the comfort of one's own home.* This care differs in many important ways from organized or family-centered day care in which one or more adults care for a number of children simultaneously in a setting outside of the child's home.

OUR CHILD-CARE DILEMMA

Our son was born when I was 42 years old and after 17 years of marriage. My husband, Jerry, and I were thrilled when I was finally able to become pregnant. By the time our son was born, we were more than ready to give him the best we had to offer and that included spending a great deal of time with him. Finding a way to balance work and family was important to both of us. I wanted to continue my satisfying career as a counseling psychologist but not at the expense of our son. My husband and I both wanted to ensure that our son received the best care possible

while we were at work. In my private practice over the past 15 years, I have helped countless families deal with child-care issues. My professional experience helped prepare me for what we were about to face as a family.

Our Choice

During pregnancy, I toured a number of high quality day care centers and was struck by what I saw. All of the children were being physically well cared for, but I wasn't sure their emotional and developmental needs were being met. All too frequently, I saw children with blank stares who looked shut down or lost, or who were wandering about as if in search of adult attention or a focus. I saw too many infants sitting in bouncy seats rather than being held. I saw toddlers being encouraged to participate in group activities when they needed to be held or comforted. Unfortunately, the child-care workers had their hands full dealing with a room full of children. Personalized care was not possible.

Many opportunities for learning by these very young children were being lost. Opportunities for being nurtured and held, for learning a new word, or for exploring something that just caught the child's eye were bypassed. I saw children essentially being socialized by their young peers rather than adults. I saw too many runny noses. The fine people offering the care were often so busy setting out snacks, putting down beds for naps, or settling a spat that their time to give individual attention was limited.

I was trying to convince myself that these settings provided good enough care because, at that time, I falsely assumed that in-home care was not attainable for us. Like many parents, I thought hiring an in-home caregiver was out of our reach. Based on the stories I had heard, I assumed that the cost of in-home child care was prohibitive and the problems associated with finding a good in-home caregiver were insurmountable. I had some very mistaken notions about in-home child care, but I didn't know it at the time.

When the time came to make a decision about child care, I took some time to reflect. I realized that I had to find something better for our child than organized or family-centered day care. I wanted to find a way to have our child cared for during his early years by an individual caregiver in the comfort of our own home. Infants and young children are in the process of developing important cognitive, social, motor, language, behavioral, and emotional skills that serve as the foundation for lifelong learning. Hiring an in-home caregiver helps ensure that your child does not have to compete with too many other children and that his critical needs are met.

Our Discovery

· · · · · · · · · · · · ·

We discovered that there are many excellent, affordable, caregivers out there.

Once we decided to hire an in-home child caregiver, what we discovered truly surprised us. *We found that there are many excellent caregivers out there, especially if you are willing to hire several part-time rather than one full-time caregiver if full-time coverage is needed.* I had always been told that good caregivers were hard to find. This has not been our experience. I have found many wonderful child caregivers for ourselves and for our friends.

We also discovered that in-home care was affordable. In-home child care is not just for the affluent. Many people falsely assume that it costs more than organized day care. This is not necessarily so, especially when you are paying for the care of two or more children. *There are many strategies any family can employ to make in-home child care affordable.* A whole chapter (Chapter 4) is devoted to helping you.

What Led Me to Write This Book

When I originally developed many of the ideas and materials in this book, I had no intention of publishing them. I had developed them for our own use so that our son could receive the kind of child care I felt he needed. The idea of writing a book sprang out of a conversation over lunch with my dear friend and professional colleague, Leslie Martyn-Gennari, M.S.W. I had mentioned to her that I was in the process of finding a replacement for one of our son's caregivers who was with us during his first year of life. We loved Betty and were sad about her leaving. We were also thrilled for her; she had just become engaged to be married and was planning to move.

Leslie commiserated with me and commented on how much effort and work would be required on my part to replace her. I responded that I didn't expect it would be all that difficult. I expected to find someone within about 2 weeks. After all, I had developed all these wonderful strategies and materials for placing ads, screening, interviewing, and then hiring a caregiver. I explained to her that I had found, with the materials I had developed, that it only took a small amount of time the sec-

ond time around because we already had a workable system in place. We had discovered, for example, that knowing where to look for excellent caregivers was critical. Once we had identified the best places to look in our own community, we could go back again and again to find another qualified individual.

I explained to Leslie that the first time around you need to put more time into such activities as finding the pools of potential in-home child-care applicants in your own community (see Chapter 2) and adapting the Child-Care Agreement Form to fit your own situation (see Chapter 9). Once you have developed your own workable system, adapting the materials included in this book and optional computer diskette containing all the book's forms (see Appendix A for ordering information and Appendix B for instructions on using the computer diskette) to fit your own needs, the time involved in hiring a new caregiver is considerably reduced. I went on to explain that a number of friends and acquaintances had been borrowing my materials and had been giving me feedback that they were very easy to use and timesaving.

It was then, during this discussion, that the idea of publishing these materials for a wider audience was born. Leslie encouraged me to write a book. Both this book and my prediction expressed to Leslie came to pass. By my son's birthday, less than 2 weeks later, I had hired Betty's replacement, Kevin. Kevin is wonderful, and his care of our son, like Betty's, has been excellent.

Contained in this book is almost everything you will need to know to successfully find, screen, interview, hire, employ, and manage live-in or live-out, in-home child caregivers. *One of the problems we all face when we become parents for the first time is a lack of knowledge about what it will really be like to care for our children. It is difficult to know what our children are going to need in terms of care until we experience it directly. These materials were developed while I was in the heart of the experience of overseeing my young son's child care.* They grew out of the real needs we as a family had, our real life challenges, worries, concerns, and problems. I want your family to gain from our efforts and experiences.

Your Opportunity

• • • • • • • • • • • • •

You too can find excellent caregivers for your child.

I learned that my skills and knowledge as a counseling psychologist were invaluable to me in knowing what to look for, what questions to ask,

and how to maintain a good employer-employee relationship. It became more clear to me why others lacking this training found the challenges of in-home child care overwhelming. There were no guidebooks focused exclusively on in-home child care. There were no experts to turn to for help. I was forced to develop my own guidelines and materials. The plan I developed has worked well for us and others time and time again, and it can work for you too. If you apply the information contained in this book, you will most likely find excellent caregivers for your child.

Making the Leap

....

Many people feel uncomfortable having someone work in their home <u>until</u> they try it.

For many people, the idea of hiring an in-home child caregiver brings up the same kinds of apprehensions people have before hiring their first housecleaner. I remember how uncomfortable I felt before we hired our first cleaning person. The idea of having someone else in the inner sanctuary of our home made me apprehensive. Would they respect our privacy? Would they care for our belongings in a respectful manner? Would they do a good job? Was it really ok to let someone else clean our bathrooms? Would it cost too much? Wasn't this a luxury only the rich could afford?

I enjoyed cleaning our home, but we needed help. I no longer wanted to spend big blocks of my precious, limited time on the weekends cleaning. After I hired our first housecleaner, I had a hard time imagining life without her. It felt wonderful to come home from work to a clean, sparkling home on those days when Lil had been there. I always loved the fresh smell of the kitchen when I opened the back door and saw the newly polished floor. It felt wonderful to then have time on the weekends to be with family and friends and for special interests and activities.

When it came time to hire our first caregiver, I felt a lot of the same worries and concerns. Likewise, they quickly vanished once our son's first caregiver, Shan, was on the job. We have discovered over and over again, with each new caregiver, that if we seek out and select someone with the right qualifications (see Chapters 6 through 13), they respect us, our child, our family, and our home. They do their job without violating our privacy. They share intimate aspects of our life with maturity, responsibility, and respect.

MOVING BEYOND STEREOTYPES

You will notice that I use the term child *caregiver* rather than *nanny* throughout this book. I purposely avoid the use of the term *nanny* because it evokes certain images that I want to avoid: female, unmarried, young (18 to 28 years old) or middle aged (40 to 60 years old), and someone who has chosen to care for children to earn a living or as a means to visit America. In addition, many people assume that only families who are well off financially can afford a nanny. Because these images are only stereotypes, I wanted to use a term, other than *nanny*, to encourage you to expand your thinking about in-home child caregivers.

My images of in-home child caregivers are quite different from the standard nanny stereotypes. Contrary to popular opinion, I have found that some men as well as some women can be excellent caregivers for children. Fine caregivers can be single or attached, young or old, and come from many different walks in life.

The best caregivers we discovered didn't set out to care for children as a means to earn a living. Our caregivers have been wonderful individuals who care about children, who happened to be at a place and time in their life when caring for a child, our child, made sense. Some have done it because they needed work while others have done it for other reasons. They have been retirees looking for a way to make a meaningful contribution. They have been graduate students in human services who have needed part-time work to support their studies. And, still others have been competent professionals from another country wanting a job, wanting to practice their English, and wanting to expand their horizons.

When I think of in-home caregivers, I think of my son's shining eyes and excitement when they arrive each day. I think of the delicious meals prepared for our son. I think of the laughter, the delight and concern for our son that we share together. I think of the toys they have mended, the nicknames they have given him, the books they have read together, and the songs they have taught him. I think of the laundry folded and the kitchen cleaned while I am away. I think of the friendships we have forged, our family with their families. I think of the peace of mind both my husband and I feel when we leave for work. It is like leaving our son in the care of "one of us," in good hands, knowing he'll be loved and cared for until we return. I think about how lucky we are to have these wonderful caregivers in our life.

Our friendship continues with each caregiver even after they leave because we have grown so attached to each other. Each caregiver, over time, becomes my son's friend, my friend, our friend. Just the other day, my son said, "Mommy, I have a pal." I asked him who his pal was and he said, "Kevin." Kevin, a graduate student in social work, is one of our son's

caregivers who has been with us since our son's first birthday. Over the past 2 years, he has become like a member of our family.

CREATING A VILLAGE THROUGH IN-HOME CHILD CARE

More and more families are looking outside the family for help in caring for their children. Each year, unprecedented numbers of mothers of infants and young children are employed in jobs that take them away from the home and caring for their young. Being a "stay-at-home parent" is no longer an option for many in today's economy. Furthermore, many mothers of young children have productive, fulfilling careers that contribute immensely to their own personal satisfaction, to their families, and to society as a whole.

When I visualized myself as a mom, I saw myself as a working mom, at least on a part-time basis. I had found my own career deeply satisfying, and I wanted to find a way to be with my son as much as possible while also continuing to work. Although my choice is not for everyone, it is important that women and their families have the opportunity to choose what is best for them, whatever that might be. I have found that excellent in-home child care makes it easier for women with jobs because, more than any other form of child care, it decreases the stress placed on her, the child, and the entire family.

In the past, grandparents and extended families often lived nearby and were readily available to assist parents in the raising of the children. Now, many grandparents themselves are working outside of the home and are unavailable. We live in a highly mobile society, and grandparents nowadays often live in another state or community. Parents therefore are having to turn to nonfamilial caregivers for help.

In the best of all worlds, children would be raised in the heart of a loving, extended family and community. I deeply believe in the African saying that "it takes a whole village to raise a child." It is only in very recent history that children have been brought up almost exclusively in the nuclear family. As nuclear families become more and more separate from the extended family and the community, our children suffer. They are robbed of the experience of being exposed daily to a variety of other loving adults. In the past, these adults were aunts and uncles across the street, grandparents nearby, the parents of other children at school, teachers who followed their progress into adulthood, friends who knew their parents as children, neighbors young and old, local shopkeepers, the family doctor, and community leaders. All of these individuals played an important part in helping a child grow up right.

Our son's caregivers serve an important function in our family's

modern version of the extended family and the community. Our extended family lives out of state and we have had to find creative ways to provide our son with a "village." His caregivers have been like the village elders or the loving aunts and uncles who step in to nurture and teach him important things when we are not there. Our son, as a result of this, is a very secure, happy, sociable little boy. He knows he is loved and cherished by many people besides Mom and Dad. He is comfortable in new social situations because he has interacted with loving in-home caregivers since he was 8 weeks old. He is growing up in a very enriched social environment.

Because we have this help, both my husband and I are able to spend lots of quality time with our son. Because our in-home caregivers help us with the laundry, preparing meals, and keeping the house straightened while our son is napping, I am able to spend 2 full weekday mornings with our son before I leave for work. Jerry, my husband, is also able to spend 1 full weekday with him. During these times, we are able to focus exclusively on him without having to do household chores at the same time. Children, especially preschoolers, need lots of time like this with their parents.

Enhancing Your Child's Social Development

One of the advantages of in-home child care is that you, the parent, remain in control of who your child interacts with and when. A common complaint about children in day care is that they are too aggressive. They are forced to learn, very early on, how to aggressively hold on to their toys or how to push a bully away. Many children in these settings learn to push, bite, and grab, observing their peers and, in the words of one of my clients, "the laws of the jungle." The staff try to deal with this situation the best that they can, but they are often overwhelmed trying to meet too many different conflicting needs at once.

It is important that children have an opportunity to interact with each other, but not before they are developmentally ready to benefit from this experience. Infants and toddlers are vulnerable physically and emotionally, and in-home care offers them a safer, more secure environment. It protects them from other young children who become aggressive because they are being asked to share something that is very important to them at the moment: a cherished caregiver or the only toy of its kind in the room.

Many kids over the age of 2, on the other hand, are ready to learn how to share and benefit from selective, time-limited experiences with their peers. Many two- to three-year-old children are ready to start preschool, starting out once or twice a week for 2 to 3 hours at a time. This limited exposure to peers allows them the opportunity to develop social

skills without becoming overwhelmed. Four- and five-year-old children can benefit from more contact. Like all things, however, what is best for other children may not be best for your child. You get to be the final judge of this for your child.

Although preschools, in general, provide higher quality care than day care centers because they are time-limited, the staff are generally better trained, and they offer daily learning activities, this is not always the case. There are some high quality day care programs that are more like preschools, and there are some preschools that are more like day care centers. Whatever you select for your child, carefully assess and observe what actually is being offered.

· · · · · · · · · · · · ·

Have in-home care make up the major portion of child care for children under the age of 5.

Regardless of what other forms of child care you select to supplement your in-home care after the age of 2, I recommend that children under the age of 5 receive the major portion of their care in their own home by an attentive, loving parent or in-home caregiver. Taking this action ensures that your child will receive one-on-one care during the most critical time in his development: the first 5 years of life. One-on-one care provides your child with a teacher of his very own along with the emotional nurturance and bonding he needs to establish a firm foundation of positive self-esteem.

Recognizing and Meeting the Demands of Child Care

· · · · · · · · · · · · ·

Caring for young children is demanding.

To provide the kind of care that young children need, caregivers need to be willing to set aside their own needs to attend to the countless needs of the child. Children thrive when their caregiver gets down on their eye level and experiences the world through their eyes. Children have physical and emotional needs that require attention, often minute-by-minute, especially when they are very young. There were many days

when my son was very young that I had to set aside some of my needs like eating or showering to attend to him: I was busy feeding, diapering, holding, and soothing.

I couldn't visualize what it would be like to be so busy caring for a newborn or toddler until I had a child of my own. I then discovered that while it has been one of the most satisfying times in my life, it has also demanded incredible amounts of energy. As children grow, while their physical needs lessen, their emotional, intellectual, and social developmental needs increase. Good caregivers of young children are busy, regardless of the age of the child.

If you ask most parents of a young child if they would like anything in their life to be different, most will respond that they feel happy and fulfilled but they would just like "more sleep." Whenever young children are awake, they require fairly constant adult attention. For many parents, going to work is less demanding than staying at home to care for a young child. My husband, who cares for our son on Thursdays, will attest to this. We both love caring for our son, but we find that after so many hours of continuous care, our energy begins to wane. We need someone else to step in so we can take a needed break.

. . . .

Hire part-time rather than full-time caregivers.

I recommend that parents hire part-time rather than full-time caregivers. As mentioned above, caring for young children is immensely satisfying but demanding. Part-time employment helps ensure that your caregiver does not get worn out by the end of the day or week.

Furthermore, it is unrealistic to expect child caregivers to provide consistently excellent care on a full-time basis. Like parents, they need breaks from the continuous demands of a little one. Caring for a child 9 hours a day, 5 days a week is incredibly demanding. Part-time caregivers are more likely to be rested and relaxed. I want our child to receive more than custodial care, and that requires an attentive, involved caregiver. Children often become fussy when their caregiver or parent is tired. A fresh caregiver, who is scheduled to take over before you or whoever is caring for your child becomes exhausted, will decrease the number of fussy periods on everyone's part throughout the week.

Part-time caregivers are also easier to find than full-time caregivers. There are more child caregivers out there who want to work part-time be-

cause of other life commitments. For example, many recent retirees don't want a full-time job. Many students are only available on a part-time basis, at times when they are not in class. Caregivers who have families of their own often want to work a select number of hours each week so that they have time for their own families. It is usually easier to find several good part-time caregivers than one good full-time caregiver.

Another major advantage of hiring part-time caregivers is that it allows you greater flexibility in scheduling child care. If one of your caregivers is unavailable or sick, another caregiver can step in to help out. I realized recently that neither my husband nor I have ever missed a single professional or social event because we couldn't find someone to care for our son. When you hire several caregivers, you are more likely to have child-care coverage whenever you need it. This situation also gives your caregivers more flexibility. If one wants to go on vacation, the other caregiver can cover for them.

HOW TO MAKE GOOD USE OF THIS BOOK

. . . .

This book will save you time.

Throughout the book, I share my expertise and experience, as a mother and a psychologist, with you. I take you step-by-step through all of the important phases of finding, hiring, employing, and managing an in-home caregiver. The text and the optional computer diskette containing all the book's forms (see Appendix A for ordering information) have been designed to be user-friendly. I know firsthand what it is like to be a busy parent with a career. I know what it is like not to have time to read the daily newspaper or to feel extremely lucky on those rare occasions when you have time to take a leisurely bubble bath instead of a quick shower. I know what it is like to sometimes go for months without a pleasure trip to the mall without a stroller. I know how precious time is when you have too little of it. *To help you out, I've developed many forms and materials that will save you a lot of time now and down the road.*

Some of the most useful forms are the Job Application Form (Chapter 8), the Child-Care Agreement Form (Chapter 9), the Job Interview Form (Chapter 11), and the Job Reference Form (Chapter 13). These forms and many others take the work out of hiring your own child caregiver.

Preparing in Advance

....

Read this book before the arrival of your baby.

Before the arrival of your baby, I recommend that you read this book from cover to cover at a leisurely pace so that you are familiar with its ideas and content. It will help you anticipate and prepare for your child-care needs. Then, when you are ready to start your search for an in-home caregiver, you will have a working knowledge and ready access to everything you will need.

Or, if you don't have time to read from cover to cover, and many of you won't, you can skim through the chapters containing the information and materials you need the most. *This book was designed so that you can either read it from cover to cover, perhaps skimming through sections of less importance to you, or use it as a resource book, allowing you to go directly to the information or materials you might need at a particular moment in time.*

Many parents are so worried that they will not have a suitable child-care arrangement in place by the end of the maternity leave that they select the first minimally acceptable child-care arrangement that comes along. They are afraid that they won't find something better or that the child-care opening will no longer be available if they do not act quickly. Or, they get so discouraged and anxious after a few calls or days of looking for an in-home caregiver that they give up and turn to a very expensive child-care placement service or select a group day care arrangement. Child-care decisions under these circumstances are based on fear rather than on reality and what is best for the child and the family. By reading this book and educating yourself, you will prepare yourself to make good, sound child-care decisions.

Conducting Thorough Background Checks

I attribute part of our success in finding excellent caregivers to the fact that I developed a system for conducting an investigation of each applicant's background before hiring (see Chapters 8, 11, 12, and 13). When you call references and conduct background checks (criminal record, child abuse and neglect, driving record and automobile insurance, academic records, and coursework in emergency resuscitation procedures for children), you can be confident you've done all you can to hire a competent, trustworthy individual.

Although conducting background checks and calling references might sound like daunting tasks, they can be easily done with the materials contained in this book. The background search materials are set up so that the job applicant, not you, completes and mails in the necessary forms. Little time, on your part, is required. You will also find that the reference checks are easy to conduct. You merely follow the script and the recommended questions in Chapter 13. Conducting these checks will bring you peace of mind because you will have a great deal of information about the caregiver before hiring.

Tailoring This Book to Fit Your Needs

. . . .

The materials and forms in this book are available on a computer diskette and can be adapted for your own unique situation.

Although you can photocopy directly from this book, I encourage you to adapt the materials and forms, all of which are available on the optional computer diskette (see Appendix A for ordering information), to suit you and your family's needs. There may be suggestions or ideas I offer that you disagree with or view differently. I expect that. *Always remember, this is your child, your family, and your life. It is important that you listen to your own inner wisdom and do what you think is best.* No one else, not even an expert, has the "right" answer for you and your child. Nonetheless, I hope that some of what I have to offer is helpful to you and your family.

. . . .

Remember that I am not a lawyer and this book is not intended to provide legal advice, but rather suggestions and forms that will give you a solid starting point. You will need to ensure that any suggestions you follow or forms you use are consistent with the laws and regulations in your location and time.

For example, discrimination laws vary from place to place; in some states or localities it may be illegal to hire or take employment actions based on a caregiver's sexual orientation or lifestyle preference (such as whether he is a smoker). Some, but not all, discrimination laws exempt

those who have only a few employees. Because of these variations among localities, and because laws and interpretations change, you will need to seek legal advice from a competent professional in your area.

THE DESIGN OF THE BOOK

This book is designed to be both practical and encouraging. It is designed to be quick and simple to use but also entertaining and conducive to reflection. It is designed to be useful to all parents, whatever their situation, but also personal.

The structure of the book reflects this design. My personal experiences are set off in boxes in italics, so they can be read separately or as part of the whole, depending on your needs. Important points are also italicized and sometimes boxed, again to make it easy both to quickly skim and to read more slowly and reflectively.

Each chapter provides step-by-step instructions at the beginning and reinforces them throughout, with numerous forms providing detailed instructions and checklists and with explanations and personal experience providing the rationale for recommendations.

Word Choice

Child/Children. To simplify the book and make it easily adaptable for all situations, the singular form *child* is used throughout instead of *children,* unless the plural form is required by the logic of the sentence. The materials and suggestions are nonetheless applicable whether one is providing care for one or several children.

He/She. To counter stereotypes, the chapters alternate the use of *he* and *she*, with every other chapter referring to only one gender throughout for both the child caregiver and the child. For example, this introduction uses *he* throughout and Chapter 1 uses *she*. To make the forms and checklists easier to tailor to your situation, however, the terms *s/he* and *his/her* were used.

SUMMARY

I hope that you find this book useful. In all of the chapters, I share my personal experiences with in-home child care and the strategies we discovered and developed that made it work so well for us. I also include the challenges and pitfalls.

In-home child care will require more effort on your part at the outset. It will take more time than it takes to visit several day care centers or homes. On the other hand, you will discover that taking the time to find a good in-home caregiver will be time well invested. We have discovered over and over again that the effort we put in up front was well worth it. Once you have a good in-home caregiver in place, you will be rewarded with greater peace of mind and the sure knowledge that your child is receiving quality care.

Our children are the future of our families; we need to invest in them wisely. This book is designed to help you do just that.

In-Home Child Care

A Step-by-Step Guide to Quality, Affordable Care

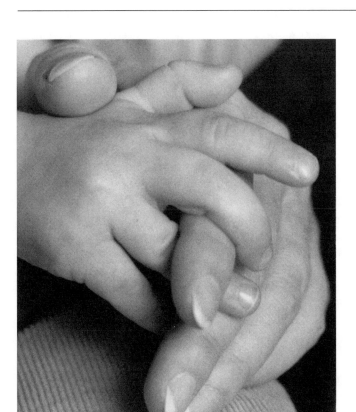

Introduction: Why In-Home Child Care is the Best Alternative

"What are the advantages of hiring someone to care for our child in our own home? While I am at work, I want my child to receive the best child care possible."

THE SPECIAL ADVANTAGES OF IN-HOME CHILD CARE

One of the overriding advantages of in-home child care is that *you* remain in charge of your child's overall care. Because you are the employer, you can delineate how you want things handled. You are able to ensure that your child's developmental needs and well-being take precedence. For example, if you want your caregiver to read to your child her favorite books while sitting in her lap, you are able to encourage this activity. Or, if you don't want her to watch endless hours of TV, you can specify that. *It is much easier to remain in charge of your child's care when she is being cared for on your own turf, in your home.*

Ensures High Quality Care

Research has found that in-home caregivers, along with fathers and grandparents, offer the highest quality of nonmaternal child care for infants, while child-care centers provide the lowest quality. As reported in the *APA Monitor* (Azar, 1995), the National Institute of Child Health and Human Development released in 1995 the first set of its findings of the largest and most comprehensive study of early child care to date. *The researchers concluded that one-on-one care, regardless of the child-care setting, was best predictive of high quality caregiving for infants.*

This study defined child care as any care other than that of the mother. The data collection on more than 1,364 infants began in 1991 with 1-month-old infants. In 1994, the researchers completed their 36-month data collection. These same children, from 10 different sites across the country, will be followed through the first grade by a team of over 24 researchers, mostly psychologists.

At 6 months, about half of the infants were observed in their child-care setting. The child-adult ratios ranged from 1:1 to 8:1. Caregivers were rated according to the level of care they provided, including highly sensitive care (23%), moderately sensitive care (50%), emotionally detached (20%), and highly insensitive (3%). This study also found that higher quality caregiving of infants occurred in child-care arrangements

where there were fewer children and lower child to adult ratios (e.g., 1:1 versus 4:1).

This study's findings pertaining to toddlers and older preschoolers have not yet been released but will undoubtedly shed important light on the child-care needs of young children.

When you select in-home child care, you are selecting the best form of child care possible because you can ensure that your child receives one-on-one care. If your child can't be cared for by you or your partner or her grandparents, then an in-home caregiver is the next best choice.

SECURES EMOTIONALLY HEALTHY CARE

In-home child care not only protects your child from the disruptiveness of day care, but it also allows healthy emotional bonds to be developed that will nurture your child for years to come.

Ensures Good Caregiver Selection.   You can match the caregiver to your child and family. You select and hire the caregiver. Making the decision yourself gives you many advantages over day care. There, you are expected to accept whoever is assigned to care for your child, whether you like her or not. Or, whether she likes your child or not.

When you select your own caregiver, you can make sure that she is a good fit for your child and your family. You can ensure that her philosophy about caring for children and her values are compatible with your own. Chapter 6 helps you identify important qualities to look for in selecting your caregiver.

Because you are doing the interviewing and hiring, you can be sure to select someone who possesses all the necessary qualifications as well as some extra talents or skills. For example, you might want to hire someone who is bilingual and willing to teach your child a new language. Or, perhaps you want someone who can teach your child to swim, to appreciate music, or to love books.

. . . .

All of our caregivers have brought special talents. Shan sang many children's songs to our son and enthusiastically introduced him to the Chinese language. Feng Fa made wonderful, nutritious food and contributed to our son's love of vegetables. Kevin is a talented artist, and our son loves it when Kevin draws him a favorite new storybook character. These drawings are placed in a cherished notebook that our son carries with him everywhere.

Secures Low Turnover and High Consistency of Caregivers.
Another bonus is that you have greater control over the high turnover rate of child caregivers, a major problem in the day care industry. You can require a commitment before hiring.

· · · · · · · · · · · · · ·

When we hire a caregiver, we are careful to select someone who is available to care for our child for at least 1 year if their performance remains satisfactory. We look for someone who is available to make a commitment to stay on the job because continuity of care is very important to us.

Furthermore, you can ensure that your child's care is consistent each day. In day care centers, children may be exposed to a number of different caregivers throughout the day as new workers step in to relieve the staff during breaks and shift changes. These constant changes undermine the child's development of an emotional bond with those providing the care.

Promotes a Healthy Emotional Bond.   One-on-one care allows for the development of a special bond with the caregiver. *The opportunity to form a loving, emotional bond with the caregiver is the most important reason for selecting in-home child care.*
Consistency and predictability are especially important for young children. With one-on-one, in-home care, your child receives full attention and care from the same individual, day in and day out. Your child discovers that this is someone, who, like her parents, she can count on to meet her needs. This relationship will help your child accomplish a very important developmental task, that of developing basic trust in significant relationships. She will come to discover that there are people she can trust outside of the family.
This relationship also allows your child to form an emotional attachment with the caregiver. Out of this attachment grows affection, warmth, and love, the most important ingredients in any child-care arrangement. Regretfully, group day care workers often have too many children to attend to, which interferes with their ability to become emotionally attached to any one child and for the children to emotionally bond with them.
The love relationship or attachment between a child and her caregiver is critical and serves as the essential foundation for a child's learning and development (Greenspan & Greenspan, 1985; Greenspan &

Greenspan, 1989). It is only in the context of a safe, loving bond that infants and young children learn about their world and learn how to love. Without this bond, children can lose interest in learning and exploring their world and their development can become interrupted or delayed. For example, a child cannot learn how to soothe herself when upset or how to regroup after a temper tantrum if the parent or caregiver is not available to soothe them or teach them ways to calm down. We all know adults who simply fall apart and are unable to self-soothe under stress or fly into a rage like a 2-year-old having a tantrum. Obviously, these individuals missed some very important learning in the context of a loving relationship in their early years.

The price we pay for not being emotionally available to children in their early years is very steep. Adults who are unable to love and relate to others and themselves in caring, respectful ways were once children emotionally deprived of the most essential ingredients for learning how to do this: love and an emotional connection.

Permits a Lasting Emotional Bond.   Your child is able to maintain an ongoing relationship with former caregivers. When your in-home caregiver's employment ends, you also have the option to stay in touch. This option is certainly not possible in organized day care.

· · · · · · · · · · · · · ·

Our son's former caregivers have been just as interested as we have in maintaining a relationship. We love inviting them over for special events in our home like our son's birthday celebration. They will sometimes call and stop by to say hello. They want to see how he is growing and developing. Our son loves it when Shan, for example, stops by to play and brings him a container of her special Chinese shrimp, his favorite. We love seeing her and her husband.

Gives Your Child the Home Advantage.   Your child gets to enjoy the benefits of being cared for in the comfort and safety of her own home. It is a real plus for a child to be able to sleep in her own bed, play with her own toys, and be cared for in her own home. Children, especially infants, feel most secure in the familiar environment of their own home. *As a parent, you remain more in charge of your child's environment because you can ensure that it is clean, safe, and stimulating.*

In group day care, children's play outdoors is often limited to a fenced-in yard. With in-home care, your caregiver can take your child for

long walks or to a park. As your child gets older, she can take her on special outings, like to the zoo or to special children's events. Likewise, you can better protect your child from aggressive youngsters or situations that might be harmful or over-stimulating. And, perhaps most important to kids, they will not have to be awakened to be transported to day care. They, like their parents, will like this advantage especially on cold, dark, winter mornings.

PROVIDES PHYSICALLY HEALTHY CARE

In-home care also gets your child off to a physically healthy start in life.

Reduces Exposure to Infectious and Communicable Diseases. In-home child care is medically safer for your child and your family. Children in group day care are exposed to more infectious and communicable diseases, as much research has shown.

A January, 1997 article in the *St. Louis Post-Dispatch* reported that many children attend day care when they are sick, citing a recent Gallup poll in which 34% of mothers admitted that their child sometimes went to school or day care sick (Stovsky). This practice increases the risk of spreading infection.

One recent study, for example, showed that day care centers pose a significant health risk to children, particularly those under the age of 2. The incidence of common minor illnesses is dramatically increased in this group. This study of 2,568 randomly selected children was conducted to find the relationship between the form of day care and respiratory infectious diseases. *Based on their findings, the researchers of this study estimate that 41% of colds, 50% of ear infections, and 85% of pneumonia cases in 1-year-old children are directly attributable to day care exposure* (Louhiala, Jaakkola, Ruotsalainen, & Jaakkola, 1995).

Although most of these illnesses are minor, they can lead to complications, hospitalizations, and surgery. The frequency of ear infections is particularly bothersome because the resultant hearing loss can lead to speech delay at a critical time in the child's development.

The risk of more serious illness, such as hepatitis and meningitis, may also be increased in children attending day care (Arnold, Makintube, & Istre, 1993; Ferson, 1993). In addition, bacterial infections acquired in day care centers tend to be more resistant to commonly used antibiotics, making treatment more difficult (Osterholm, Reves, Murph, & Pickering, 1992; Schwartz, Giebink, Henderson, Reichler, Jereb, & Collet, 1994).

Anyone in contact with the child is also more at risk because there is a ripple effect from the increased frequency of illness associated with day care attendance. Siblings, parents, and others in close contact with the child risk exposure to these illnesses. This factor can be of major significance for the pregnant mother, who may be exposed to a disease potentially harmful to the fetus (Ferson, 1993).

The situation can place a hidden financial burden on your family. *It has been estimated that parental lost time from work, because of these illnesses, costs families using a day care center $1,623 per year, per child under the age of 3.* This cost is in addition to the costs for medication, doctor visits, and other direct medical costs (Nurmi, Salminen, & Pönkä, 1991).

Because of these health risks and the resultant hidden costs, many parents select in-home child care. Also, when your child cared for at home becomes ill, you do not have to miss work. An in-home caregiver, unlike caregivers in day care centers or family-centered day care, will even care for your sick child.

Guarantees Good Nutrition. With in-home care, you have greater control over what your child eats and when. You can ensure your child's particular nutritional needs are met on a schedule that suits your child.

I have been astonished at the poor quality of food offered to children in many day care homes, centers, preschools, and camps. Typical snacks are often processed foods containing too much sugar, refined white flour, or high amounts of fat (e.g., apple juice, fruit gelatin, cookies, crackers, and chips). At home, I can make sure that our caregiver gives our son a healthy array of fresh fruits and vegetables and wholesome food. When your child is cared for outside your own home, you generally have no control over the foods offered once your child graduates to table foods.

. . . .

One of the many special services our caregivers provide is preparing special homemade meals for our son. This service reduces my stress considerably because my work schedule often doesn't allow me time to prepare nutritious meals on the days I am working. My son has grown so fond of Chinese food that I have arranged with our Chinese caregivers to bring food for him. They prepare extra food the evening before they work when they prepare their family's evening meal. I pay them an extra fee to cover their costs. You may be able to make similar arrangements with your caregiver, or you can have her prepare your child's meals during nap times.

Your child can also eat on a schedule that suits her. Like many children, our son might be hungry for a full meal at an unlikely time, like 10:00 A.M. or 4:30 P.M. Likewise, he might not be hungry or interested in eating at more established times, such as when a day care center offers lunch or a snack. I like being able to make sure that he eats healthy, nutritious meals and snacks when he is hungry.

Ensures Good Sleep.   With in-home care, your child's day is scheduled around her own sleep schedule versus a fixed schedule for a group of children.

Children's nap schedules can change dramatically over time. Healthy sleep patterns in children evolve when children are allowed to sleep when they need to rather than having to accommodate to a preset group schedule. *With in-home care, your child's own schedule is honored.*

Meets Your Needs

FITS YOUR SCHEDULE

In-home child care is designed and scheduled to meet your child's and family's needs rather than the needs of someone else. In day care, families are expected to accommodate to the provider's business hours, daily schedule for the children, and regulations whether or not they are compatible with the needs of the child or the family.

For example, some day care centers and preschools inappropriately require children to be toilet trained by an unrealistic age, like $2\frac{1}{2}$ or 3. Although some children can accomplish this feat, many are unable to do so. Consequently, unnecessary pressure is imposed on children and their parents as they scramble to accommodate. Or, many organized child care programs will require full-time attendance without regard for whether this is needed or appropriate. Again, the needs of the provider take precedence over the needs of the child or the family. With in-home care, you are able to establish how things are done, based on *your* needs.

Having the caregiver come into your home gives you much greater scheduling flexibility. Your caregiver can be available when *you* need her versus when the day care center opens or closes. If your meeting runs late or you are caught in traffic, you don't have to worry. You can arrange with your caregiver in advance to cover for you when such unanticipated delays occur. These types of situations can be very stressful for parents with children in day care. In-home care provides a solution to this common problem.

Also, inconveniences and annoyances associated with child care outside of the home, such as having to awaken your child so she can be dropped off or picked up, are avoided. If your child is sick, you are not required to miss work to care for her. Your caregiver is there for your child, in sickness and in health.

Day care center's business hours typically correspond to standard working hours despite the fact that many family work schedules are not standard and often involve long commutes. According to a June 1995 *New York Times* article, "A study released last month by the Federal Department of Labor reported that nearly one in five full-time workers, or about 14.3 million people, worked nonstandard hours in 1991, and that more than 1,000 different work schedules are in use in what is increasingly a 24-hour national economy. And those numbers have probably grown since then, as more companies emphasize global operations that require people working around the clock" (Hays, 1995).

A special advantage of hiring part-time in-home caregivers is that it allows you greater flexibility. It makes it much easier to have coverage whenever you need it, whether it is during the daytime or evening or during the week or weekends. This benefit is especially helpful to parents who travel.

Many families also bring their in-home caregiver with them on vacation. Although we have not, I have friends who have, and they report that it works out very nicely for everyone. It allows them time to relax without having to care for their children every minute, especially in the evenings.

· · · · · · · · · · · · · ·

My husband and I want to minimize the overall amount of time our son is not with one of us. To accomplish this goal, I work 3 long days at the office instead of 5 normal workdays. I also go into work around noon on 2 of these 3 days and work through the evening. On these days, our son is with the caregiver only about 6 hours because my husband takes over and cares for him at 5:30 P.M. In-home care allows us this flexibility in scheduling, and it also minimizes our child-care costs.

I am usually able to arrange for one of our in-home caregivers to come in for several hours during one of my days off if I have a special meeting or doctor's appointment. Because our caregivers work part-time, one of our caregivers is usually available.

SAVES YOU TIME

Because it is designed to meet your needs, in-home care is more convenient and will save you a lot of time.

The most important convenience is that it will save you time on chores that can be performed by the caregiver. During the early years, children sleep a lot. Our son napped anywhere from 6 hours a day when he was 6 months old to 2 to 3 hours at age 3. During nap time, your caregiver can assist you with many household chores, like doing laundry, helping prepare food, or doing dishes. It makes it more possible for us to have some time to relax at home after a long day at the office.

Another timesaving advantage of in-home care is that you do not have to spend additional time commuting to and from your child's day care home or center. For many parents, the time surrounding going to and from work is often the busiest time during the day. And, as many parents can attest, getting young children dressed for an outing is often time-consuming and challenging. *It is much more convenient to have the caregiver come to you and not have to fit in dropping off and picking up your child into an already tight schedule.* This benefit means that you can sleep in a little longer and get home a little earlier. The time saved can be better spent relaxing with your child, perhaps reading books together, at the end of the day.

In addition, you do not have to take time to pack your child's belongings for the day. Although this benefit may seem minor, it represents one more chore added to the list of countless things busy parents have to do when they have young children. It reduces time and stress not to have to pack a day pack, and it is a relief to know that everything your child might need throughout the day is readily on hand when she is cared for at home.

GIVES YOU VALUE FOR YOUR MONEY

In-home care can cost the same or just slightly more than a quality day care center and costs less than what such a center charges for the care of two or more children (see Chapter 4). Day care fees do not take into account many of the hidden costs of organized day care, such as costs associated with transportation and parental lost time from work because of illnesses related to day care and their associated medical costs. Also, in-home caregivers are able to provide several hours of assistance with household chores daily at no additional cost to parents. *You get a lot more for your money with in-home child care.*

BOX 1.1. *Advantages of In-Home Child Care*

Your child receives personal, one-on-one care.

You remain in charge of your child's overall care.

Research shows in-home child caregivers offer the highest quality of care.

You get to select and hire the caregiver.

Your child is protected from the high turnover rate of day care workers and exposure to too many different caregivers.

You have greater control of who your child interacts with and when.

One-on-one care allows for the development of a special bond with the caregiver, which serves as the essential foundation for a child's learning and development.

Your child is able to maintain an ongoing relationship with former caregivers.

Your child gets to enjoy the benefits of being cared for in the comfort and safety of his/her own home.

In-home child care is medically safer for your child and your family.

You have greater control over what your child eats.

Your child's day is scheduled around his/her own sleep and feeding schedule versus a fixed schedule for a group of children.

In-home care is designed and scheduled to meet your child's and family's needs rather than the needs of the child-care provider.

In-home care is more convenient and will save you a lot of time.

Although in-home care costs the same or slightly more than a quality day care center, it costs much less than such a center if you have two or more children.

SUMMARY

In my personal and professional opinion, in-home care is the best child-care alternative. There are many, many advantages (Box 1.1). Our family has benefited so much from this child-care arrangement that we can't imagine selecting any other option. Perhaps the greatest benefit has been having our son's caregivers in our life. There is an old saying that when you take a child by the hand, you hold the heart of that child's mother. Our son's wonderful caregivers have certainly done that. In-home child care puts love back into child care.

References

Arnold, C., Makintube, S., & Istre, G. R. (1993). Day care attendance and other risk factors for invasive *Haemophilus influenzae* type b disease. <u>American Journal of Epidemiology, 138,</u> 333–40.

Azar, B. (1995, June). Data released from child-care study. <u>APA Monitor,</u> p. 18.

Ferson, M. J. (1993). Infections in day care. <u>Current Opinion in Pediatrics, 5,</u> 35–40.

Greenspan, S., & Greenspan, N. T. (1985). <u>First feelings: Milestones in the emotional development of your baby and child from birth to age 4.</u> New York: Viking.

Greenspan, S., & Greenspan, N. T. (1989). <u>The essential partnership: How parents and children can meet the emotional challenges of infancy and childhood.</u> New York: Viking.

Hays, C. L. (1995, June 8). Increasing shift work challenges child care. <u>New York Times,</u> p. B5.

Louhiala, P. J., Jaakkola, N., Ruotsalainen, R., & Jaakkola, J. J. K. (1995). Form of day care and respiratory infections among Finnish children. <u>American Journal of Public Health, 85,</u> 1109–12.

Nurmi, T., Salminen, E., & Pönkä, A. (1991). Infections and other illnesses of children in day-care centers in Helsinki II: The economic losses. <u>Infection, 19,</u> 331–35.

Osterholm, M. T., Reves, R. R., Murph, J. R., & Pickering, L. K. (1992). Infectious diseases and child day care. The Pediatric Infectious Disease Journal, 11, S31–S41.

Schwartz, B., Giebink, G. S., Henderson, F. W., Reichler, M. R., Jereb, J., & Collet, J. (1994). Respiratory infections in day care. Pediatrics, 94, 1018–20.

Stovsky, Renee. (1997, January 29). My child, my job: Sick children put working parents on the spot. St. Louis Post-Dispatch, p. E1.

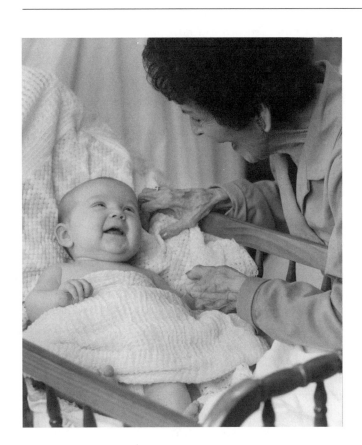

Identifying Pools
of Potential Applicants
in Your Community

"I love the idea of having an in-home caregiver for my child, but I have no idea how to find one. I have heard it's almost impossible to find someone good."

In the process of searching for caregivers for my son and others, I have been repeatedly amazed at the number of excellent people out there. I seemed to be most successful when I looked not for a professional nanny or child-care worker but rather for individuals who loved children and who just happened to be at a time or place in their lives when caring for a child was an appealing job option. This is not to say that career caregivers are not important to consider, simply that I encourage you to consider noncareer caregivers. They can be the best.

●●●●●●●●●●●●●●

Our son's caregivers have included both a male and a female graduate student in social work, a single mother whose children had left for college and who wanted a second job working evenings and weekends, and two wonderful women from China. The first Chinese woman, Shan, a 52-year-old mother of a college student, worked for years as an eye doctor and medical school faculty member in China. She cared for our son during his first year and a half until she developed health problems. She continues to work for us on a part-time basis. The second, Feng-Fa, also earned a university degree in China and worked for years as a secretary in a medical college while raising her two children. Both of these women's husbands are scholars who came to this country to work in a university. In addition to being bright and capable, all of our caregivers have been committed, deeply caring individuals who have contributed a great deal not only to our son but to our family as a whole. Their support has been invaluable, especially since our extended family lives out of state.

A good place to begin is by erasing any stereotypes you might have about child caregivers. The process of finding an excellent caregiver outlined in this chapter involves some novel as well as some tried-and-true approaches. If you are willing to stay open, you will discover options available to you that you might not have previously considered. This approach will offer you a greater number of potential candidates and increase your likelihood of finding someone excellent.[1]

---

[1] Keep in mind when you make any hiring or employment decision that federal and state laws prohibit an employer from excluding any individual based on that individual's classification. Therefore, you may not exclude someone from consideration based on their age over 40, sex, race, national origin, disability, or religion.

There are many effective ways to reach potential caregivers: You can place an advertisement in a newspaper, put an announcement on a bulletin board, or, best of all, connect with your network of family, friends, and business associates. Chapter 3 offers guidelines for employing each of these methods, along with sample materials. Before selecting your methods of advertisement, however, determine who you would ideally like to employ. This decision, in some cases, will determine what method you will use to advertise the position.

We all have images in our mind of the ideal caregiver for our child. You might picture, for example, a warm, soft, grandmotherly type rocking your baby and smelling like freshly baked bread. Or, you might imagine an energetic 23-year-old woman who loves taking your youngster down the slide on her lap at the park. Although it is important to use these fantasies to help guide you in finding what you want, do not let your fantasies limit your options. Just as there is no perfect child or partner, there is no perfect caregiver. Nonetheless, there are many people out there who make wonderful caregivers. To discover these jewels, remain open at least initially to your many options, particularly non-traditional ones.

Students, retirees, relatives, friends, neighbors, stay-at-home parents, housecleaners, and immigrants are just some of the categories of caregivers to consider in your search. These groups are discussed in the rest of the chapter, but you might also want to brainstorm with your partner or friends to identify additional categories of individuals available in your own community. Remember, too, that men can be excellent caregivers.

A NOTE ON MEN AS CAREGIVERS

An untapped resource of child caregivers are men. Men traditionally have not been considered for this role, but this situation is going to change, I believe, as men become more and more involved in the care and raising of their own children. It is now more socially acceptable for men and fathers to feed, diaper, and nurture babies and children. Many men are wonderful caregivers. I predict that as more and more men discover the enriching aspects of caring for children and as society finds this more acceptable, many are going to want to become child caregivers.

. . . .

Currently, we have a male graduate student in social work who cares for our son on a part-time basis. I love that my son is exposed to two very different, loving, nurturing males, his Daddy and Kevin. I take great plea-

sure in watching Kevin care for our son. Kevin is a tall man, and it warms my heart to see our son perched in his arms while Kevin gently kisses the top of his head. There is no better training ground for our son to learn how to become a well-rounded, nurturing male. If he has children of his own someday, perhaps stepping into the role of the involved, caring father will be easier for him.

Our society's children are often denied exposure to a variety of male role models. Children's relationships with adult males, outside of the family, are often limited to the competitive environment of sports. Both the male caregiver and the child can benefit from the caregiving arrangement: They will deeply enrich each other's lives as the nurturing side of masculinity is allowed full expression.

Because the serious problem of child sexual abuse is most typically perpetrated by men, many parents naturally feel anxious about employing male caregivers. However, parents can take steps to safeguard against this possibility, such as doing very careful background checks and then monitoring the relationship between the child and the caregiver. It is always wise to proceed carefully when selecting *any* caregiver and to observe how your child is doing under his care. Despite the very real problem of child abuse, it is important to keep in perspective that the vast majority of men would not intentionally harm a child. Most men, like women, feel very protective of children.

Another commonly expressed concern about hiring men is their comparative lack of experience with children. However, there are many male applicants who have cared for nieces and nephews, grandchildren, and their own children. Even if one's experience with children is more limited, caring for children, like many things, can be learned. I believe that we, as parents, are the best ones to teach and instruct a caregiver on how to care for our child. In fact, I prefer employing someone who is less experienced but motivated to learn than someone who is very experienced and set in their ways. Conveying to a caregiver how you want things done does not have to be a time-consuming endeavor: I have found that I am always passing along new information to my caregivers.

A good way to reach male caregiver applicants is to make it known that men are welcome to apply. To feel more confident about hiring a man, parents might want to rely on their own personal network of family, friends, and associates. A good recommendation from someone you know well, who knows the applicant well, is reassuring.

On several occasions I have had male students respond to my childcare announcement. I have felt comfortable considering them and relying

on their personal and employment references because being a student at a good institution is usually a serious endeavor and the college or graduate school application process is typically quite thorough. Male retirees who have cared for their own children or grandchildren are often good candidates also. One can speak to their former work references to assess their suitability for the position.

STUDENTS

Advantages

Mature college and graduate students can be excellent caregivers. The cost of tuition has skyrocketed, and many students hold down part-time and even full-time jobs to help cover costs. Students preparing for careers in the helping professions, such as psychology, social work, education, the ministry, physical or occupational therapy, medicine, or nursing, can make excellent candidates. These career choices often reflect a genuine desire and interest in working with people. Many working in these fields find caring for a child a meaningful form of employment. They would much rather be reading books to a child than working in a bookstore or waiting on tables.

A student's schedule will often fit well with the needs of a family. Because most students are single, they are often available to watch your child on weekends and evenings too.

• • • • • • • • • • • • • •

It has been wonderful for me and my husband to have graduate students watching our son every Saturday evening so that we can go out as a couple. Both of us are quite busy during the week, so it is especially nice for us to have a regularly established time on the weekend to enjoy each other's company.

What to Consider

You may need to hire at least two part-time student caregivers if you need full-time coverage. Many students' schedules are open during the day at various times during the week. This may work nicely with your schedule, especially if you have some flexibility.

• • • • • • • • • • • • • •

I have found that having several part-time caregivers, rather than one full-time caregiver, works better for everyone for a number of reasons. Caring for a child is very demanding. It is ideal when it can be shared by a number of enthusiastic adults. It helps ensure that no one becomes overwhelmed and exhausted and that your child receives optimum care. Because our son has had loving, close relationships with a handful of different adults besides us, he is friendly, open, and self-confident in new relationships as well.

20

Look for an emotionally mature student who will grow from rather than be held back by this type of work. Ideally, you want to find someone who can remain committed week-in and week-out over the long haul because it is difficult for both the child and the family if there is a rapid turnover. Many undergraduates in their late teens and early twenties are just beginning to spread their wings and enjoy their newly acquired freedom, and they are not ready to make such a commitment to a family. If you do consider undergraduates, the key is to select someone who is highly motivated and has the skills, patience, and perseverance child care requires.

In general, graduate students, especially those in the helping professions, tend to be more settled than undergraduates. They are older, more mature, and typically have been at the top of their class. Many are very bright, responsible, and hardworking. Because of cuts in financial aid, many graduate students today are employed in minimum-paying jobs outside the university. They often have to work and find taking care of children to be rewarding.

How to Reach

Good ways to reach student job applicants include the following:

1. Student bulletin boards outside departmental offices or where students congregate such as in the student union

2. Student newspapers

3. Student mailings

4. University job placement offices

5. Contacts with a departmental chairperson or director of student affairs at a particular school (e.g., a school of social work or seminary)

The sample letters and advertising materials in Chapter 3 will help you accomplish this part of the process in a timely manner.

1. Bulletin Boards. College officials in departmental or student services offices are often glad to post your job notice on a nearby bulletin board or bring it to the attention of particular students. Many will allow you to fax the information so that you don't even need to leave the comfort of your own home or office. This is a nice bonus for busy parents.

To ensure that your notice is promptly posted on as many bulletin boards throughout the campus as possible, however, it is best to make a trip to the campus to do it yourself or ask a dependable relative or friend on campus to do it for you. College bulletin boards have a life of their own, as any student can attest to, and you may want to check every week or so, if you haven't been receiving inquiries, to make sure your notice hasn't been removed. It is also helpful to date your announcement so students and college officials know that it is a current announcement. Otherwise, it is likely to be removed by someone making room for new announcements. To prevent an interested party from removing the entire announcement from the bulletin board, put tear-off sections on the bottom of the announcement with information on whom to contact.

2. Newspapers. In my experience, advertisements in student newspapers, while fairly inexpensive, are not as effective as bulletin boards. Newspaper ads are generally brief, and I have found that I end up having to spend more time screening the applicants by telephone. A bulletin board notice provides more information, which helps potential applicants determine on their own if they are well-suited for the position. Arranging the placement of an ad in a student newspaper can also be quite an adventure. Many of these offices are run by student volunteers, and it can sometimes be difficult to reach the office by phone because there may not always be someone there to answer your call. Also, I have had ads misplaced or not published at the times promised. In addition, most student newspapers are not published during academic breaks.

Although a student newspaper ad has its drawbacks, it does reach a larger and broader cross section of the student body.

. . . .

I have had the most success when I call and get information regarding the cost and publication dates first and then immediately follow that up with a letter, ad, and enclosed payment. I write on the envelope "Newspaper Ad Request Enclosed" to catch the editor's attention. Because many student newspapers operate on a shoestring budget, payments for advertising are welcomed.

3. Mailings. Many graduate-level programs, like schools of social work, departments of psychology, or seminaries with large groups of incoming students from out of town, mail orientation packets with housing, student services, and job opportunities information to help students make a smooth transition to their new life at the university. If you are looking to employ someone at the beginning of a fall, winter, spring, or summer term, you can inquire if the school provides such a mailing to their incoming students and if they would include your job position information in their packet. Program officials are sometimes glad to do this, at no or little cost to you, because they know it will be ultimately beneficial to their students.

22

• • • • • • • • • • • • •

I have had great success with this approach. Each time I have tried it, I have received over 25 calls from interested, graduate-level social work students from around the country.

4. Placement Offices. Most universities and colleges have job placement services that provide listings of job opportunities for students. Call the school and ask to be directed to the appropriate office offering this service. You can also ask how to have your job opening posted. In addition, if your position is for a live-in caregiver, you can list it through the school's housing office.

5. Contacts. Student applicants can also be sought through a particular academic department. Approach departments that prepare students for careers in the helping professions. Because department chairpersons are often very busy, it is usually best to write a letter and enclose copies of your job announcement. You can ask them to place your announcement on the student bulletin board in the departmental office or forward it to students who might be interested.

Another pool of potential caregivers is the partners of students. I have found that the partners of seminarians, for example, are often seeking full- or part-time employment. Whether they have children of their own or not, they may be a potential resource for you. The best way to reach these individuals is through the same channels.

RETIREES

Advantages

There are many retirees who would very much enjoy caring for your child. For some, this is an ideal time in life to care for a child. Retirees usually have more time on their hands, and many want to contribute something important. Helping to nurture and care for a young child can be a deeply meaningful and fulfilling endeavor. Individuals in this age group have a greater appreciation for this opportunity. Many bring to the job a good sense of what is most important in life and a wisdom that has been finely tuned by life experience. If you are ever in doubt about what this age group has to offer, visit a hospital setting and watch them at work. Volunteer organizations in hospitals are often staffed by energetic, committed, caring retirees. These are just the type of individuals who also make great child caregivers.

A special category of retirees, those who have lost their partners, may find caring for a child especially appealing. The intimate contact with your child and family can provide them with just the kind of human warmth and closeness lacking in their lives. Everyone, especially your child, will benefit from this arrangement.

What to Consider

My recommendation to parents to employ two part-time, rather than one full-time, caregivers also applies here. Caregiving can be exhausting for anyone. Having a caregiver work 2 to 3 days a week or 4 to 5 hours a day may be ideal. That way, caregivers can have plenty of time off to rest and enjoy their own lives. Also, a part-time position provides just the right amount of supplemental income desired by many retirees.

One potential drawback to hiring someone who has parented in the past is that sometimes they think they know better than you how to care for your child. If you are ever concerned that a caregiver is not following your wishes, it is very important to discuss the issue. If the caregiver is unable to assure you that your wishes will be followed, employ someone else. Remember, though, this problem can occur with a caregiver of any age.

How to Reach

A good way to reach retirees is through your own network of family, friends, and business associates. People you come into contact with through your neighborhood, religious or social organizations, or doctors' offices can also offer you leads. Look around, ask around, and don't be afraid to approach a retiree you like and ask if he is interested in applying for the position. When you are in social situations with your child, it is apparent who is drawn to and delighted by children. These are the people that approach your child, smiling, chatting, and waving. If you and a retiree don't know each other but know someone in common, you can ask

your mutual acquaintance if he thinks this individual might be interested in and skilled at caring for a child. *Networking, in my experience, is often the least costly and most effective way to find a good caregiver.*

RELATIVES, FRIENDS, OR NEIGHBORS

Advantages

Many parents turn to the extended family to help care for their children. This arrangement can be ideal because family members are more likely to have a personal investment in the child's life. One might make arrangements with a close relation, such as a parent or sibling or a more distant relative. Parents often feel a greater peace of mind with a family member they have known for a long time.

What to Consider

Bear in mind, however, that a family member will not necessarily make a better caregiver. A relative should possess the same qualities you would expect in a nonfamily caregiver. For example, evaluate how a potential caregiver treats his own children and grandchildren. Have his children or those he cared for in the past done well? It is always a red flag when a caregiver's own children have emotional, behavioral, or interpersonal problems. Although the caregiver may not have contributed to the development of such difficulties, it is an important factor to consider before hiring someone.

I recommend, whenever possible, that parents pay their relatives a salary for their services. I encourage this practice for several reasons. One, in certain circumstances, it may be required by state law. Two, it helps ensure that the caregiver is compensated at least in part for their invaluable contribution. And, three, it makes it easier for parents to stay in charge of their child's care. It helps to reduce the role confusion that occurs when you hire a relative or friend.

Another group of potential child caregivers are friends and neighbors. The friendship and caring that already exists between you can be enhanced when helping to raise your child is added to the equation. You have the added bonus that your child may develop a lifelong friendship with this person. Children and adults alike benefit immensely from this relationship.

....

I have very fond memories of my own childhood caregivers. I remember with special fondness Mrs. Yorks and Bobbie Shoaff, who became close friends of our family over the years. Seeing them and their families has always been a special part of returning home to the small community where I grew up in Northern Minnesota.

One major drawback can exist when hiring a friend, neighbor, or family member to care for your child. You, the parent, are required to wear two different hats: that of employer and that of friend or family member. This situation can be awkward and downright difficult at times because of boundary or role confusion. It is much easier to request what we want and to establish guidelines with an employee than with a family member or friend. These two types of relationships are very different.

Hiring a family member or friend as caregiver requires special efforts on both parties' parts to establish a clear and separate parent-caregiver relationship. Both parties need to respect that the child-care relationship is hierarchical (employer/employee), with the parent in the position of authority. The parents always need to have the final say on how the child is to be cared for, and there needs to be a clear understanding and agreement that this will be respected. Openly discuss this issue with the caregiver at the very beginning when you are establishing the child-care agreement. Do not hire someone who won't respect your authority.

STAY-AT-HOME PARENTS

Advantages

Stay-at-home parents are excellent resources for parents looking for someone to come into their home to care for their child. Many need the supplemental income that this arrangement offers, and it affords them the best of both worlds: an income and what they desire most, the ability to raise their own child full-time. In this situation, the caregiver may bring his child with him to your home, or the child may come to your home after school.

This arrangement is an especially appealing option for parents with more limited funds for child care. Generally, the salary paid to the caregiver is less because he is dividing his time between his child and yours.

Obviously, this situation works best with a caregiver with only one child, although there are always exceptions, based on the age and needs of the children involved.

· · · · · · · · · · · · · ·

My brother and sister-in-law had such an arrangement for the first year of their daughter's life and were very pleased with the care their daughter received. They took great care at the outset to clarify their expectations, an especially important thing to do in this type of situation. Their caregiver was a college graduate with a child about a year older than their child.

What to Consider

If you are entertaining this option, keep in mind that arrangements need to be made to accommodate the caregiver's child. His child may need a quiet place to nap and space to keep toys and play safely. Before hiring, it is also essential to meet and to observe the caregiver's child interact with yours so that you can assess his readiness to share his parent. It will also allow you to see how skilled the caregiver is in meeting the needs of your child while also caring for his own.

It is advisable to discuss and negotiate in advance what arrangements will be made in the event that his child becomes ill. Will he stay home to care for his child, or will he make other arrangements with his partner or another so that he does not miss work? If his child is in the infectious stage of an illness, do you want him to notify you immediately and make arrangements so that your child is not exposed? You may also want to establish in the written child-care agreement that you never want the children left without his supervision.

How to Reach

Probably the best way to find someone for this type of arrangement is through your own network of family, friends, and business associates. Have you met someone in your childbirth class, at your church or synagogue, or at the neighborhood park who might be interested? Do you know any stay-at-home parents who are excellent parents and may need a supplemental income?

HOUSECLEANERS INTERESTED IN BECOMING CAREGIVERS

Advantages

Over the years, I have known many families who have hired their housecleaner to care for their child. A special bond often develops between families and household employees, and this sometimes leads to this kind of arrangement. This possibility is always worth considering if you like your housecleaner and feel he would be a good caregiver. Some housecleaners are delighted to be asked, and they welcome the opportunity to work for one family rather than many. Also, if you only need someone part-time, they can work for you when you need them and fill the remainder of their time cleaning homes.

IMMIGRANTS

Advantages

In most urban areas in the United States and in many smaller communities, a sizable number of individuals have recently immigrated to this country, and you may be able to find someone who has obtained Immigration and Naturalization Service (INS) Employment Authorization documents from the U.S. government, providing them with the legal authorization to work.

Before coming to the United States, many immigrants have worked in fields such as medicine, education, or business and have been highly accomplished. Whether they are on a professional level or not, many are upwardly mobile, highly motivated, and hard-working individuals. Some, because they are in the process of learning English or do not possess the U.S.- required professional credentials, are not able to obtain employment in their chosen field. Many are therefore eager to work, especially in jobs that will allow them to practice their English.

Working as a child caregiver in a home can be an ideal position as they adjust to their new life in this country. It helps them establish a solid work record and a network of support, and it gives them time to learn about and acclimate to our culture. The benefit to your family on a number of different levels can be immense.

OUR PERSONAL STORY

Our son's first primary caregiver, Shan, came to this country from China a year before we hired her. She was a student in a nearby English language school. We were extremely pleased with Shan, who retired as a faculty member in a Western-style medical school before coming to the United States. Her husband came to this country as a visiting scholar, and their daughter was an honors student at a local university. Shan is very bright, loving, and wonderful with our son. He adores her: His eyes light up when he sees her. She became like a member of our family. We still lovingly refer to her as "Mommy #2," even though she only works for us occasionally now because of a health problem, and we feel a special bond with her entire family. A special occasion, like a holiday or Mother's Day, would not seem complete without Shan and her husband. Shan's care extended beyond our son; she was generous in her care of all of us. Because she had been a working mother too, she understood how difficult it can be sometimes, and she did many things to make my life easier. Just her words of support on an especially busy day meant a great deal to me.

Shan has had many opportunities to practice her English with us, and she continues to improve. She had a good grasp of English when we hired her, and she has continued to pursue her studies at the English language school. I have always made an effort to speak just a bit more slowly, and we both let each other know if we are not understanding each other. She brought a dictionary to work so she could look up new words or ones she didn't understand. At the beginning, she had to look up words several times a day. A year later, this was only necessary several times a month. Now, 3 plus years later, I can't recall the last time she had to pull out her dictionary.

We both had quite a chuckle after her first day when I asked her to keep track of the number of "bowel movements" our son had each day. She was not familiar with the term and I had a hard time explaining. All I could think of were slang terms, and I thought it was too early to introduce those. She left that day with the word "bowel movement" written on a piece of paper to check the meaning with her family. We both chuckled the next day when she returned, assuring me that she now understood.

At the beginning when there was something important that I wanted to make sure she understood completely, like how to respond in a particular emergency, I would give her a pamphlet, a short article, or instructions in writing, which she would translate. Her family or English teachers would help if necessary. Because she was eager to become proficient in reading and writing English, she saw this as an opportunity to perfect her skills. This year, Shan wrote a letter to our son in response to the Valentine he had sent her. I was amazed and impressed with her written mastery of the English language.

One of the special advantages of hiring two Chinese caregivers is that our son has been introduced to a whole new language and culture. Both are excellent cooks, and our son clearly knows the difference between American and Chinese cuisine. If given a choice, he will choose Chinese food every time. I have never had to worry about him getting enough variety and vegetables in his diet. After he was well-established on solid foods, I made a financial arrangement with Feng-Fa to bring a selection of foods from her family's evening meal for him each day. This arrangement has worked wonderfully for us. Our son loves her cooking, and on my busy work days, I do not have to worry about finding the time to prepare a nutritious, well-balanced meal for him. When I tell him that Feng-Fa is coming the next day, he cheerfully responds, "OK." She is wonderful, and her delicious food is an extra bonus.

Both Feng-Fa and Shan agreed, when they accepted the job, to teach our son the Chinese language as part of their job assignment. I marvel when they talk to him in Chinese and he understands. He does not speak Chinese yet, but he clearly understands some of what they are saying. He indicates this by sometimes responding appropriately in English.

Over the time that Shan has worked for us, I have recommended several of her friends to other families seeking a caregiver for their children. Everyone has been very pleased with these arrangements. When Shan tearfully told me that she had developed health problems and had to stop being our son's primary caregiver, she already had Feng-Fa in mind to take her place.

What to Consider

Box 2.1 provides information on how to order the U.S. Department of Justice *INS Handbook for Employers*. This handbook is short and easy to read and gives you instructions on how to verify someone's employment eligibility. The Immigration Reform and Control Act of 1986 requires employers, including household employers, to hire only individuals authorized to be employed. ***When you hire a child caregiver, whether they are a U.S. citizen or not, you are required to verify their employment eligibility and retain on file a one-page form (I-9) that is completed by both the employee (section 1) and employer (section 2).*** Box 2.1 contains the information you will need to comply with this law.

BOX 2.1. *Employment Eligibility Verification Requirements*

··

All employers, including household employers, are required by The Immigration Reform and Control Act of 1986 to hire only individuals authorized to be employed. To determine an individual's employment eligibility, both you and the potential hire must complete a one-page form (Form I-9). Both parties provide information and signatures. By law, the employer must retain a copy of this completed form on file and present it for Immigration and Naturalization Service (INS) inspection, if requested.

You can obtain a copy of the *Handbook for Employers: Instructions for Completing Form I-9* (INS M-274), which contains two copies of Form I-9, by calling or writing your nearest INS office. Written requests for a copy can be made "To the Attention of Employer Sanctions."

Carefully read the *current* version of the handbook, because there could be changes in the law. The handbook answers many commonly asked questions. You can also write the office with your questions. If you write, provide your phone number, and your local office will then respond to your request for information by phone.

Copies of Form I-9 can also be ordered from the United States Department of Justice, Immigration and Naturalization Service, Division of Consumer Affairs Outreach by calling (800) 870-3676. Their fax number is (202) 633-4708.

If you have direct questions about the I-9 process, you can call their Employer Hotline at (800) 357-2099 or (202) 633-4483. They request that you fax any questions involving significant details to (202) 633-4708. Two documents providing useful information on the I-9 process can also be requested from this office. They are the "Employer Information Bulletin 96-03: The I-9 Process in a Nutshell" and the "Employer Information Bulletin 96-09: Information about the Form I-9."

It is important to already have the handbook and Form I-9 on hand when you hire because you are only allowed 3 business days for completion of Form I-9 or, if you plan to hire for less than 3 days, the I-9 must be completed the first day of employment. If you need additional copies of Form I-9, you can make photocopies of it, although you are required to photocopy *both* sides of the form. The back side of the form contains the lists of acceptable documents that establish employment eligibility and identity.

How to Reach

Immigrant communities are often very close-knit and supportive of their members. If you are looking to hire an immigrant, one of the best ways is through networking with a member of that group. If you know such an individual or someone who knows someone, you can ask them to help you. Word usually travels fast in these ethnic communities because of their relatively small size, and this form of networking is often effective.

. . . .

We discovered an amazing thing with our immigrant caregivers. We essentially have been guaranteed ongoing child care by someone in their close network of families and friends. Once we had established trust, they not only found new caregivers for us but for our friends as well.

Another way to reach immigrant caregiver applicants is to place an announcement at an English language school or contact a local agency that helps immigrant families resettle. Many urban areas have such support organizations. Or, some immigrant communities become involved in a particular church. You can contact the church and ask how you might advertise your job opening to its members.

AU PAIRS

Advantages

Another option is to hire an au pair from Europe. Au pairs are typically 18 through 26 years old and speak English as a second language. They are usually required to possess the equivalent of a high school degree and have some experience caring for children. This experience might include babysitting or helping care for a younger sibling. An au pair will provide child-care services for up to 45 hours per week while living with the American host family. The family is expected to treat the au pair like a family member, rather than an employee, including him in family meals, activities, and outings, and providing a private room and weekly stipend.

What to Consider

Before arriving, the au pair typically receives 8 hours of infant and child safety training and 24 hours of child development coursework. Au pairs are *not* child care professionals and except for this training, their skills, experience, and training can vary greatly.

Before hiring an au pair, talk to as many families as possible who have tried an au pair because I have heard many mixed responses. Entering this arrangement with realistic expectations on both sides is an important factor for it to be successful.

How to Reach

There are several agencies that, for a fee, recruit and screen au pairs, plus provide some additional services. Box 2.2 includes the names, addresses, and phone numbers of several of these agencies. You can contact these agencies for written materials and information.

PROFESSIONAL CHILD CAREGIVERS

Advantages

Individuals in this group are typically more experienced in caring for children, and some have had formal child-care training, usually on the college level. An advantage of hiring a professional child caregiver is that they generally have more expertise and experience. They have chosen caring for children as their career choice and usually enjoy taking care of children.

What to Consider

Hiring a professional, however, is not a quick fix: It requires just as much thought and planning as hiring any other caregiver. You still need to carefully screen anyone you plan to hire, conducting a background check (see Chapter 12) of schools attended and previous employers. An individual may market himself as a child-care professional but have little actual experience or training. To be careful, you can, for example, require the applicant to present their official academic transcripts to you so that you can verify what courses related to child care were completed and what grades were received. If you specifically want to hire a professional, verify that the applicant is indeed a professional.

It is also important to realize that hiring a professional caregiver is no guarantee that you are hiring the best caregiver for your child. That

BOX 2.2. *Au Pair Agencies*

··

Au Pair in America
102 Greenwich Avenue
Greenwich, CT 06830

(203) 863-6147 or (800) 928-7247 ext. 6147
Fax (203) 863-6180

EF Au Pair
One Memorial Drive
Cambridge, MA 02142

(800) 333-6056
Fax (617) 494-1389

EurAupair
250 North Coast Highway
Laguna Beach, CA 92651

Eastern Region:
(800) 901-2002
Fax (703) 518-5033

Western Region:
(800) 713-2002
Fax (206) 828-1987

Southern Region:
(800) 618-2002
Fax (404) 814-0996

Midwestern Region:
(800) 960-9100
Fax (612) 476-7612

World Wide Web Address: http://www.euraupair.com

depends on the individual. Professional child caregivers may appeal to those parents wanting someone who is more experienced. Because a professional nanny has had specialized training or experience, he may have more definite ideas about how to care for children. Make sure, therefore, that the caregiver's style and philosophy of raising children is compatible with your own. Just as there are "a thousand ways to skin a cat," there are a thousand ways to care for a child.

For example, some caregivers and parents believe that an infant should not be picked up or responded to every time he cries, fearing that this will produce a demanding, spoiled child. They believe it is better in the long run to sometimes let the child cry it out. You, on the other hand, may believe like I do that infants cry to communicate their needs, and it is important to respond with food, a diaper change, or comforting.

If you suspect that the caregiver is set in his ways and that those ways are different from your own, you can try to assess if this is likely to develop into a problem by asking previous employers if the caregiver was flexible and willing to respect their wishes. Most professional caregivers are very sensitive to this issue and will try to respect your wishes whenever possible.

Because of their college coursework and experience, professional caregivers usually charge more for their services. Don't assume that you cannot afford the services of a professional caregiver. The price differential for a professional caregiver is sometimes just a bit higher than the going rate for other caregivers.

How to Reach

The best way to find a professional caregiver is to ask your family, friends, and acquaintances if they know someone they can recommend. Perhaps there is another family whose children have grown and are no longer in need of the caregiver's services. Another avenue is to contact a local college or university with a program in early childhood education. Students, including those preparing to graduate, might be interested in your job offer. Professional caregivers and nannies also advertise their services in local newspapers.

SUMMARY

Hiring the right individual will greatly enhance your life. There are many wonderful people out there to help you care for your child, and you can find them. Stay open to individuals you might not have previously considered, and try not to get discouraged too quickly. The time and effort you put into this search in the beginning will be well worth it over the long haul. Believe me, I know firsthand the value of excellent in-home caregivers.

3

Advertising Your Child-Care Position

"I'm already so busy that I just don't see how I can find the time to look for an excellent caregiver. Besides, what if I spend a lot of time advertising and don't find anyone?"

Advertising the child-care position is one of the most important steps in arranging in-home care, but it can be one of the most difficult emotionally. At this stage, there are many unknowns: You are spending time without knowing what kind of response you will receive from calls, fliers, and ads. But don't get discouraged. I found that if I were patient, I eventually received positive responses. I think many people give up their search for an excellent in-home caregiver too soon because they find this stage of the search too anxiety producing. Don't give up. Nothing is more important than finding an excellent caregiver for your child. It is helpful to remind yourself that you are taking the necessary steps to find the best for your child and that the time spent and the effort expended are worthwhile.

Taking the time to find the right caregiver for your family is a wise investment: In the long run, it will save you time and worry. In addition, you can make the process of finding a caregiver efficient by choosing appropriate advertising strategies and following through patiently on them. This chapter includes the advertising methods and materials that I have found most effective. A variety of methods are offered, and sample materials are given for you to copy or adapt for your own use, allowing you to devote a minimum amount of time. You can copy directly from this book or use this book's timesaving optional computer diskette containing all the book's forms (see Appendix A for ordering information).

SAMPLE JOB ANNOUNCEMENTS AND ADS

To advertise your child-care position, you can develop a job announcement flier to distribute to potential applicants and to anyone who may be able to help you find a caregiver. This announcement can also be placed on bulletin boards at nearby colleges or institutions of higher education, English language schools, churches, or local libraries.

Sample job announcements, which can be adapted to meet your specific needs, are offered in Boxes 3.1–3.3. Headings such as "Attention Active Retirees," or "Attention Students," or "Part-time Position for Caring Individual" can attract different types of applicants.[2]

---

[2] In some states or localities, it may be permissible to advertise for a nonsmoker. Check your local laws, or call your local chapter of the American Lung Association.

BOX 3.1. *Sample Job Announcement For Non–Live-In Child Caregiver*

Job Opening For Child Caregiver

<u>Description:</u>   Assist parents in caring for a 6-month-old infant

<u>Time:</u>   Monday through Thursday, 9:00 A.M. to 4:00 P.M. (24 hours a week, plus occasional evening and weekend hours at mutually agreed upon times)

<u>Where:</u>   In home of family in the Towns Square area (a smoke-free work environment)

<u>Salary:</u>   Negotiable, but based on the standard rates in our community

<u>Position Available:</u>   Immediate opening. We are looking for someone who is available on an ongoing basis, as opposed to a time-limited basis.

<u>Job Requirements:</u>   **Individual who is loving and sensitive to children, emotionally mature, and responsible. Some experience caring for infants is required.**

- For further information, please call Martha at (822) 878-6262. If I am unavailable, please leave a message on my answering machine after 5 rings. Please speak slowly, and leave your name, number, the purpose of your call, and the hours when you are available.

Job Opening for Live-In Child Caregiver

<u>Description:</u>   Assist parents in caring for a 6-month-old infant and a delightful 4-year-old, who is in preschool part-time

<u>Time:</u> Monday, Wednesday, and Friday, 8 A.M. to 5 P.M. (27 hours a week)

<u>Where:</u> In lovely home in Westley (a smoke-free environment)

<u>Salary:</u> $___ a month, plus room and bath, with plenty of privacy; must have a car and a good driving record

<u>Position Available:</u> Beginning April lst; must be interested in holding this position for at least 1 year.

<u>Job Requirements:</u> **At least 6 months experience in caring for an infant.**

- We are a loving, child-oriented family searching for someone who is committed to providing excellent care for our children.
- During your hours off, your privacy and free time will be respected.

For further information, please call Martha at (822) 878-0007. If I am unavailable, please leave a message on my answering machine. Please speak slowly, and leave your name, number, the purpose of your call, and the hours when you are available.

BOX 3.3. *Sample Job Announcement for Live-In Child Caregiver (Barter Arrangement)*

··

Small Furnished Apartment Available in Exchange for Child Care/Household Assistance

Located in a lovely home near Jefferson University

Large one-room apartment (14′ x 24′), fully furnished, including all utilities (heat and air conditioning)

Shared kitchen and bath

In exchange for 10 hours a week to care for 3-year-old child, and for assistance in household and yard tasks (at mutually agreeable times)

Located in beautiful neighborhood; plenty of privacy; ideal for single, mature student

Child-care experience and love of children required

Must be able to live and work in a smoke-free environment

FOR INFORMATION, APPLICATION, AND INTERVIEW, CALL: Rebecca at (822) 990-0065 (answering machine is on after 10 rings). Please speak slowly, and leave your name, phone number, purpose of call, and times when you are available.

Please do not remove this announcement from the bulletin board. If you are interested, please tear off the information tab with our phone number below. Thank you.

Child care/Apt. Exchange Call: (821) 990-0065	Child care/Apt. Exchange Call: (821) 990-0065	Child care/Apt. Exchange Call: (821) 990-0065	Child care/Apt. Exchange Call: (821) 990-0065

Sample ads for newspapers or newsletters are listed in Box 3.4. These ads have been written using as few words as possible to save on cost at publication.

To save time and postage, fliers can be sent by fax to many offices such as job placement services, newspaper offices, and university student services. You can phone in advance, with a request that they place your job announcement on their bulletin board, and then fax the announcement with a cover letter.

When developing ads or announcements, creatively express your needs and requirements in a positive, brief fashion designed to capture the attention of the reader. Then, be patient and wait for responses, being sure not to give up too quickly.

SAMPLE LETTERS ANNOUNCING YOUR CHILD-CARE OPENING

Many of us prefer finding a caregiver through our own network of family, friends, and business associates or through a particular school, church, or synagogue. Hiring someone who is not a total stranger can lessen your fear about hiring an unscrupulous person. Most child-care placement services are costly, and they cannot provide names of individuals who are associated with your own social network. Before advertising the position to the general public or before consulting a child-care placement service, use your personal contacts.

Begin by informing others that you are looking for a caregiver to work in your home, and then follow up with a letter. The sample letter in Box 3.5 can be used as a guide. Several copies of the job announcement (see previous section) can be attached to the letter. Personalize the letter with information about your child, and include other pertinent details to capture the reader's interest.

Creating these announcements need not involve a great deal of time, especially if a personal computer is available. If you do not have a computer, write one letter, make copies, and distribute them.

Begin by compiling a list of friends and acquaintances; include other parents of young children who might have leads on potential caregivers. A list of names for holiday card-giving can serve as the basis for your networking name list.

Contact the people on your list in person or by phone, and ask for help. Inquire whether you can send them a copy of your job announcement. You may need to spend only 1 to 2 hours on the phone making these calls. Because this is the age of the answering machine, be prepared to leave a brief informative message so that your contact will not need to reply, unless she can give you the names of potential applicants. Send the

BOX 3.4. *Sample Job Ads for Caregiver*
•••

CHILD CARE: Loving person, nonsmoker, in-home care for toddler, part-time; days. (822) 778-9912

NANNY: Live-in, loving, responsible, patient, nonsmoker for caring parents of preschoolers. (822) 873-9009

CHILD CARE: Seeking retiree who loves kids; mornings in our home, must drive. (822) 990-5556

CHILD CARE: Experienced, loving, responsible person to care for infant in home; full-time; nonsmoker. (822) 993-0008

NANNY: Live out; experienced care of 3 children in loving home; nonsmoker; full-time; references required. (822) 332-9976

BOX 3.5. *Sample Letter for Family, Friends, and Work Associates*

••

Bob and Mary Miller
1312 Greenacre Drive
Anytown, U.S.A. 66611
(222) 439-9066

Date

Dear Family and Friends,

As you know, we are engaged in a project that is dear to us: finding someone wonderful to come to our home 25 hours a week to help us take care of Laura, who just turned 8 weeks old. Laura is so sweet right now. She is a healthy baby and loves to cuddle. We would appreciate your help in finding an excellent caregiver for Laura. We hope to hire someone by May 1 because Mary returns to work on May 15.

Please pass along our enclosed job announcement to any good candidate you know who might be interested. Do you know any responsible, active retirees, college or graduate students, or adults who would be good caregivers? If so, would you ask them if they might be interested in applying? Extensive child-care experience is not required, although it is of course preferred. An open-mindedness for learning and an enthusiastic attitude are qualities we value.

We are especially looking for someone who loves children and would be available to work for us for at least 1 year, assuming of course that everyone is happy with the arrangement.

We appreciate your help. If you know someone, please call us or encourage that individual to contact us directly at the above number. Thank you so much for your help. Laura has a lot to learn before she will be able to speak for herself, but we know she would want us to thank you too.

Sincerely,

Bob and Mary Miller

members of your network the letter and job announcements to remind them of your job opening.

Sample letters that can be sent to churches or synagogues, organizations, and universities are found in Boxes 3.6–3.9. Consider contacting the following institutions:

- Local churches or synagogues that have a large membership of retired persons or immigrants

- Support organizations that work with immigrant families or active retirees

- English language schools

- Seminaries

- Public and private colleges and universities in your area that target programs in the helping professions, such as education; nursing; social work; psychology; counseling; physical, occupational, speech, art, and music therapy; and premedicine; and schools' offices of student affairs, career development, and job placement

43

BOX 3.6. *Sample Letter to Send to a Church or Synagogue*

Martha Levinson
892 51st Street
Anycity, U.S.A. 33890
(222) 492-9365 (Home)
(222) 493-9012 (Work)

Date

Rabbi Robert Cohen
Temple Beth Shalom
88th and 4th Avenue
Anycity, U.S.A. 33896

Dear Rabbi Cohen,

I would appreciate it if you would post the attached job opening announcement on the bulletin board in the Temple. I am looking for a mature, responsible adult who loves children and is interested in providing part-time care in my home during daytime hours for my 22-month-old son.

My son is delightful and needs a nurturing caregiver who would enjoy reading to him, taking him to the park, and introducing him to the many new and exciting wonders in life. If you know any members of the congregation who might be interested, would you share this information with them?

Thank you so much for your help.

Sincerely,

Martha Levinson

BOX 3.7. *Sample Letter for an Organization or English Language School*

··

Robert and Michelle Masters
210 South Road
Anycity, KI 96390
(226) 847-0138 (Home)

Date

Ms. Phyllis Moore, Director
International Families Resettlement Center
6200 Page Street
Anycity, KI 96390

Dear Ms. Moore,

Attached are copies of the announcement of the in-home child-care position that I spoke to you about yesterday. Our 2 1/2-year-old son, Nathan, is a wonderful child. He loves to play outside and is curious about everything he sees. We are looking for someone who is caring, responsible, and patient, someone who will encourage Nathan to explore all the corners of his new world.

I know that your organization assists families who are eager to settle here and to find work. *We are looking for an adult who enjoys caring for children and whose command of the English language is at least fair to good.* We would be patient and glad to help the individual practice and develop his or her English language skills. This person, naturally, would need to possess bona fide work papers.

Would you please share this information with anyone who would be suitable for the position? Also, would you please post one of the attached job announcements on your center's bulletin board?

Thank you so much for helping us.

Sincerely,

Robert and Michelle Masters

BOX 3.8. *Sample Letter for a Department Chairperson at a University or College*

••

Sam and Rebecca Friedman
8403 Curving Street
Collegetown, ST 90052
(420) 677-9214

Date

Louise S. Brachter, Ph.D., Chairperson
Graduate Program in Clinical Child Psychology
Brooksville University
Campus Box 231
Collegetown, ST 90052

Dear Dr. Brachter,

We would like to request your help in finding graduate students in your department who might be interested in applying for a part-time job to care for our 4 1/2-year-old daughter in our home. This work will involve both daytime and evening hours. Perhaps you are aware of incoming students who are looking for part-time employment. Our home is located 5 minutes by car from the university. We plan to hire at least two caregivers and aim to work around their academic schedules. We will pay $ ___ per hour.

Our daughter, Meredith, is a bright, curious, and inquisitive little girl. We are looking for a mature, caring, and energetic caregiver. I know that the students in your program are top notch, and we would be delighted to have the opportunity to interview anyone interested.

Would you please post our job announcement (attached) on the departmental bulletin board and also give the information to any students who might be interested?

Thank you for your help.

Most sincerely,

Sam and Rebecca Friedman

BOX 3.9. *Sample Letter to a University, College, or Seminary Office of Student Affairs, Job Placement, or Career Development*

John and Sally Marvin
810 East Bay Street
Riverdale, PE 83238
(993) 967-7653 (Home)
(993) 962-7568 (John's Work)
(993) 847-8546 (Sally's Work)

Date

Dan Zolaf, M.Div.
Director of Student Services
Holy Word Seminary
210 East Road
Riverdale, PE 83237

Dear Mr. Zolaf,

We are writing to inquire if you would please post our attached job announcement on the student bulletin board. We are aware that many of your students seek part-time jobs, and we believe that this position would be ideal for one of them. If you know any students or students' partners who might be interested in a child-care position, would you please share this information with them? Our home is less than 20 minutes by car from the seminary, and the work hours can be adjusted to accommodate a student's schedule.

We have two children, a 15-month-old daughter and a 3 1/2-year-old son. They are wonderful children, and we would like to find a qualified person to help us care for them on a part-time basis in our home during daytime and evening hours. This position will be shared with another caregiver, each working 15 hours per week.

We very much appreciate your help. Thank you.

Gratefully,

John and Sally Marvin

4

How to Make In-Home Child Care Affordable for Your Family

"We'd love to have in-home child care, but we just can't afford it. Day care is expensive enough."

For many families, the cost of child care is a major concern. Many parents mistakenly assume that they cannot afford in-home care, falsely concluding that it is more expensive. Until I researched child care, that's what I assumed. However, when I checked out the real costs involved, I was pleasantly surprised by what I discovered.

The cost of an in-home caregiver for a single child is generally only slightly more than the cost of a quality day care center and can cost comparatively less if you are having to pay for two or more children. In other words, for essentially the same cost, you can receive one-on-one care for your child in the comfort of your own home versus care in a day care center with countless other children.

My own research revealed that in-home care would basically cost my family the same as organized day care. Granted, I could find day care arrangements that cost less, but I was not willing to place my infant son in a situation where the care or the facilities were substandard or where four or more children were under one adult's care. So, before you decide that you can't afford in-home care, compare the actual costs, both monetary and non-monetary, to determine what you actually receive for your child-care dollar.

COMPARING COSTS AND BENEFITS

A good place to start is to find out the standard fees for both in-home child caregivers and other child-care options in your community. There are a number of ways to find this information. You can begin by calling friends and work associates with young children, or call a local child-care placement service and explain that you are trying to find out the going rate for in-home child care. Friends will often volunteer how much they pay their in-home caregiver, and placement services can quote the standard fees for their nannies. You can then call organized day care centers and family-centered child caregivers who care for children in their homes for information on their fees and services. Ask a lot of questions about how many children are cared for per adult and what kind of attention they are given, so that you will know exactly what you will receive.

Calculating Costs

When you have gathered your information and are ready to calculate the true costs, consider both how much you are actually spending per hour and what you receive for your child-care dollar.

The cost of an in-home child caregiver will vary in different regions of the country. An article in the January 1997 issue of *Better Homes and Gardens* reported that the average cost per hour is $5.40 for a live-in nanny and $6.30 for a non-live-in nanny (Atkins, p. 24).

In our community, a moderately-sized Midwestern city, the current pay range for in-home child caregivers is $6.00 to $8.00 per hour with the higher fee range generally reserved for the care of more than one child or for caregivers with a college education or more experience. A local child-care placement service who quoted the above fee range also told me that their non–live-in nannies make at least $250 a week ($1000 for a 4-week month) and that most of their nannies work a 50-hour week (which means they're actually making a minimum of $5.00, not $6.00, an hour).[3]

When you consider the loving, personal care you get for this cost and when you take into account the hidden costs of day care, the cost of one-on-one, in-home child care can be essentially the same as the cost of care in a reputable day care center.

To calculate the true cost of day care per hour, estimate the number of hours you will actually use it. In many day care centers you are required to pay a flat rate whether or not you use the services on a full-time basis. Or, many offer part-time care for a higher fee. For example, one well-regarded child care center in our community for infants and toddlers charges a flat rate of $1000 per month for full-time care of an infant. The center is open $10\frac{1}{2}$ hours per day (7:30 A.M. to 6 P.M.). If you use their services less than $52\frac{1}{2}$ hours per week, you are actually paying more per hour. For example, if you use their services 40 hours a week, you would essentially be paying $6.25 an hour, compared to $4.76 an hour for the full $52\frac{1}{2}$ hours. This same center offers a flat daily rate of $53.00 per child for part-time care, which means you are paying $5.04 an hour for a $10\frac{1}{2}$ hour day. If your child is there less time, you are again essentially paying more per hour (e.g., $6.62 an hour if you only use the center 8 hours).

In addition, the costs increase when you have more than one child in a day care center. In the center noted above, you would be paying $8.47 an hour for two children ($4.76 for an infant and $3.71 for a toddler) based on the full $10\frac{1}{2}$ hour day).

In this fairly typical center, for $8.47, an amount slightly higher than what you would typically pay an in-home caregiver in our community to watch 2 children, your first child, an infant, would be cared for by 3 caregivers watching a total of 9 youngsters (a mixture of infants and toddlers) and your second child, a toddler, would be cared for in another room by 3 caregivers overseeing 15 other toddlers besides yours.

---

[3] Remember, you will have to pay at least the minimum wage, and you may need to take into account overtime pay. There are laws about overtime pay that apply if you employ a caregiver more than 40 hours per week. To find out about these requirements, call your state department of labor. Their phone number is in the state government section of the phone book.

Doesn't it make more sense to hire an in-home caregiver who will, for essentially the same fee, be available to pick up your infant whenever he needs to be comforted or fed rather than compete with the needs of 8 other children with only 3 caregivers? Likewise, wouldn't you want your toddler to be able to ask for help in playing a game without having to share the 3 day care workers with 15 others? For the same or less money, wouldn't you also want to reduce your children's exposure to cold and flu viruses that run rampant in these centers? In-home care would further save you money because doctor's visits and medications are costly. Likewise, wouldn't you want your toddler to be able to see his younger sibling throughout the day? With organized day care, siblings of different ages are often separated. With in-home care, your children can be together. In other words, for similar costs, you receive greater benefits, both for your child and for yourself, by using in-home care.

Estimating Benefits

Consider exactly what you are getting for your child-care dollar: In-home child care can provide assistance in running your household and freeing up your time that day care just cannot provide. For example, an in-home caregiver can often provide several hours each day of household assistance while your child is napping.

....

As a 6-month-old, my son slept 6 hours during the daytime. At age 1, he slept about 4 hours. At nearly 3, he was still taking a 2 to 3 hour nap each afternoon. When you pick up your child from a day care center or from another family's home, you don't arrive home to a clean kitchen, a salad prepared for dinner and baked potatoes in the oven; laundry washed, folded, and put away; or your stroller wiped clean from a messy Sunday at the zoo.

In-home child care can also save you on transportation costs, in terms of money and time. A hidden cost in child care outside the home is transportation. Even if you only have to transport your child 3 miles each way each day, this actually costs you an estimated $9 per week or $450 per year (based on the 30 cents standard mileage method used by the Internal Revenue Service for business travel). Transporting children is often stressful and a drain on parent's time, especially during rush hour. Having an in-home caregiver may save you an hour or more each day, de-

pending on the distance traveled. That's enough time to cook a family meal or mow the lawn or sit down at the end of a long, hectic day and read the newspaper or take a relaxing bubble-bath. Probably the number one complaint of parents with young children is not having enough time for themselves. In-home child care is a good way to get more time for yourself in a way that also benefits your child.

Another cost-saving, stress-reducing advantage of in-home care is that parents don't have to take time off from work when their child becomes ill. Your in-home caregiver is there for your child even when he is sick. As mentioned in Chapter 1, it has been estimated that it costs families using a day care center $1623 per year, per child under the age of 3, for parental lost time from work because of infectious diseases (Nurmi, Salminen, & Pönkä, 1991).

In-home care will not only save you this money, it will protect your child and family from illnesses contracted at the day care center and days of feeling miserable.

. . . .

During our son's first 3 years of life, my husband and I did not have to miss a single day of work because he was ill.

Most importantly, take into account the emotional and financial advantages in the long run of your child receiving higher quality child care. As mentioned in Chapter 1, data from the National Institute of Child Health and Human Development released in the spring of 1995 revealed that higher quality caregiving to infants most typically occurs in child-care arrangements where there are fewer children and low child to adult ratios. Furthermore, the study found that in-home caregivers, along with fathers and grandparents, offered the highest quality caregiving for infants and that child-care centers offered the lowest. It concluded that "regardless of the type of care, adult-child ratios of 1:1 best predicted high-quality caregiving . . . " (Azar, 1995). We can assume that children are more likely to thrive and be the happiest when the care they receive is excellent. Happy, secure children are more likely to develop into happy, secure teenagers and adults. How can one put a price on this care?

Although it is true, in general, that an in-home caregiver for a single child can sometimes cost slightly more per hour than other forms of child care, it is not that much more when you take into account the countless benefits like these and the hidden costs of day care. In addition, you can lower the cost of child care overall by thinking creatively and planning carefully.

STRATEGIES TO LOWER COSTS

The following are some strategies you might consider in your efforts to make in-home child care more affordable for your family. The key to success in this area is being flexible and creative. Even if these suggestions do not fit your situation, perhaps this list will help stimulate other workable ideas of your own.

Everyone's job and work schedule is different. Some places of employment are very family-oriented and willing to work around the needs of an employee raising children. Don't be afraid to ask for what you need: Your employer may allow you to switch your hours to accommodate your child-care needs. Other employers are not so flexible. In that case, perhaps your partner's job offers more flexibility, allowing him or her to provide more of the child care and thus keep the costs down.

Whatever your situation is, remain optimistic. Many families of young children face this challenge every day and discover countless ways to afford high quality in-home care for their children.

Consider the following possibilities:

- Jointly hire a caregiver with another family to care for the children in both families, sharing the costs and rotating homes.

- Arrange your work schedule with your partner so that you can each care for your child 1 day a week. If you and your partner both work 4 instead of 5 days a week, with each of you caring for your child 1 day per week, you will only need a caregiver for 3 days. If both of you work full-time, you could each work four 10-hour days instead of five 8-hour days to make this possible.

. . . .

My husband and I both rearranged our work schedules so that together, one of us was available to care for our son 3 of the 5 work days. We each put in longer days at work on those days the other was home caring for our son. We also did paperwork at home on our child-care days, logging in hours during our son's nap time. Thus, we only had to employ a part-time caregiver 2 days plus 1 evening during the week. Although our work schedules are more flexible than most parents, there are many creative ways to arrange for child care to keep the costs down.

- Rearrange parental work schedules so that one parent goes in early (e.g., 7:00 A.M. to 3:00 P.M.) and the other goes in late (noon to 8:00 P.M.). In this way, you will only have to employ a caregiver for 3 or 4 hours per day.

. . . .

My husband and I have this type of arrangement 2 days a week. He leaves for the office at 7:00 A.M., and I leave around noon. He returns home at 5:30 P.M., and I arrive home around 9:00 P.M. I am available to be with our son during these mornings (the caregiver is also there part of the time assisting me in light household chores), and my husband cares for our son during the evenings. Although our time together as a family is limited on these days, we make up for it on other days of the week.

- Hire a parent with a child (a relative, for example) who will care for your child along with theirs.

- Turn an extra bedroom or space in your home into a room or apartment for a caregiver and offer free room in exchange for child care and household assistance. Graduate students often make very good candidates for this arrangement. See Chapter 18 for information on such barter arrangements.

  I don't recommend that you offer meals with the arrangement, however. As a busy mother, I find that my meal preparation time is limited and having to cook for a caregiver also would be an unwanted stress. Your live-in caregiver can prepare their own meals and assist you in preparing meals for your child and family. In the same vein, I ask my daytime caregivers to bring their own lunch to work. In this way, I don't have to worry about having the right food on hand.

- When your child is a little older, hire a competent neighborhood teen 2 or so hours each day after school so that your regular caregiver can leave earlier.

  This practice could save you considerable money over a year's time because teen babysitters charge less. Further, the federal social security law exempts workers under the age of 18, including babysitters, from employment taxes unless they are not in school and household employment is their main occupation. For any extensive use of teenagers, check with your state or federal department of labor.

  In general, however, I do not recommend young teens for children under the age of $1\frac{1}{2}$ years.

- Arrange for a family member or friend to care for your child for a portion of the week so that your child only requires a part-time caregiver.

- Sign up for a "parent's day out program." Many churches and community centers offer these programs for toddlers and preschool children, and the cost is usually quite low. The programs are usually time-limited (e.g., 2 hours per day).

··············

At age 2, our son was enrolled in a 2-hour morning program 1 day a week, the day my husband was "on duty" all day until 6:00 P.M. This gave him a much-needed break in what otherwise might have been a long day. Best of all, our son loved "his" chance to "go to work." This program cost just slightly less than what we would have had to pay a caregiver. We used this program, however, not for its cost-saving advantages but for its original intention: to give parents a needed break and to offer children a positive social learning experience.

- If your child is 2 or older, enroll him in a high quality preschool for part of the time, using an in-home caregiver for the remainder of the time. Your caregiver can pick your child up from preschool on his way to work. Depending on the cost of the preschool, this may or may not save you money.

- Make arrangements with a friend or neighbor to swap child care. You watch their child part of the time in exchange for their caring for your child at other times. During the remainder of the time, you can employ an in-home caregiver.

- Decrease your overall expenses in order to increase your family's discretionary income. For example, you can bring your lunch to work, use grocery coupons, buy off-brand items, and shop sales for food, clothing, household items, and gifts. Or, give up one luxury expense, such as eating out frequently.

- Lastly, you can consider downsizing your lifestyle so that you can decrease the need for one or both of you to work full-time. With part-time work, the number of hours you need to employ someone will be decreased. You also will have the added benefit of spending more time with your child during these wonderful, precious years.

SUMMARY

If you are creative, flexible, and willing to make some concessions, you can afford high quality in-home child care. You will be deeply rewarded for your efforts. It is very gratifying to leave for work knowing that your child is happy and well cared for the entire time you are away. Remember, the opportunity to provide one-on-one care for your child in your home is limited: Before you realize it, he will be developmentally ready for preschool and other forms of care outside the home.

57

References

Atkins, Andrea. (1997, January). The affordable nanny. <u>Better Homes and Gardens,</u> pp. 24, 26–27.

Azar, B. (1995, June). Data released from child-care study. <u>APA Monitor,</u> p. 18.

Nurmi, T., Salminen, E., & Pönkä, A. (1991). Infections and other illnesses of children in day-care centers in Helsinki II: The economic losses. <u>Infection, 19,</u> 331–35.

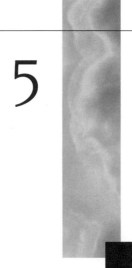

5

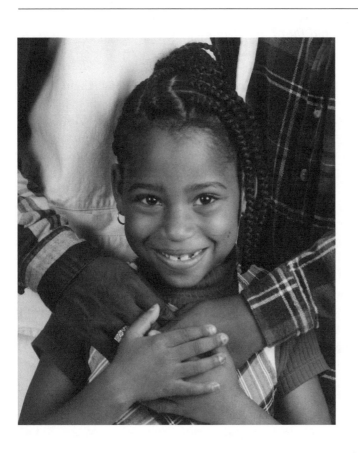

Making Your Child-Care Position Appealing to Applicants

"What can we do to attract good applicants? I have heard that caregivers are so much in demand that I am afraid we won't be able to find a good one."

Good caregivers are in demand, but you can attract them to your position by showing them what you have to offer. This chapter lists suggestions to make your job opening more appealing to highly qualified applicants. These suggestions are offered to give you an edge with good candidates. No family will be able to provide all of these benefits, but offering some will certainly help you attract fine individuals.

- Handle the application and interview process in a friendly, professional manner.

    How you handle yourself at the outset conveys an important message. It tells the applicant that you treat employees with respect, that you are organized, prompt, responsible, and friendly. One of the biggest worries job applicants have is that they won't like their new boss. The tone you set early on in this relationship can allay their fears on this matter. It will encourage excellent candidates to seriously consider your job opening because they will want to work for you.

- Conduct the interview in a quiet environment, without interruption.

    Job applicants appreciate a calm, relaxed interview that allows time for sharing all the necessary information and for discussion. For example, we arrange to speak with candidates at times when we are not caring for our son. We want to devote our full attention to the applicant and convey that selecting a caregiver for our child is a serious endeavor. Excellent candidates will take notice of this and other steps taken to manage the process well.

- Maintain a clean, organized home.

    Your home will become the caregiver's place of employment. She will spend many hours each week in this setting. Everyone likes to work in a pleasant environment. Although homes with children are often filled with toys and child-related paraphernalia, your job offering will be more appealing to good candidates if your home is organized, clean, and attractive.

- Maintain a happy, healthy atmosphere in your family.

- Be good, loving, attentive parents.

- Offer more salary or benefits.

    Although it is not necessary and there are other cost-free benefits you can offer, you can also make your child-care position more appealing by offering special benefits or financial incentives like the following:

    Pay within the high end of the salary range in your community.

    Offer to pay the employee's portion of payroll taxes (this currently represents a 7.6% increase in wages).

    Pay a portion or all of the employee's health insurance.

    Offer additional time off with pay for vacation or sick leave.

    Offer additional paid holidays.

    Promise a bonus after a period of employment (e.g., a $500 bonus at the end of each year of employment).

- Show flexibility and an interest in the caregiver's personal as well as work needs and concerns.

- - - - - - - - - - - - -

One of our caregivers wanted to change the work schedule so she could attend a class and also work around her child's schedule. She wanted to arrive later in the morning and leave a little earlier. We agreed to make the change because we not only wanted her to accept the job, we also wanted to convey sensitivity towards her needs.

- Express appreciation.

- - - - - - - - - - - - -

One of the ways I like to express my appreciation is to do something special for a caregiver that I know she will appreciate. One of our caregivers wanted an opportunity to practice her English. I frequently invited her to go on a morning walk with me and my son. We would walk to a neighborhood bakery 20 minutes away, stop for a cup of coffee, and then return home. This break gave us plenty of time to converse and allowed me to get to know her better. She is lovely, bright, and has a delightful sense of humor. Our walks together forged a friendship between us. Even now, she looks for extra ways to repay me for this opportunity, and we both receive much pleasure in giving to each other and to my son.

Qualities to Look for in a Caregiver

"I know what qualities I don't want in a caregiver. I'm just not sure, because we've never hired someone before, what qualities I do want and which are most important."

Excellent caregivers are warm and affectionate, respond to both physical and emotional needs, interact with children in a manner that stimulates cognitive development, and, according to a recent government study on child care, also tend to possess nonauthoritarian beliefs about childrearing (NICHD Early Child Care Research Network, 1996). "The caregiver with nonauthoritarian beliefs believes that children are basically good, learn actively, and should be allowed to disagree with their parents if they feel their own ideas are better, rather than believing that it is more important to teach children to value obedience and authority" (p. 283). Certain qualities, such as sensitivity towards children, are required, while other qualities, such as a good sense of humor or a fun-loving attitude may be desirable but not essential.

This chapter lists the child caregiver qualities that I believe are *required* in Box 6.1. Review the list and see if you agree. Perhaps you can add qualities that *you* feel are mandatory.

Box 6.2 lists other *desirable but not required* qualities or qualifications that one might look for in a child caregiver. The list and questionnaire in Boxes 6.1 and 6.2 were developed as an exercise to help you identify, discuss, and then decide what other caregiver assets you as a family value the most. The results of this exercise can then be used to fill in the "Personalized List of Important Caregiver Qualities" in Box 6.3. This personalized list will reflect your family's personality, values, and specific needs. Participation in this exercise will help you focus on what qualities to specifically look for during the interviewing process and when calling applicants' references.

It is important to select a caregiver who possesses the qualities *you and your partner* value most. Select a caregiver whose personality is a good match for you, your family, and your child. If you are an outgoing, fun-loving, boisterous family, for example, you may prefer someone possessing similar qualities. Likewise, if you are intellectuals, you might like a caregiver who shares your love of reading and pursuit of knowledge and can bring this to your child. Or, if your child has special needs, you will want someone who can offer what is needed. For example, if your child is shy, a quiet yet self-confident caregiver might be a good match, or you might want to look for an adult capable of heavy lifting if your child is physically handicapped and requires a great deal of lifting. Think about your particular child and family situation, and identify what type of characteristics in a caregiver would be most beneficial.[4]

---

[4] Also, remember that the requirements for a caregiver position must not necessarily exclude persons with disabilities if a reasonable accommodation (within the situation of your household) would permit them to perform the essential functions of the job.

BOX 6.1. *Required Qualifications for Child Caregivers*[5]

••

In relation to children:

Is loving, sensitive, and genuinely interested in children

Is responsive to both physical and emotional needs

Talks, interacts, and engages in activities that stimulate cognitive development

Is patient, gentle, and calm

Can be firm, yet kind, when discipline is necessary

Has realistic expectations of children based on their mental age and level of development

Has a minimum of 6 months child-care experience (can include babysitting and caring for one's own children, younger siblings, or relatives if this involved having full responsibility for the child while care was being provided)

In relation to others:

Gets along well with others

Respects self and others (e.g., can say *no* and respects other's *no's*)

Handles conflict constructively (listens and responds calmly and respectfully versus angrily or in a blaming manner)

Respects others' privacy

As a person and as an employee:

Is emotionally mature, responsible, honest, and trustworthy

Is punctual

Is flexible in finding solutions to problems

Is capable, with a reasonable accommodation, of lifting, bending, stooping, chasing, and carrying a physically active child

Possesses sound judgment and is intelligent

Has background training in emergency resuscitation procedures for children and has the ability to remain calm in a crisis or an emergency

Honors parental wishes for child care

Is able to work in a smoke-free environment without smoking breaks

Is available to hold the position for a minimum of 1 year if performance remains satisfactory

[5] Reminder: To make sure you comply with your local laws, check with your state department of labor or your state attorney general's office.

BOX 6.2. *Child Caregiver Qualities Questionnaire*

••

This questionnaire contains a list of desirable but perhaps nonessential child caregiver qualities or qualifications. It was developed to help you and your partner identify what nonessential qualities in a caregiver you value the most. It will assist you in completing your own "Personalized List of Important Caregiver Qualities" in Box 6.3, that you can use, along with the "Required Qualifications for Child Caregivers" (see Box 6.1), to guide you in selecting the right caregiver for your family.

Before interviewing applicants, you and your partner can independently complete this questionnaire and then compare and discuss your responses. Together, you can fill in your "Personalized List of Important Caregiver Qualities," which will contain those qualities that you as parents value most highly. Keep this information on hand when you interview applicants and when you contact references. See if the applicant's references spontaneously mention any of the desired qualities, or use your list to inquire about them. Taking these steps will help you stay focused on the most important qualities during the selection process.

Using the scale below, circle the response that best describes the degree of importance of each child caregiver quality or qualification:

	1	2	3	4
	Doesn't Apply	Slightly Important	Moderately Important	Very Important
Personal Attributes:				
• Enthusiastic	1	2	3	4
• Fun-loving	1	2	3	4
• Good sense of humor	1	2	3	4
• Intelligent	1	2	3	4
• Assertive	1	2	3	4
• Wise	1	2	3	4
• Self-confident	1	2	3	4
• Quiet	1	2	3	4
• Enjoys helping others	1	2	3	4
• Outgoing	1	2	3	4
• A good listener	1	2	3	4
• Financially responsible	1	2	3	4
Work Habits:				
• Hard-working	1	2	3	4
• Neat and orderly	1	2	3	4
• Well-organized	1	2	3	4
• Open to new ideas and eager to learn new things	1	2	3	4

(Continued on following page)

66

BOX 6.2. *Child Caregiver Qualities Questionnaire* (*Continued*)

	1 Doesn't Apply	2 Slightly Important	3 Moderately Important	4 Very Important
• Does things that need to be done without having to be asked	1	2	3	4
• Takes pride in a job well done	1	2	3	4
• Takes an interest and pride in a child's development	1	2	3	4
Background:				
• Well-educated	1	2	3	4
• Professionally trained in child care	1	2	3	4
• Has completed coursework in child development	1	2	3	4
• Has completed coursework in emergency medical procedures for children	1	2	3	4
• Bilingual	1	2	3	4
Other Qualifications:				
• Is available to work full-time	1	2	3	4
• Is available to work part-time	1	2	3	4
• Is available to live-in	1	2	3	4
• Is available to live-out	1	2	3	4
• Is capable and willing to care for more than one child	1	2	3	4
• Has car and is willing to use it to transport your child	1	2	3	4
• Is willing and able to transport your child in your car	1	2	3	4
• Is willing and able to do light cooking	1	2	3	4
• Is willing and able to assist with light cleaning and household chores	1	2	3	4
• Is proficient in the language spoken in your home	1	2	3	4
• Is willing to teach your child a second language	1	2	3	4
• Possesses less authoritarian beliefs about child rearing	1	2	3	4
Special Talents, Skills, or Interests:				
• Enjoys intellectual pursuits	1	2	3	4
• Creative	1	2	3	4
• Artistic	1	2	3	4
• Musical	1	2	3	4
• Athletic	1	2	3	4
• Spiritual	1	2	3	4

BOX 6.3. *Personalized List of Important Caregiver Qualities*

Fill in the qualities that you and your partner think are most important, based on your responses and discussion of the questionnaire in Box 6.2.

_____

_____

_____

_____

_____

_____

Although it is important to hire someone who possesses the qualities that you consider essential, it is also important to be realistic and not expect perfection. No one is perfect; we all have our strengths and weaknesses. It is unrealistic to expect to find someone who possesses all the qualities you desire.

No matter how thorough one might be in obtaining information about a caregiver, it is very difficult to know all there is to know about a caregiver through interviews or references. Trust your instincts and select the best qualified person. Even then, you will probably feel anxious because you are placing someone incredibly dear to you, your child, in another's hands. Feeling anxious or worried are normal responses in this process.

. . . .

I recall very clearly how anxious I felt shortly after hiring our son's first caregiver, Shan. I knew she had all of the essential qualifications we wanted but I was nonetheless worried because she was a stranger to us. My son was only 6 weeks old, and he was so tiny, so vulnerable. Now, quite a while later, I can say we made an excellent decision in hiring her. There were many things about her that I didn't know and could not have known then. Only time has allowed us to see her great capacity for love, her gentle nature, and her sincere desire to help us. Despite my initial anxieties, my intuitive instincts told me that she would be an excellent caregiver. I was right.

During the selection process, remind yourself that if a caregiver doesn't work out as planned, you can hire someone else. You owe it to yourself and to your child to replace the person if they are not providing satisfactory care. Reminding yourself that you have this option may help you overcome the normal fears associated with hiring someone to care for your child.

Reference

NICHD Early Child Care Research Network. (1996). Characteristics of infant child care: Factors contributing to positive caregiving. <u>Early Childhood Research Quarterly, 11,</u> 269–306.

7

Your First Phone Contact with an Applicant

"Won't I need to meet with each applicant? It seems like the screening process will take a lot of time."

Your first phone conversation with an applicant, if handled properly, can save you a great deal of time in the long run. This call is your first opportunity to gather vital screening information while establishing a positive relationship with someone who may become a very important person to you and your family. Making a good first impression is important. It encourages excellent candidates to take the next step and apply for the position. On the other hand, this first call can also help you to screen out unacceptable candidates, thus freeing you to focus your efforts on suitable candidates only.

The primary purpose of this first call is to screen applicants, verifying that they possess the essential qualifications before you invite them to formally apply for the position. If done properly, this call will save you considerable time; it helps ensure that you don't waste your time on individuals not suitable for the job. The purpose of this call is *not* to gather extensive information on each caller. That will be done at a later date when they complete the job application form (see Chapter 8) and are formally interviewed (see Chapter 11).

Set aside some time (ideally 30 minutes) for the call. The actual time used, however, may be very brief if the individual does not meet your basic job requirements. It is best to make this call when you are not distracted by other responsibilities, like caring for your child. If the person calls at an inconvenient time, you can offer to return the call at a mutually agreeable time.

The "Initial Phone Call Form For In-Home Child-Care Applicants" in Box 7.1 is set up so that parents can quickly screen applicants. You can place this book in front of you during the call and take notes on a separate sheet of paper. The form's sections are numbered to assist you in note-taking. Or, you can use the book's optional computer diskette containing all the book's forms (see Appendix A for ordering information), adapt the form to suit your needs, and take notes directly on your copy. Your notes will be very helpful to you later when you are keeping track of information from several different applicants.

During this call, pay attention not only to the direct information the applicant is giving you about herself but also to the indirect or nonverbal messages, and make notes of your first impressions in the space provided at the end of the form. For example, an applicant who calls with screaming children in the background is giving you very valuable information about her own household. Or, the tone of the caller's voice will tell you such things as her level of enthusiasm for the job or her degree of self-confidence. Or, you may assess the individual's expertise with English if she is bilingual or her use of improper grammar if she is a native speaker.

BOX 7.1. *Initial Phone Call Form for In-Home Child-Care Applicants*

Date: _____

Applicant's Name: _____

Address: _____

Phone Numbers: _____(H) _____(W)

Best Times to Call: _____

INTRODUCTION AND OVERVIEW OF THE POSITION

Sample Script:

"Thank you so much for calling and showing an interest in this position. My husband and I are both employed, and we have a 3-year-old daughter, Jane. We are looking for someone with experience caring for preschool children who can care for her in our home 32 hours a week, Mondays through Thursdays, from 7:30 A.M. to 3:30 P.M., beginning the first week of September. The salary for the position will be $_____ per hour, which is $_____ per week."

"Jane's current caregiver is returning to school full-time, so we are looking for her replacement. We were very pleased with her and will miss her. We are looking forward, however, to having a new person on board. Jane, a social little girl, asks at least 20 questions an hour, and has developed very nice connections with her caregivers in the past. Our previous caregivers have become like family to us, and we are looking for someone special who is a good match for all of us."

This is a good time to mention important information that may make a difference to the applicant, such as the following:

"We are also preparing as a family for a new baby. I am expecting a child in 6 months."

"We are planning to move across town to the Kirkland area next summer."

IMPORTANT QUESTIONS TO ASK

• Obtain information about how the applicant came to apply:
"How did you learn about this job opening?"

• Ask about availability:
"If hired, would you be available to start work the first week of September?"
"Would you be available Mondays through Thursdays, from 7:30 A.M. to 3:30 P.M.?"

(Continued on following page)

- Obtain information regarding other job requirements:
  "Do you have your own car, a current driver's license, and insurance so that you can transport Jane to and from special activities?"
  "Do you have a green card or working papers?" This is an important question to ask an immigrant applicant.
  "Do you have experience caring for infants? If so, can you tell me about it?"

- Ask about factors that might disqualify a candidate:
  "Can you work in a smoke-free environment during the entire workday without a cigarette break?"
  "We want to prevent our child from experiencing unnecessary loss caused by a high turnover of caregivers. Assuming you were able to perform the job satisfactorily, would you be available to hold this job for at least 1 year?"

- Obtain basic information about the applicant and his/her level of interest in the job:
  "Can you tell me about yourself and your interest in this position?"

You can then ask follow-up questions about background experiences and training in child care and any other questions that will help you determine whether you want to invite this applicant to formally apply for the position.

Remember, keep this call as brief as possible, obtaining only the most necessary information, because a lot of background information will be provided on the job application form.

Generally, don't invite someone for a job interview until after s/he has completed the job application form and read the child-care agreement: You risk wasting your time with unsuitable candidates if you invite them to interview before they have more information about the job and you have more information from them.

DISCUSS SALARY

Sample Script:
"As I mentioned earlier, the salary for this position is $_____ per hour, which is $_____ per week. Would this be acceptable to you if we offered you the position and you were interested in taking the job?"

(Continued on following page)

_____ (Check) This applicant indicated that this salary offer was acceptable.

If the salary offered is unacceptable but you are still interested in the applicant and willing to negotiate further, you can ask, *"What salary amount did you have in mind?"* and then discuss this amount with him/her.

It is helpful to keep in mind that you do not have to make a firm decision about a negotiated salary at this time. You can say, for example, *"Your salary request is higher than we planned on paying, but I am willing to consider it. I would want to get to know more about you and what you would have to offer before deciding if your request would be agreeable to us. If you are interested, you could apply for the position, and then we could negotiate the salary if you are offered the position. Are you interested in this arrangement?"*

ASK IF THEY HAVE ANY QUESTIONS OR SPECIAL NEEDS

• *"Do you have any questions about us or the job? Are there any special needs that you have?"*

INVITING THE APPLICANT TO APPLY FOR THE POSITION

If, at this point, you have determined that you would like to invite the person to apply for the position, you can ask if s/he is interested. You could say, for example, *"Are you interested in applying for this position?"* If s/he is interested, you can explain, *"We are asking all applicants to complete a job application form so that we can best determine if you have the background and child-care skills we are looking for. We will call you within 1 week of receiving your completed application to let you know whether we have decided to consider you further and to ask you to come in for interviews."*

If the applicant is interested in applying, you can obtain the correct spelling of his/her name, the address, phone numbers, etc., filling this information in at the top of the form.

If you are <u>not</u> interested in this applicant, you can thank them for calling and explain, *"At this time, I am doing a preliminary screening of all applicants by phone. If we decide that we would like you to complete a job application and come in for an interview, I will get back to you within 24 hours. Thank you so much for your time and expressing an interest in us."*

(Continued on following page)

ENDING THE CONVERSATION AND THANKING THE APPLICANT FOR CALLING

"Thank you so much for your time and showing an interest in our position."

OPENING THE APPLICANT FILE

To keep things organized, you can then place this form and all further correspondence related to this applicant in a file with his/her name on it.

MAILING OUT THE APPLICATION PACKET

If you and this applicant are interested in beginning the formal application process, you can then mail the applicant a packet of application materials including (1) the Job Announcement (see Boxes 3.1–3.3), (2) the Job Application Form (see Box 8.1), and (3) the Child-Care Agreement Form (see Box 9.1).

Place an extra copy of the Child-Care Agreement Form in the applicant's file so that you have a record of the exact document the applicant received and the date it was given to him/her. If you ever need to check what information your caregiver was given, this copy will be readily available to you.

Document below what materials were sent when.

DOCUMENTATION OF APPLICATION MATERIALS SENT

_____ (Check) An application packet containing ___ the job announcement, ___ job application form, and __ child-care agreement were mailed on _____.

_____ (Check) An extra copy of the child-care agreement has been placed in the applicant's employment file.

FURTHER COMMENTS ABOUT THIS APPLICANT

Write notes on any initial impressions, concerns, strengths, or weaknesses of the applicant you observed in this first phone call. List any of your concerns you will want to investigate further during the job interview and with job references.

Your initial reactions, no matter how minor they may seem, can offer valuable insight into a candidate. By paying attention to these reactions, you can identify personal characteristics that otherwise may not be obvious until much later.

The "Initial Phone Call Form For In-Home Child-Care Applicants" in Box 7.1 will help guide you through your first phone call with an applicant. Its use will help ensure that you ask the essential questions and cover all the important information so that your job selection process gets off to a good start. You and your partner may want to review this form in advance to tailor it to your particular needs. The data you gather during the initial phone call and document on this form will then become an important part of your job applicant's file.

. . . .

A NOTE ON IMMIGRANT APPLICANTS

I always make special accommodations for applicants who are in the process of learning English. I have found that many immigrants feel uncomfortable speaking on the phone until they are fairly confident and competent in speaking English. Many prefer to speak in person and usually function much better with eye-to-eye contact. For these reasons, I usually get enough information over the phone to determine if the person has the basic requirements for the position, and then I immediately schedule an interview. I also do not ask the applicant to complete the application form until after the first interview. Again, this accommodation is because many immigrants' written English language skills are not on an equal basis with those of native speakers. They may, nonetheless, be excellent candidates, and I want to do everything I can to encourage them to apply. I also want the interviewing process to go as smoothly as possible for them. Sometimes I will initially speak to an applicant's partner, if his English is more advanced, and welcome him to accompany the applicant to the job interview.

The Job Application Form

"There is so much I would want to know about someone before I could trust them to care for my child. How can I gather all this information without having to spend time that I don't have?"

This chapter's "Job Application Form for an In-Home Child Caregiver" (Box 8.1) will enable you to gather essential information about an applicant quickly and efficiently. It can be abbreviated or tailored to meet your needs. When it is completed, you will have well-organized, written information on an applicant's academic, employment, and child-care qualifications and background, and on the applicant's philosophy about caring for children. It also contains important questions that will help you screen out unsuitable applicants. Many of these questions are easier to ask in questionnaire form than in person. This format ensures that this vital information is gathered in a sensitive manner for both the parent and the applicant.

The completed application serves as an excellent screening device. It will help you decide whether you want to invest further time in the applicant by inviting him for an interview. Suggestions on how to use the completed application as a screening tool are included in Chapter 10.

A real bonus of the application form is that time is spent by the applicants, not you, providing the necessary information and demonstrating their suitability and interest in the job. Busy parents can reserve their very limited time for those candidates who possess the best qualifications.

The completed application form will also help you make the job interview productive and positive. Not only will it help you prepare for the interview and determine what additional background information you would like to obtain or explore further, but it will also allow you to be more relaxed during the interview because you will already know a lot about the applicant. The interview can therefore be more spontaneous, providing an opportunity for you and the applicant to get to know each other.

One of the major benefits of having a completed application form is that it helps ensure that you have a broad base of information on the individual who will be working or living in your home and caring for your child. This information, which can be verified by other supporting information such as criminal record and child abuse and neglect background checks (see Chapter 12), will bring you much peace of mind. It helps ensure that you know who you are hiring.

The last section of the application form, "Additional Background Information," contains important questions that will help you screen out individuals with a history of serious problems or with a criminal or child abuse record. If an individual lies on this section, there is a very good chance you will discover the problem when you call his references or conduct the criminal record or child abuse and neglect background checks.

As mentioned previously, you will need to make sure that any suggestions or forms that you might use in this or any other chapter in this book are consistent with the laws and regulations in your location and time. I am not an attorney, and this book is not intended to provide legal advice, but rather suggestions and forms that will give you a good place to start. Because laws vary among localities, and interpretations of these laws can change, it is wise to get competent, legal advice from a professional in your area.

In summary, the "Job Application Form for an In-Home Child Caregiver" in Box 8.1 will provide essential information on each job applicant. You can use the completed form as a screening device, inviting only those candidates possessing the best credentials for an interview. This process will also screen out less serious applicants who will not be motivated to complete the form. Many important questions that are difficult to ask in person are included. Using this form will make it possible for the actual job interview to be more relaxed because the most critical background questions will already have been addressed. You may copy the form from this book or adapt and print it on your personal computer, using this book's optional computer diskette containing all the book's forms (see Appendix A for ordering information).

BOX 8.1. *Job Application Form for an In-Home Child Caregiver*

EMPLOYER'S NAME: _____

ADDRESS: _____

_____

PHONE NUMBER: _____

Please print or type. Write N/A (not applicable) in the blank if a question does not apply to you. Use additional paper for any questions requiring further space, explanation or clarification, indicating the specific question to which you are responding.

We are an equal opportunity employer.

IDENTIFYING INFORMATION:

Name: _____ Date: _____

Home phone: _____ Business phone: _____

Present Address: _____
_____ ZIP: _____
Dates From/To? _____

Permanent Address: _____
_____ ZIP: _____

Permanent phone: _____

Previous Address: _____
_____ ZIP: _____
Dates From/To? _____

On a separate sheet of paper, please list the full address of each additional place you lived in the past 5 years and the dates you lived at each location.

For access purposes, please list any other names you have used if your work records are under another name:

_____

Please provide your driver's license information if driving will be part of your job duties:

Driver's license number: _____ State: _____

(*Continued on following page*)

Note: All employers, including household employers, are required by The Immigration Reform and Control Act of 1986 to hire only individuals authorized to be employed.

Are you authorized to be employed in the United States? _____

Person to contact in event of an emergency:

Name: _____ Relationship: _____

Address: _____ Phone: _____

Military service:

Dates of Service: _____ Branch of Service: _____

Highest Rank: _____

Academic preparation:

• **High School**

Name: _____ Location: _____

Class Rank: _____

• **G.E.D.**

G.E.D. Test Score: _____

Issuing State: _____

• **Vocational-Technical Training**

School Name: _____ Location: _____

Area of Study: _____ Certificate Earned: _____

• **College/University**

Name: _____ Location: _____

G.P.A.: _____ Major: _____

Degree Earned: _____

Name: _____ Location: _____

G.P.A.: _____ Major: _____

Degree Earned: _____

(*Continued on following page*)

83

- **Other Relevant Academic Training or Course Work**

Please describe:

_____

_____

- **Extracurricular Activities and Honors**

Please describe:

_____

_____

Previous experience working with children (Private, Professional or Other Organizations):

<u>Name</u>   <u>Address</u>   <u>Dates</u>   <u>Assignment</u>   <u>Colleague/Supervisor</u>

_____

_____

_____

_____

_____

Hobbies, special skills, interests, qualifications, talents:

_____

_____

Background training in emergency resuscitation procedures (CPR) for children (Please also note any recertification):

Type of training and location: _____

_____

        Dates: _____

Type of training and location: _____

_____

        Dates: _____

(Continued on following page)

Job references (nonrelatives only please):

Please list at least 3 references who have known you well, preferably in the last several years. Include at least 2 employment references and someone who has known you for at least 5 years.

Name and Address   Business or   Relationship   Phone
                   Occupation   (Employer,
                                 Coworker)

1. _____
   _____
   _____
   Length of Relationship (include dates): _____

2. _____
   _____
   _____
   Length of Relationship (include dates): _____

3. _____
   _____
   _____
   Length of Relationship (include dates): _____

4. _____
   _____
   _____
   Length of Relationship (include dates): _____

I authorize the release of any or all information regarding my person, past or present employment, or any other aspect, whether personal or otherwise, and do hereby further release and agree to hold harmless any individual, company, organization, or entity from any and all liability or damage whatsoever that may develop from furnishing such information to my potential employer identified above at the top of this application form.

_____   _____   _____
Signature   Date   Witness

(Continued on following page)

Present employment:

Company Name and Address: _____

_____

_____

Phone: _____

Job Title and Description: _____

_____

Number of Hours per Week: _____

Dates of Employment: _____

Supervisor's Name: _____

Previous employment:

Please list all jobs held in at least the past 3 years, using additional pages if necessary. Or, please attach a current resume.

1. Company Name and Address: _____

_____

_____

Phone: _____

Job Title and Description: _____

_____

Number of Hours per Week: _____

Dates of Employment: _____

2. Company Name and Address: _____

_____

_____

Phone: _____

Job Title and Description: _____

_____

Number of Hours per Week: _____

Dates of Employment: _____

(Continued on following page)

Language proficiency:

Do you speak English as a second language? ___ Yes ___ No
If so, please indicate the level of your fluency (i.e., average, above average, below average, or like a native) in speaking, reading, and writing English.

Speaking: _____

Reading: _____

Writing: _____

Do you speak, read, or write any other languages besides English?
___ Yes ___ No

Please indicate which languages you are skilled in (including your native language if other than English) and your level of fluency in speaking, reading, and writing.

Languages: _____

Speaking: _____

Reading: _____

Writing: _____

Would you be willing to teach my child a second language?

_____

On a separate sheet of paper, please describe (1) your philosophy about raising children, (2) your philosophy and approach to disciplining children, and (3) why you are interested in this position.

Would you be available to work at the following specified times? (Please note *yes* or *no*.)

_____

_____

_____

(Continued on following page)

ADDITIONAL BACKGROUND INFORMATION:

Instructions: Please answer all questions. Give an explanation for any *yes* questions on an attached sheet of paper, and write the number of the question at the beginning of each explanation.

      Yes No

I. ___ ___ Have you ever been convicted for any reason by any law enforcement authority either in the United States or outside this country, excluding misdemeanors?

2. ___ ___ Have you ever engaged in any undetected criminal activity (e.g., buying or selling drugs or stealing)?

3. ___ ___ Have you ever been expelled from any school?

4. ___ ___ Have you ever had excessive absences from work or been counseled on the job for tardiness or excessive absences that were unrelated to any disability?

5. ___ ___ Have you ever been fired, dismissed, or asked to resign from any job?

6. ___ ___ Have you ever stolen any money or material goods from any job?

7. ___ ___ Do you currently abuse a controlled substance (e.g., marijuana, cocaine, or LSD)?

If driving will be part of your job responsibilities, please answer items 8-11.

      Yes No

8. ___ ___ Have you ever had your motor vehicle license suspended or revoked?

9. ___ ___ Have you received any driving citations, tickets, or summons in the past 2 years?

10 ___ ___ Have you been involved in any traffic accidents in the past 5 years? If so, please explain how many and if you were considered "at fault."

11. ___ ___ Has your automobile insurance ever been canceled, or have you ever been denied insurance by any company?

12. ___ ___ Have you ever found yourself feeling angry at a child under your care?

(Continued on following page)

Yes   No

13. ___ ___ Is there any aspect of the job as described in the en-closed Child-Care Agreement that you would be un-able to fulfill (with or without a reasonable accommo-dation) for any reason whatsoever?

14. ___ ___ Have you ever been in a situation where you felt spanking was the best way to handle a discipline prob-lem?

15. ___ ___ Is there any information about yourself we did not ask about that you would like to voluntarily share with us?

16. ___ ___ Have you ever been placed on permanent record in any state for child abuse or neglect?

17. ___ ___ Have you ever felt exhausted caring for a child?

18. ___ ___ Can you work in a smoke-free environment during an entire workday without a cigarette break?

19. ___ ___ Will you be able to work the hours requested with reg-ularity and predictability, as required by the job?

20. ___ ___ Are you able to lift, bend, stoop, chase, carry, and en-gage in other physical activities necessary to care for an active, young child, with or without reasonable ac-commodation?

I have received and read the Child-Care Agreement specifying the responsibilities and duties of this job.

I understand and agree that I could be dismissed for any false or misleading statements or omissions contained in this application.

I understand that any employment with you would be entered into voluntarily and that I could resign at any time. Similarly, my employ-ment could be terminated for any reason and at any time without pre-vious notice.

_____   _____

Signature   Date

At a later point, you may be requested to undergo a complete or partial background search involving criminal, driving, and automobile insurance; child abuse and neglect records; academic transcripts; and emergency medical training for children certification. You may also be asked to provide verification from your physician that you do not have an infectious or communicable disease.

9

The Child-Care Agreement Form

"If I go through all this trouble hiring someone, I want to make sure she will take good care of my child. How can I let her know in advance what I will expect?"

THE ADVANTAGES OF USING A CHILD-CARE AGREEMENT FORM

A child-care agreement form provides both the caregiver and the parent clear guidelines. By putting your expectations in writing in the form of a child-care agreement, you give the child caregiver a clear understanding of the job requirements and expectations at the time of hiring. If these are not explicit and in writing, there is a greater chance for misunderstanding and upset.

The child-care agreement can be attached to the application form so that the applicant is fully informed of the job's parameters before investing time in completing the application. This step will ultimately save you time because you will not spend time interviewing applicants who are not truly interested in or suitable for the position.

Another advantage of developing a child-care agreement is that it will help you clarify what you want and expect from the caregiver. There are many different ways to care for children that reflect one's child-care philosophies and values. One of the advantages of having a caregiver come into your home is that you have greater control over the quality of care. For example, you can ensure that your child is not exposed to inappropriate television programs, inadequate attention, or harsh discipline. You can also ensure that your child *is* exposed to books, music, healthy meals, adequate exercise, and attention from a caring adult. Taking time to develop your own child-care agreement will be time well invested. The agreement will serve as the basic foundation of your employer-employee relationship.

MODIFYING THE CHILD-CARE AGREEMENT

The child-care agreement will change as your child gets older. For example, you will want to specify that you do not want your infant under 1 year of age to be placed on the tummy (a risk factor for sudden infant death syndrome) or that you want sunscreen to be put on your baby when she is at risk for sunburn, but only after 6 months of age. Caring for children involves acquiring a great deal of information that at times can be quite detailed. The child-care agreement allows you to pass along the

most vital information in a format that is easily understood and available for later review.

Box 9.1 contains a sample child-care agreement with an addendum that can be attached for live-in caregivers. The sample agreement states reasonable expectations of a caregiver of a single child. The content of an agreement may vary somewhat according to the number of children or the particular needs of the family. You may use this sample agreement as is, tailor it for your situation, or develop your own. Many parents err in either asking too little or too much of their caregiver. I offer this agreement as a sample that has worked well for us and has been positively received by all our job applicants and caregivers.

I use the child-care agreement with my caregivers as a job description, to facilitate communication and understanding, and not as a legal document per se. Some parents, however, may elect to draw up a legal document for the caregiver to sign. If you decide to take this step, you can use the sample agreement as a foundation and ask your family attorney to review the document and build indemnification (liability) and other protections into the document.

As with this book's other forms, you can either photocopy the child-care agreement directly from the book or from the book's optional computer diskette (see Appendix A for ordering information) and adapt it to suit your needs.

NEGOTIATING THE CHILD-CARE AGREEMENT

On occasion, one may need to renegotiate the child-care agreement. For instance, some child caregivers take a position that they "don't do housework." This issue often evokes strong feelings on the part of both parents and caregivers and needs to be addressed. I think it is best to take a middle ground on the issue. It is very important for parents not to take advantage of caregivers and unrealistically expect them to do housecleaning while also caring for a child. On the other hand, it is reasonable to ask a caregiver to assist with light household chores like tidying a child's room or doing laundry, light cooking, or dishes during the large blocks of time each day when a child is napping.

• • • • • • • • • • • • • •

An Example

I do not expect a caregiver to do anything else while watching my child. I do, however, expect assistance with light household chores during our son's

naptime (which has varied from 2 to 6 hours daily) and after a nice meal break. Nevertheless, this aspect of the child-care agreement is always negotiable, and the salary can be set accordingly. For example, I employed one caregiver who was interested in providing child care but with limited household responsibilities. Instead of assisting me with household tasks, she wanted to use the time to do homework. Because I felt confident that she would provide excellent care for our child, I renegotiated the agreement to accommodate her request. I have discovered that my willingness to be flexible to accommodate my employees' needs always pays off in the long run. I have found that if I am willing to make concessions for them, they are in turn willing to do the same for me. This particular caregiver also asked me if I would be willing to change the time she was to report to work each day so that she could attend an English language class. I was able to do that, and she then felt good about accepting our job offer.

It is much easier to establish rules and expectations at the time of hiring than at a later date. If you wait or are not explicitly clear, there is a great risk that your caregiver will resent you because her expectations may differ greatly from your own. All of the excellent caregivers I have employed have told me that they really appreciated receiving my detailed child-care agreement. They said that it reassured them that their employment was going to be handled in a professional, organized manner. They felt reassured knowing exactly what would be expected of them.

As mentioned earlier, the sample child-care agreement can be tailored to meet your needs: Develop a document that suits you and does a good job of representing your wishes and needs. Do not be afraid to spell things out in even greater detail if you wish. Make reasonable requests, however. If you are in doubt, you can ask friends with children (preferably parents who have hired caregivers in their home) if they would review your agreement. It is sometimes difficult, before you have children and employ caregivers, to anticipate what arrangements are reasonable.

(Note: The forms mentioned in this agreement can be found as follows: "A Report on Our Child's Day" in Box 17.1, an "Emergency Information Sheet" in Box 16.4, a "Consent Form For Emergency Medical Care" in Box 16.2, and a "Monthly Time Sheet And Pay Form" in Box 18.2.)

BOX 9.1. *Child-Care Agreement Form*
••

Employer's Names: _____

Child's Name and Age: _____

_____

Address: _____

_____

Phone Number: _____

This position involves caring for the following child:

_____

Our child has the following special needs:

_____

_____

_____

_____

    The following agreement clarifies our expectations so that you will know, in advance, what we are looking for and to help you decide if you are well-suited for this position. Furthermore, this document contains information about our household and other helpful information. If you have any questions or require additional information, please give us a call.

    We want to offer this position to someone who is available to work with us for a minimum of 1 year, assuming satisfactory job performance. Please do not apply if you are unable to make that commitment. Thank you for your time and your interest in applying for this job.

Salary: $_____ per hour/$_____ per hour overtime (for work in excess of 40 hours per week)/$_____ per week

    You will be paid at the end of each month (unless other arrangements are made with us). Your earnings will be reported for tax purposes. You will be required to fill out the necessary tax and other required employment forms when you begin employment. Your portion of the payroll taxes owed will *not* be deducted from each paycheck. We will pay these payroll taxes (Social Security and Medicare

(Continued on following page)

BOX 9.1. *Child-Care Agreement Form* (Continued)

taxes) for you as a job benefit, which are equal to 7.6% of your wages.

You, of course, are responsible for filing your own federal and state income tax returns and paying any income taxes owed. We respectfully will not agree to withhold any federal income tax from your paychecks (an allowable option for household employers) because of the extra paperwork involved.

We will give you a "Monthly Time Sheet and Pay Form" to keep track of your hours. Please fill out this form before leaving each day and turn it in to us on your last workday of the month.

Transportation:

We expect that you will provide your own transportation to and from work. However, if your car breaks down or you are afraid to drive because of bad weather, we will be glad to help you if possible. If we are unable to assist you, we expect you to find another means of transportation, such as getting a ride from a friend, hiring a taxi, or taking public transportation.

Food:

We would appreciate if you would bring your own food, snacks, and beverages each day. We have found that this simplifies things for us and ensures that your nutritional needs are met. We want you to feel at home in our kitchen and throughout our home. If you need space to store some of your food items, please let us know. On most days you will have time for a quiet, restful meal during our child's nap.

Duties:

1. Care for our child on the following days and times:

_____

_____

These hours may change in the future, with your prior approval.

Our child's well-being and safety will always need to be your foremost concern. You will not be expected to do any other chores while caring for our child unless (1) you are comfortable doing so while monitoring him/her or (2) s/he is asleep. Likewise, we do not want you to be preoccupied with other activities, such as talking on the

(Continued on following page)

BOX 9.1. *Child-Care Agreement Form* (Continued)

phone, doing homework, or watching TV, while caring for our child.

Activities. As our child gets older, you may introduce him/her, on a limited basis, to educational TV programs or videos that are appropriate for young children. We do not want him/her exposed to endless hours of television, videos, or media involving violence or adult topics (including talk shows, newscasts, violent cartoons, TV shows, or movies).

We want you to make *his/her* needs a priority and engage in the following type of activities with him/her: floor level play and activities such as running, jumping, climbing, walking, reading, singing, dancing, and drawing. *We want you to talk and interact with our child in a calm, pleasant, patient, and joyful manner. Most of all, we want you to have fun together!*

This job requires an individual who is capable of lifting, stooping, bending, carrying, and other physical activities necessary to care for an active young child. You will be required to work in a smoke-free environment during the entire workday without a cigarette break.

Care. We will also expect you to feed, diaper, and bathe our child as well as ensure that s/he gets adequate sleep and rest. It is very important to us that our child be exposed to healthy, nutritious food. We will always have fresh milk, juice, fruits, vegetables, meats, grains, legumes, and breads available. *To prevent scald burns, please check the temperature of foods and liquids before serving them to our child.* Please do not give our child candy or sweets without our permission.

Please do not introduce our child to any new foods or beverages without our explicit permission. Also, please do not give our child any prescription or nonprescription medication unless specifically instructed to do so by one of us in writing or over the phone. If you are ever in doubt about something, please check with us first.

If we need you to administer medication, we will leave written instructions, whenever possible, to help prevent error. We will also expect you to document in writing the time and the amount of medication administered on a form that we provide entitled "A Report On Our Child's Day." A list of foods that can cause choking are listed on our refrigerator door. Please do not allow our child to have access to these food items.

We expect you to keep our child clean, washing his/her hands and face throughout the day. On occasion, we will request that you bathe our child. *Please check the temperature of the water before*

(Continued on following page)

BOX 9.1. *Child-Care Agreement Form* (Continued)

placing our child in the bath tub. To help prevent scalding, our hot water heater is set below 120° F. We also expect you to change his/her diaper frequently throughout the day whenever it becomes wet or soiled.

You will be expected to complete the form "A Report on Our Child's Day," which documents his/her intake of food and liquids, sleep, elimination, and periods of fussiness.

General. One of the major reasons we have our child cared for in our home is that we believe it provides more opportunity for nurturance and attention to physical, emotional, cognitive, and social needs. The role you will play in this area is very important, and we will count on you to help us provide excellent care for our child during these formative years.

As our child grows and develops, we will want you to engage in activities that stimulate and nurture his/her all-around development. We will sometimes suggest special activities for you to do with our child. We will also share brief written materials about our child's current stage of development and special needs. We will expect you to read these materials (while our child is napping, for example) and will also welcome any of your ideas and suggestions on promoting healthy growth and development.

Because there are many different ways to care for a child, there may be some occasions when we disagree on how to handle a particular situation involving our child. We will expect that you will honor our wishes in *all* situations. Please know, however, that we are open to your ideas and feelings on any matter and we will expect you to communicate openly with us. Perhaps through discussion, we can negotiate an alternative way of handling things so that we both feel comfortable. Of course, there may be some issues that we as parents will not feel are negotiable, and we will expect you to honor our wishes. If you are not able to do so, please speak to us about this right away.

We do not want you to ever hit or spank our child or make hurtful comments as a means of discipline. We do not want you to speak to our child in a manner that may harm his/her self esteem. This includes name-calling (e.g., "you're a big baby") and derogatory comments, such as "you're bad" or "you're lazy." As we go along, we will share with you discipline strategies that we are comfortable with and that are effective. In general, we want you to discipline with kindness and firmness, not harshness.

(*Continued on following page*)

BOX 9.1. *Child-Care Agreement Form* (Continued)

We want you to be calm and patient in helping our child accomplish new developmental tasks such as walking, talking, toilet training, and confronting fearful situations. Please do not pressure or force our child to do something new that is uncomfortable or frightening for him/her. Also, please do not tease or belittle our child about his/her shortcomings in new skill areas. We believe that s/he will accomplish these new tasks at his/her own pace. Finally, we want our child to feel good about his/her body, and we do not want you to tell him/her that exploration or touching of private body parts is bad or wrong.

2. Assist us in housekeeping chores.

Housekeeping chores will include activities such as the following: picking up toys and straightening our child's room, doing laundry, washing dishes and wiping off kitchen countertops, helping prepare a meal, ironing, mending, and light housecleaning as needed, such as emptying a waste basket, sweeping a room, or wiping the interior shelves of the refrigerator.

This household assistance will only be expected if our child is not requiring your attention, is asleep, or is with an adult family member. There will be 2 to 6 hours each day in which our child will be asleep. Although we will sometimes leave a list of things needing done if you have time, we would also greatly appreciate if you would do things that you see need to be done as time allows.

We expect you to keep things picked up throughout the day so that the house is as orderly and tidy, if not more so, as when you arrived. We will continue to employ our regular housecleaner and be involved in caring for our home along with you. If we are home and available to care for our child while you are here, we may prefer to be with him/her and have you help out in this other way.

3. Learn and stay updated on how to perform emergency infant and child resuscitation techniques.

Depending on how recent and extensive your training, we may require you to take additional training in this area. In this event, we will pay for the course but not for your time attending the course. Or, we may ask you to view training videos on this topic. We will provide the videos but expect you to view them while our child is napping or on your own time.

In addition, we keep written summary materials on important emergency medical procedures for children. We expect you to read

(Continued on following page)

BOX 9.1. *Child-Care Agreement Form* (Continued)

and review these materials on a regular basis. These materials are stored in a file and are kept beneath your time sheets.

Vacation/Sick Days/Illness/Holidays:

You will receive 1 paid vacation day per number of days worked per week for each 6-month period worked. In other words, if you work 3 days weekly, you will be entitled to 3 paid vacation days at the end of each 6-month period. We request that you give us at least 1 month's notice of your plans to take vacation so that we can make alternative arrangements for our child's care.

We plan on being away _____ weeks each year although this may vary from year to year. We will give you at least 1 month's notice of our travel plans so that you will have adequate time to plan for this time off. You will not be paid for these days that we are on vacation unless you plan to use part or all of this time for your paid vacation.

You will also receive 1 paid sick day per number of days worked per week for each 6-month period worked. In other words, if you work 4 days a week, you will earn 4 sick days at the end of each 6-month period. You will be paid for all earned sick days that are not used. If you are ill, please give us as much advance notice as possible. If you know the day or evening before that you might have to miss work the following day because of illness, please let us know at that time.

If you are sick with a less serious contagious illness like a cold or the flu, we want you to let us know as soon as possible and before caring for our child. We may ask you to take sick leave or wear a face mask to prevent the spread of infection. Likewise, if you develop a more serious contagious illness that would pose a serious health risk to our child, we require you to inform us immediately.

To prevent the spread of infectious disease, please wash your hands after changing a diaper, using the restroom, and before and after handling food or feeding our child. In general, we expect you to wash your hands with soap frequently throughout the day. Please only use clean, disposable tissues to wipe our child's nose and dispose of them immediately.

We will try to inform you when our child is sick so that you can take the necessary precautions and stay as healthy as possible.

If you become pregnant while caring for our child, you need to talk with your physician about your risk of exposure to infectious disease in the child-care environment. Some childhood illnesses do not pose

(Continued on following page)

BOX 9.1. *Child-Care Agreement Form* (Continued)

a problem unless you are pregnant, and a physician can list these for you.

After we hire you but before you care for our child, you will be required to undergo an infectious and communicable disease medical checkup to make sure that you are not a carrier of a disease like hepatitis B or tuberculosis.

The following days are *holidays* that you will *not* be required to work.

Memorial Day
Independence Day
Labor Day
Thanksgiving Day
Christmas Eve and Christmas Day
New Year's Day

You will receive 1 paid holiday per year for each day worked per week. In other words, if you work 5 days a week, you will receive 5 paid holidays per year.

We hope that you will be willing to be flexible and accommodate our special days and occasions, and we want to be able to do the same for you. If you have a special event in your life, please let us know and we will try to accommodate you. Give us as much advance notice as possible if you wish to change your work schedule. We will also try to extend the same courtesy to you.

Other Expectations and Requests:

Please do not have someone else watch our child for you, even for a minute, without first asking for our permission. The only exception to this rule is in the event of an emergency.

Please do not ever leave our child unattended unless s/he is asleep, and then we expect you to listen for the monitor and check periodically. Especially, please do not ever leave our child unattended, even for a few seconds, in the bathtub or in a bathroom, near a body of water, on a bed, or the changing table. Please do not ever place him/her on a countertop or any surface where s/he might fall and injure him/herself. Do not ever leave our child, awake or asleep, in our home alone or in a car unattended, even for a minute.

Please take every precaution to ensure that our child is safe at all times. Please remember that small objects and certain foods are very dangerous for young children because they can very easily

(*Continued on following page*)

BOX 9.1. *Child-Care Agreement Form* (Continued)

choke. Please protect him/her from open toilets, electrical outlets and cords, hanging cords, drawstrings on clothing, stairways, and poisonous substances, such as household-cleaning products, medications, and vitamins. When needed, there will be child safety locks on all of our floor-level cabinets and stairway safety gates. Please make sure they are latched shut at all times. Please protect our child from falls from windows, stairs, playground equipment, and furniture. Do not ever allow our child to stand up in a grocery cart (one of the most common causes of serious head and neck injuries in children). Make sure s/he is buckled up in the cart and sitting at all times.

Please protect our child from sunburn by using protective clothing, applying sunscreen, and keeping him/her in the shade during the midday hours. The stroller has a sunshade. Please make sure it is in use at these times.

Please do not take our child in a car without our prior permission. If you would like to take him/her somewhere special like the zoo or shopping center, please discuss this with us in advance. This provision does not include walks in the neighborhood or to the park.

(Check one of the following:)

_____ You will be expected to transport our child in (check one) _____ your vehicle _____ our vehicle.

_____ You will not be expected to transport our child in a vehicle.

Explanation (List other forms of transportation expected, and state how the needs for transportation might change over time. For example, you might write, "In 6 months, we will expect you to transport our child on the subway to and from his/her piano lessons."):

_____

_____

_____

If you use your own car for transporting our child, we will reimburse you at the rate of 30 cents per mile (the standard mileage method used by the IRS for business travel). Please keep track of your mileage and submit it with your time sheet at the end of each month. You will be expected to maintain a safe vehicle.

If you will be driving as part of this job, you will be expected to possess an unexpired driver's license and up-to-date car insurance. You will also be expected to undergo a background driving record check and verification of car insurance.

(Continued on following page)

BOX 9.1. *Child-Care Agreement Form* (Continued)

We expect our child to be buckled up in his/her car seat at all times if traveling by car. Before you travel with our child by car, we will demonstrate the proper placement and use of the car seat.

Please do not do personal errands or chores while caring for our child.

Please ensure that our child is wearing a safety helmet whenever s/he is on a bicycle, skateboard, or roller skates/blades.

Please do not allow our child to play in or near the street, and please require him/her to hold your hand whenever crossing a street. Safety experts recommend that children under the age of 10 not be allowed to cross the street alone.

Please do not ever lay our child, if under the age of 1, on his/her tummy for sleep (a risk factor for sudden infant death syndrome). We will show you how to place the baby on his/her back.

Please do not give our house key to anyone without our permission.

Please do not invite a guest over while caring for our child or take our child to visit someone else without our prior permission.

Please do not open the door of our home to a stranger. We will inform you in advance if we are expecting someone, like a repair person. If someone you do not know or expect comes to the door, you can simply not respond or tell them through the door when to return.

Please keep the exterior doors to the house locked at all times. Also, keep your house keys in your pocket at all times to avoid being locked out and for quick exit in event of a fire or other emergency (because our doors have deadbolt locks).

You will be expected to read and be familiar with our "Emergency Information Sheet" that provides guidelines for handling emergencies. You will be given a copy of this document. In addition, an extra copy is located in the emergency information file, which is stored beneath your time sheets, and one is posted near each phone. This sheet includes emergency telephone numbers and information regarding the location of our first-aid kit, fire extinguishers, etc.

No smoking is allowed in the house (by you or a guest). Also, please ensure that our child is not exposed to secondhand smoke. If our child is near someone smoking, please move him/her away to a smoke-free area.

If you suspect that our child is ill or becoming ill, we would like you to observe his/her symptoms, take his/her temperature, and then

(Continued on following page)

BOX 9.1. *Child-Care Agreement Form* (Continued)

....

contact us at work so that we can advise you on how to respond. Again, please do not administer any medication or treatment without our approval.

If our child requires emergency medical care or hospitalization, we expect you to respond as you have been trained in your coursework on emergency resuscitation and in accordance with the written guidelines and supplemental reading materials we will provide you.

A signed "Consent Form for Emergency Medical Care" is located in the emergency information file, which is stored below your time sheets. This form grants parental permission to provide care to a child in the parent's absence. If time does not allow you to contact us at the time of an emergency, we do not expect you to do so until our child is out of imminent danger.

If you are ever in doubt about whether to call 911 in the event of an emergency, we prefer that you call.

If you have any concerns about our child, please let us know, no matter how minor they may seem. We will need to have ongoing, open communication with you about our child's care and well-being. We will welcome your input on special games our child enjoys, effective strategies that you have discovered, and ongoing progress reports on his/her growth and development. We delight in sharing stories and information about our child.

Assuming satisfactory job performance, we want a caregiver who plans to be part of our home for at least 1 year and preferably longer and who will establish a warm, caring attachment with our child. We want our child to know that there are adults, other than his/her parents, with whom s/he can grow to trust and love. We also hope that we will be able to maintain a friendship with you even after your employment with us ends so that our child will be able to see you occasionally. We recognize the deep attachment children, caregivers, and parents can develop with each other, and we want to minimize the impact of this loss, especially for our child.

It is important to us that you feel happy in our home and enjoy working for us. If you have any needs or concerns, please bring them to our attention as soon as possible. This is especially important if something isn't satisfactory to you.

This job is an "at will" employment arrangement, which means that either one of us may terminate the employment relationship at any time or for any reason, so long as the reason is not illegal.

(Continued on following page)

BOX 9.1. *Child-Care Agreement Form* (Continued)

Obviously, we would not expect you to continue to work for us if either of us is dissatisfied. We expect, however, that each of us will be committed to making this child-care arrangement work well for everyone involved, especially our child. If problems develop, we hope that you will work with us to find mutually satisfying solutions. If this is not possible and you decide to terminate your employment, we respectfully request that you give us as much advance notice as possible and preferably 8 weeks, so that we will have adequate time to find your replacement. Likewise, we will give you a minimum of 2 but preferably 8 week's notice, as long as our child is not in any imminent danger.

Thank you for your time and showing an interest in sharing the care of our child with us.

Additional Comments:

BOX 9.1. *Child-Care Agreement Form* (Continued)

Addendum to the Child-Care Agreement for Live-In Caregivers

This addendum includes information specific to the live-in aspect of the job position. Please note that this live-in child-care position has the following additional responsibilities.

Salary and/or Room:

(Check A or B below)

_____ A. In exchange for _____ hours per week of work, you will receive the hourly/weekly salary listed on the first page of this Child-Care Agreement as well as the following:

_____ B. In exchange for _____ hours per week of work, you will receive the following:

The exclusive use of a __ foot by __ foot furnished room with __ windows containing the following furniture and items

_____

_____

_____

Bath. You will have the exclusive use of a (check one) _____ full _____ partial bath (check one) _____ with _____ without a shower and or bathtub.

(Check) _____ You will share the following bathroom arrangement: _____

Linens and Supplies.
- You (check one) _____ will _____ will not be responsible for providing your own personal toiletries such as shampoo, toothpaste, and soap.
- You (check one) _____ will _____ will not be responsible for providing your own bed and bath linens.
- You (check one) _____ will _____ will not be responsible for providing your own toilet paper for your bathroom.
- You (check one) _____ will _____ will not be responsible for providing your own cleaning and laundry supplies.

The following checked utilities are included without additional cost to you:

_____ heat,

_____ air conditioning,

(Continued on following page)

BOX 9.1. *Child-Care Agreement Form* (Continued)

_____ electricity,

_____ gas,

_____ water,

_____ garbage pickup, and

_____

Telephone. You (check one) _____ will _____ will not be expected to provide for the phone in your room, including the installation and the monthly service fee.

Use of washer and dryer but preferably not at the following times when the machine is typically in use: _____

We would appreciate it if you would not leave your laundry in the machines for extended periods of time.

Use of the following: _____

_____

Parking Arrangements. Free parking (check one) _____ is _____ not available.

Food and Meals: Check A, B, or C.

_____ A. All your meals and groceries will be provided. You will be welcome to eat all of your meals with us or prepare something to eat on your own. We keep a grocery list in the kitchen. If there is something that you need, you can add it to the list.

_____ B. You will be expected to provide your own meals, snacks, and beverages. We have found that this simplifies our life and provides us both with needed privacy around meal times.

_____ C. Other (Describe) _____

_____

Shared kitchen. You are welcome to share the following checked items in our kitchen: _____ oven, _____ stove, _____ microwave oven, _____ toaster oven, _____ toaster, _____ refrigerator, _____ pots, pans, and utensils, _____ other _____

Check the appropriate items.

_____ We prefer that you prepare your own meals

_____ in the space provided in your room

_____ in our kitchen

_____ either in your room or in our kitchen

(Continued on following page)

BOX 9.1. *Child-Care Agreement Form* (Continued)

You are welcome in our kitchen any time. You will find that it is empty at most times during the day except for immediately before and after our meals. We want you to feel at home with us. We would appreciate if you would do your dishes after use and clean up after yourself in the kitchen.

Check the appropriate items.

_____ We provide a coffee maker for your room.

_____ You will be responsible for supplying and storing your own cooking utensils in your room. Adequate space is available.

_____ We provide a microwave oven for your room.

_____ We provide a small refrigerator for your room.

_____ We provide refrigerator and freezer space for you in our kitchen.

Guests. You are welcome to have guests anytime as long as you are present. Please do not invite a guest over while caring for our child without our prior permission: Such an arrangement is usually fine with us as long as our child remains with you at all times and is the focus of your attention.

Privacy. We will respect your privacy and trust you will respect ours. When you are off duty, *your privacy will be respected.* We will not allow our child to disturb you.

A warm and friendly atmosphere in our home. We want you to feel welcome and comfortable in our home, and it is important to us to maintain a warm, friendly atmosphere. If any difficulties ever arise, we welcome the opportunity to work things out in a kind, mutually respectful manner.

Additional responsibilities. You will be responsible for cleaning your own space and are welcome to borrow our vacuum cleaner. Or, you can contract with our housecleaner to have your space cleaned on a regular basis. You will be expected to leave your space clean and in the same condition it was in when you arrived (exclusive of normal wear and tear). You will be responsible for repairing in a timely fashion any damage done to your space or to our home by you. Otherwise, if you need anything repaired in your space, please let us know and we will be glad to take care of it for you.

(Continued on following page)

BOX 9.1. *Child-Care Agreement Form* (Continued)

You will also be expected to perform the additional chores: _____

_____

_____

_____

Deposit. A $_____ deposit will be required before you move in. It will be returned to you at the time of your departure except in the event of the following: (1) You owe us hours, or (2) there is damage to your room or our home caused by you, beyond normal wear and tear. In the event of the first condition, we will deduct $_____ for every hour owed. In the second condition, we will deduct the cost of repairing the damage or replacing the item if you have elected not to take care of this.

Note: If you work for us in exchange for a place to live, this is considered a barter relationship, and we are both required by federal law to pay taxes on the monetary value of this arrangement. We can explain this situation further to you in your initial interview.

Screening Completed
Job Applications

"Now that I have all these facts about a child-care applicant, what should I look for on the completed application to help me decide whether I want to invite this candidate in for a job interview? How can I tell if he's a good applicant and deserving of serious consideration?"

The quality of the child-care applicant will be apparent when you review the completed job application form with a careful eye. You will be able to evaluate how the applicant approaches tasks (like applying for a job) and whether he has strong qualifications, based on his past experience caring for children, educational background, and philosophy about raising children. The completed job application will also help you detect the presence of serious problems, such as a history of drug abuse or a criminal record. Box 10.1 offers a checklist of questions to consider when reviewing the completed job application. This checklist is by no means exhaustive. It is designed as an aid to help you decide whether to invite the applicant for an interview.

. . . .

My Experience

The excellent caregivers that we have hired all presented a typewritten or neatly printed application. They also responded to the questions, especially the open-ended short essay questions, in a thoughtful, comprehensive manner. The manner in which they approached this task was predictive of their excellent, thoughtful, thorough approach to caring for our child and our home. I have received sloppy, rushed applications and ones containing poor writing skills, and I felt confident not considering these applicants further.

I only made exceptions for our excellent immigrant caregivers. They found the application form overwhelming because it demanded advanced writing skills. I nonetheless gave them the application to complete, explaining that I understood it would be difficult, but I needed some background information. They each asked a family member or friend for assistance and provided me with some basic information about themselves. I accepted whatever they were able to provide and what I was able to verify, relying predominantly on their personal references. With one caregiver, I needed more background information, and so I sat down with her and asked some of the more important questions in person.

As mentioned earlier, I do not ask immigrant applicants to complete the job application before the initial interview. I meet with them first and then give them the job application form to complete if I am interested in considering them further.

BOX 10.1. *Checklist for Evaluating Job Applications*

Consider the following in reviewing the completed job application:

- How did the applicant approach the task of completing the application form? Are the responses neat, legible, and complete? Does the applicant's approach to this task reflect skillfulness and a level of interest in the position? A sloppy, rushed application can serve as a fair warning of how the individual might approach child care or other job-related tasks.
- Did the applicant leave any important items blank? Did the applicant list all addresses for the past 5 years and the corresponding dates? This information will be important later when you conduct the criminal record check.
- Did you take into account the applicant's level of formal education? Some excellent caregivers have less formal education, and it is important not to exclude them from consideration because their responses are less sophisticated. On the other hand, is the applicant's use of incorrect grammar or lack of basic knowledge a serious concern?
- Does the applicant have adequate background experience in caring for children?
- Did the applicant list appropriate references, that is, at least three people who have known the applicant well in the last several years, at least two employment references, and at least one person who has known them for at least 5 years?
- Does the applicant possess compatible philosophies and beliefs to your own about raising and disciplining children?
- Is the applicant available to care for your child at the specified times?
- Are there any responses that suggest possible problems or difficulties? You can make a note of these and request further information by phone, in the job interview, or from the job references. In particular, did the applicant respond *yes* to any of the final 27 questions, many of which serve as red flags requiring careful scrutiny?
- Did the applicant answer *no* to items 20 ("Have you ever found yourself feeling angry at a child under your care?") or 25 ("Have you ever felt exhausted while caring for a child?") If so, this could indicate that the applicant is not being completely honest and may be attempting to give a false good impression. After all, feeling angry and feeling exhausted while caring for children are fairly universal experiences.

(Continued on following page)

BOX 10.1. *Checklist for Evaluating Job Applications* (Continued)

- Did the applicant answer *yes* to item 22 ("Have you ever been in a situation where you felt spanking was the best way to handle a discipline problem?") If so, how do you feel about that response?
- On paper, does this individual intuitively feel like a good match for you and your family? Why or why not? Make a list of what you like and don't like about this applicant so far. If your overall impression is favorable, invite the applicant for an interview.

11

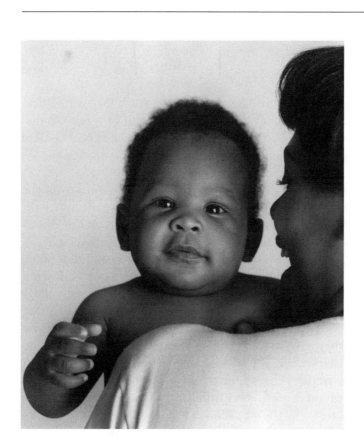

Conducting the Job Interview

"The thought of conducting the job interview totally overwhelms me. There seems to be so much to cover, I'm not sure where to start. What questions should I ask, what are the most important things to look for, and how long will it take?"

An advantage of using the "Job Application Form for an In-Home Child Caregiver" (Box 8.1) is that the job interview can be a relaxed discussion, allowing you and the applicant to get to know each other. All of the important background questions have already been covered on the job application form and in the initial phone call.

The interview, then, is your opportunity to follow up on any of the areas requiring further information and to focus on the applicant's suitability as a caregiver. You'll be able to focus on such issues as the following: Is this applicant a good match for us? Does she share compatible child-care views and practices, possess a good attitude and understanding of children, seem reliable and trustworthy? Will she be a good influence on our child, and does she have a good track record of providing quality child care?

The interview is a good time to tap into your intuitive, parental instincts. This is the time to check out if the applicant is caring, honest, mature, and reliable. Remember, you will have opportunities to verify your instincts when you contact the applicant's job references and conduct criminal and background checks. Meanwhile, during the interview, I have found that if I am relaxed, the applicant is more relaxed and spontaneously shares more important information. If you end up hiring the applicant, this meeting could be the beginning of an important relationship. Therefore, this initial meeting is crucial.

THE INITIAL INTERVIEW

General Guidelines

Ask yourself during the interview, "Is this someone with whom I would like to spend a long period of time?" This is exactly what you will be asking your child to do over and over again. If you select someone you like and feel comfortable with, your child will likely feel the same.

It is essential to interview an applicant in person and in your home. There are many personal qualities that can only be learned in a face-to-face meeting: Is her outlook on life positive, and are her people skills good? Does she seem emotionally troubled? Does she have good personal hygiene? Is she able to establish appropriate boundaries in relationships? Does she interact in a manner with both adults and children that is com-

fortable and appropriate? Is she emotionally mature? Is she overly critical of past employers and likely to develop the same attitude towards you?

Just as it is important for you to have a face-to-face meeting, it is equally important for the caregiver. She too needs to check you out to make sure your family and the job are a good match for her. To further help a caregiver decide whether to accept your job offer, you can also give the applicant several names of people who know you and your family well as references. By speaking with people that have worked for you or your family in the past, the applicant also has a better idea of what she is getting into.

To help create a comfortable, hospitable atmosphere for the applicant, I usually offer something to drink (coffee, tea, juice, or soda) before sitting down in the living room or dining room for the interview.

I also explain that we will talk first before I introduce our child. During the interview, I recommend that you have someone else care for your child. The interview is very important and will require your full attention. It is very distracting for both you and the applicant to have a child present who is also requiring attention.

It is ideal if both parents can be present for the interview. This individual will become an important person to your entire family, and it is vital that *everyone* like and feel comfortable with the person you hire.

After the interview, if you still consider the individual a serious candidate, you can give a short tour of the more public areas of your home (e.g., living room, kitchen, family room, dining room, child's room, and play areas), followed by an introduction of your child.

Conducting the Interview

To draw out the most information in the interview, it works best to ask open-ended questions, such as *"Can you tell me about yourself?"* rather than questions that elicit a *yes* or *no* or brief response. You can also invite the applicant to elaborate on a response by stating, for example, *"That's interesting, can you tell me more about that?"* or *"I'm interested in learning more about such and such, can you explain further?"*

Box 11.1 provides the "Child Care in the Home Job Interview Form," an outline with questions that can be followed during the job interview. Before the interview, you can make changes in this outline, adding or deleting questions or areas of investigation. You can photocopy the form or adapt and print it using the optional computer diskette containing all the book's forms (see Appendix A for ordering information).

You and your partner can have this outline in front of you during the interview, and one of you can take notes on a separate sheet of paper, keeping track of the applicant's responses and characteristics that either impress or concern you. The sections of the form are numbered to assist you in note taking. Keeping notes is especially helpful when you are interviewing multiple applicants. Without notes, it is easy to become confused about who said what. You and your partner can even decide in advance who will ask what questions and who will take notes on the responses.

When an interview is running smoothly, it is not uncommon to find yourselves departing from the outline into a comfortable, free-flowing discussion. Let the discussion take its course because you will learn a lot about each other. Then, as you wind things down, refer back to the outline to make sure that you have covered all the important areas.

Time

The length of this meeting is typically 1 to 2 hours. If, in the course of the interview, you learn something about an applicant that removes her from consideration, you can wrap up the interview in a briefer period of time.

Interviewing Immigrant Caregivers

It has been my experience that immigrant caregivers often like to bring along for their job interview their partner or a family member or friend who may have a greater command of the English language. I encourage this practice because it ensures that the candidate has a good understanding of the position. I think the applicant's intent is not only to have language assistance but also to check us out to ensure this is a good place of employment. I certainly respect that reason. Direct all your questions to the applicant, however, encouraging her to respond and allowing you to evaluate her level of language proficiency. The companion, though, can be helpful in explaining difficult-to-understand concepts or words.

A SECOND INTERVIEW

I have found it helpful to invite serious candidates for a second interview. In that way I can devote an entire meeting to orienting them to our child and the job while providing us yet another opportunity to observe their interpersonal and child-care skills.

In addition, some excellent candidates might make a poor impression in the first interview because of anxiety. A second interview will give

you another chance to assess their suitability for the job. Many second interviews are less anxiety producing for both the applicant and the employer.

"AT WILL" EMPLOYMENT

To protect against wrongful discharge lawsuits, this book's job application and child-care agreement forms are intended to create an *at will* employment relationship between you and the caregiver. This relationship means that you, or the caregiver, may terminate the employment relationship at any time and for any reason so long as the reason is not illegal.[6] The laws in some states may vary with regard to *at will employment*. If you live in a state like California that has a different interpretation of *at will employment*, you should speak to a competent attorney.

A TRIAL PERIOD

I also suggest that you arrange for a trial period of employment (e.g., several days or weeks) with a new caregiver. This arrangement allows you to make sure that the caregiver meets your needs and that she, likewise, is happy in the new position. It is very important to me that our caregiver like the job and our child. If she is not happy, I would rather take the time at the outset to find a more suitable individual. I have found that applicants feel relieved knowing that they can take time in the beginning to see if they like working for us and caring for our child. Agreeing to care for another's child, if one is conscientious, is a big decision and this arrangement makes it easier for both of you to make a sound choice.

---

[6] Make sure that any of the suggestions and forms you use from this or any other chapter are consistent with the laws and regulations in your location and time. This book provides a solid starting point but is not intended to provide legal advice. Because laws vary from place to place and interpretations of these laws change over time, it is always wise to consult with an attorney or the state and federal departments of labor.

BOX 11.1. *Child Care in the Home Job Interview Form*

Date: _____

Applicant's Name: _____

Name of Interviewer: _____

1. Welcome the applicant into your home and help him/her feel comfortable.

Warmly introduce yourselves and offer something to drink.

Break the ice by thanking the applicant for coming, asking questions, such as "*Did you have any difficulty finding our home?*" or making comments to generate conversation, such as "*I noticed on your application form that you're a graduate student in social work. How do you like your program?*"

2. Provide an overview of how you plan to conduct the job interview.

After you are seated, you can begin the interview with the following overview.

"*What I'd like to do today is give us both an opportunity to get to know each other better. You probably have a good understanding of what we are looking for from reading our child-care agreement. We have some good basic background information on you from your application form. We'd like, however, to learn more about you personally and what you have to offer us and, at the same time, help you get to know us so you can decide if this position is a good one for you too. While we are talking, please feel free to ask us questions as well.*"

"*After we talk, we'd like to briefly introduce you to our child. If we decide that we're interested in possibly hiring you, we'll call and invite you back for a second interview so that you and our child can spend more time together to further help us all make a good, sound selection.*"

"*If at any point along the way you decide that this is not the right job for you, please let us know. In that way, we won't take up any more time. We want this to be a job that feels right for you and that you can look forward to and feel excited about. We want you to feel like you're interviewing us as much as we're interviewing you. We want to hire someone who will feel comfortable in this position for an extended period of time, that is, at least 1 year. This, of course, assumes satisfactory job performance and the understanding that eventually our child will no longer need in-home child care.*"

(Continued on following page)

BOX 11.1. *Child Care in the Home Job Interview Form* (Continued)

3. Introduce your family and your child-care needs.

At this point, you will know a great deal more about the applicant than s/he knows about you and your family. This is a good time to share information about yourselves and the family. You can share basic facts such as the following:

- A description of your family
- Your occupations and work schedules
- How long you've lived in town and in this home
- Your short- and long-term goals as a family (e.g., plans to move or enlarge your family)
- Why you have selected in-home child care
- Your family's particular needs, special concerns, and values
- How the job responsibilities might change as your child gets older

4. Review the job position.

"Before we start, I wanted to make sure that you have a good understanding of the job position. Did you have a chance to read the Child-Care Agreement? Do you have any questions? Is there anything we can elaborate on?"

This is a good time to clarify important job expectations, such as work hours, child-care and household tasks and responsibilities, and the salary, to ensure that the applicant is willing and able to provide what you need. Much of this information is covered in the child-care agreement, but it is important to go over the issues that are of greatest concern to either of you. This will help ensure that you are both on the same wavelength and that there are not any major misunderstandings.

5. Get to know the applicant as a person and as a caregiver.

5a. *"Can you tell me about your past job and personal experiences that have prepared you for a job position like this?"*

5b. *"I noticed on your application that you have children (younger siblings, nieces and nephews, grandchildren) of your own. Can you tell me about your experiences in caring for them? How old are they now, and how are they doing?"*

5c. *"What do you like the most, and what do you like the least about caring for children?"*

5d. *"Our child is _____ months/years old. What do you think are some of the important factors to consider when caring for a child of this age?"*

(Continued on following page)

BOX 11.1. *Child Care in the Home Job Interview Form* (Continued)

5e. "What are some words or phrases that you might use to describe yourself as a person? I ask you this question so that we can get to know you as quickly as possible."

5f. "And what words would you use to describe yourself as a caregiver?"

Note: Sometimes, the applicant will use an adjective that requires clarification because it is hard to tell if it is a positive or negative quality. You can then simply say, for example, "You used the term _overly sensitive_ to describe yourself; can you explain further?"

5g. "What special qualities, skills, or strengths would you bring to this job?"

6. Assess the applicant's ability to handle difficult child-care situations.

Anyone caring for a child is likely to encounter difficult situations from time to time. In this section of the interview, you can assess the applicant's ability to think on his/her feet in challenging situations. This section is also designed to help give you information about a caregiver's approach, attitudes, and beliefs. Introduce your questions with a comment like the following:

"As parents, we are challenged from time to time with difficult situations. We recognize that there are many _right_ ways to respond to and care for children. We want to present you with some hypothetical, challenging situations involving children and ask you how you might respond."

6a. "What are some things you might try to do to comfort our _____-month/year-old child if s/he is crying uncontrollably? What would you try or consider? If all failed, what would you do?"

6b. "Suppose you are caring for our child, and s/he seems to be ill. S/he is just not his/her usual self. S/he seems fussy, in discomfort, and somewhat listless. How would you handle this situation?"

6c. "Suppose you are caring for a 2-year-old child, and s/he keeps running out into the street while on a walk. How would you deal with this situation? How would you handle this same situation if the child was 4 years old?"

6d. "Suppose you are caring for a 3-year-old, and you walk into the room and discover that s/he has passed out, is blue, and not breathing. What would you do?"

(Continued on following page)

BOX 11.1. *Child Care in the Home Job Interview Form* (Continued)

6e. *"Suppose you are caring for a 4- and a 5-year-old brother and sister. They begin to fight over their toys, and the brother hits his sister, and she responds by pulling his hair. They are both screaming and crying. How would you deal with this situation?"*

6f. *"Suppose you are caring for our _____-month/year-old child, and s/he is unable to go to sleep, and it is well past his/her bedtime. What would you do?"*

6g. *"Have you ever had a conflict with the parents of a child under your care? How did you handle this situation?"*

6h. *"You are caring for a 3-year-old, and a large thunderstorm erupts, and the child becomes terrified by the thunder and lightning. How would you handle this situation?"*

6i. *"You are caring for an 8-year-old, and s/he refuses to go to bed or obey you. How would you respond?"*

6j. *"A child's emotional bond with his/her caregiver is very important. What are some things that you might do to help ensure that your relationship with our child is a good one?"*

7. Follow up on any concerns you might have about the applicant.

This is a good time in the interview to request further information or clarification on anything that might still concern you about the applicant. For example, you can review the job application before the interview and place a check mark next to any response on which you would like additional information. Or, you can ask about anything that has come up thus far that concerns you.

This is also a good time to discuss potential problems the caregiver may have and how they might be handled. Such problems might include illness in the caregiver, difficulties getting to work because of bad weather, conflicting vacation schedules, or the need to take a refresher course in emergency medical procedures.

8. Encourage the applicant to address any of his/her concerns.

"Do you have any questions or concerns about us or the position?"

9. Provide the applicant with personal references on your family.

"It might be helpful to you to be able to talk with some of our former caregivers/employees or with individuals who know us well. Would you like us to give you some names and phone numbers of people you could call for further information on us?"

(Continued on following page)

BOX 11.1. *Child Care in the Home Job Interview Form* (Continued)

10. Ascertain the applicant's level of interest in the position.

10a. *"How interested are you in this position?"*

10b. *"If you were offered this position, do you think you would accept? When would you be available to start?"*

10c. *"If you accepted this position, how long do you think you'd be available to work for us?"*

If you are seriously interested in an applicant and they indicate they are not interested, you can ask them why and if they are willing to reconsider their decision. Perhaps you can renegotiate the terms of the job, such as the time scheduled to work or the salary to satisfy their needs.

Even if it is possible to renegotiate the terms of the position to make it acceptable, do not pressure an applicant to accept a job. It is important to respect the applicant's decision. For this arrangement to work, everyone has to feel good about it from the outset.

11. Introduce the applicant to your child.

Observing the applicant interact with your child is one of the most important parts of the job interview. One might look good on paper and possess good interview skills but not possess good interpersonal skills with children. Look for the following during this part of the interview:

11a. Does the applicant approach your child slowly and with respect, understanding that infants and young children are often intimidated by unfamiliar adults? Does the applicant seem understanding if your child is fearful? Is the applicant reassuring?

11b. Does the applicant respond appropriately to your child's cues, if given, to back off?

11c. Does the applicant seem genuinely interested in your child? Does the applicant seem to like and enjoy children?

11d. Does the applicant seem to respect your emotional bond with your child?

11e. Does the applicant seem open to your cues and information about how to successfully interact with or care for your child?

11f. Does the applicant attempt to relate at eye level with your child?

11g. Does the applicant seem gentle, caring, and patient?

11h. Does the applicant talk to your child? Is the applicant pleasant and appropriate?

(Continued on following page)

BOX 11.1. *Child Care in the Home Job Interview Form* (Continued)

11i. Is the applicant playful? Does the applicant have a good sense of humor? Does the applicant seem to delight in your child?

11j. Does the applicant seem confident and comfortable handling your child?

11k. Does the applicant seem rigid or controlling?

11l. Does the applicant encourage and respond to your child's communications?

11m. Would you feel comfortable spending an entire day with this person if you were a child?

11n. Does your child seem to like and feel comfortable with this person after the applicant is more familiar?

12. End the interview.

You can end the interview in a variety of different ways according to the decision you have reached at this stage in the process. The following are some possible options.

If you are *not* interested in this applicant:

"We very much appreciate your time and interest in this position. Unfortunately, what you have to offer is different from what we had in mind. We are sorry that we are unable to offer you the position, but we want to thank you for all your efforts on our behalf. Good luck in your job search."

If you need time to consider your choice:

"Thank you so much for your time and effort. The next step for us is to decide which applicants to invite in for a second interview. We will be able to make that decision in the next _____ days. I will call you by _____ to let you know our decision. Thank you so much for coming today. I will talk to you soon."

If you are interested in hiring the applicant and you have decided that you would like to invite him/her to come back for a second interview:

"We are very pleased that you are interested in this position. We would like to invite you back for a second interview. At that time, we would like you to get to know our child better so that we can all decide if this is a good match. Meanwhile, we will also contact your references. Would you be willing to come back for a second interview? When would you be available for this interview?"

Sometimes you will want an immediate commitment from a candidate who possesses all the essential job qualifications before s/he is offered another position elsewhere. It can take several weeks to

(Continued on following page)

BOX 11.1. *Child Care in the Home Job Interview Form* (Continued)

complete background record checks, and an excellent child caregiver might be offered another position in that intervening period. If you are interested in hiring someone on the spot but want to check out the job references and background records first:

"We want to offer you this position but want to take time to ensure that your job references are satisfactory and that there are no problems uncovered in your background records check. Would you be interested in accepting this job now, with the understanding that the final, official offer will be made following these background checks?"

"Would you be willing to immediately call the individuals you listed as job references on the job application form, let them know we will be calling, and ask them to speak openly with us about you?" (Note: You can then check the job application form with the candidate to ensure you have up-to-date phone numbers and information on how to best reach their references.)

"Would you be willing to complete and submit the paperwork for the background record checks in a timely fashion so we can get you on board as soon as possible?"

"Initially, will you work on a trial basis for _____ day(s)/week(s), allowing us both time to ensure this is a good arrangement?"

Arrange a tentative starting date, and give the candidate the paperwork for the background checks (see Boxes 12.1–12.10). You can then contact their references (see Box 13.1), and if these reports are not satisfactory, you can immediately discontinue the hiring process. If they receive good reference reports, you can proceed, waiting for the completion of the background records checks before officially hiring. Once they are hired, have them complete Form I-9 (see Box 2.1).

Congratulations, you have just completed an important step in the hiring process: the job interview.

12

Investigating an Applicant's Background

"How can I be sure that the person we hire is who he professes to be and not someone with a history of serious problems?"

This concern probably crosses every parent's mind as steps are taken to hire a child caregiver. Many parents worry that the person they hire will turn out to be someone other than he seems or professes to be, causing serious harm to the child and family. *This fear is understandable, but you can take steps to minimize such problems and confidently hire a caregiver by conducting a thorough background investigation and reference check.* Furthermore, you can conduct the investigation yourself for only a small investment of time and money.

This chapter shows you how to conduct a thorough investigation of an applicant's background so that you can hire a caregiver with peace of mind. Naturally, you may need to adapt the information in this chapter to the situation and laws in effect in your community at the time when you are conducting your investigation.

In any case, it is a good feeling to have supporting documents on hand that verify that the individual you wish to hire has a clean record. This knowledge combined with information from personal references (see Chapter 13) will give you the collaborative information you need to confidently hire the caregiver of your choice.

CONDUCTING THE INVESTIGATION YOURSELF

If you conduct the investigation yourself, not only will you know it was a thorough investigation, but you will know the applicant better by having gone through the process together. The applicant actually does the legwork, while you oversee the process. And the process is simple.

. . . .

The information, instructions, and forms in this chapter have been specifically designed for busy parents; all the legwork has already been done for you in the development of these materials.

Simply photocopy the forms and instructions contained in the chapter or print them off your personal computer with the help of this book's optional computer diskette containing all the book's forms. Then give these simple forms and instructions to the child-care applicant to complete and mail in. Only 1 to 3 hours are generally needed to do the paperwork required for the searches, but *this time is spent by the job applicant, not you*. You merely oversee the process.

There may be no reason to pay an agency to do these background searches. The background checks will require little time on your part and save you considerable money, and, at the same time, you will be sure that a thorough search was indeed conducted because you will be overseeing the entire process. You will be able to view the official documents firsthand and verify that a record check was completed. I have heard of situations where parents paid for background checks through child-care placement services that were not thorough or were never conducted.

To conduct the investigation in a fair and professional manner, pay your applicant for the few hours of time he spends going through the process and for the minimal processing fees usually charged by the state or institution conducting the search or providing the documentation. You should also reimburse him for the infectious and communicable disease medical examination. These costs will be considerably less than the hundreds of dollars typically charged by investigative agencies and child-care placement services for conducting a background search, and you will ensure goodwill.

Everyone will benefit from going through the process. It builds trust. In addition, the applicant will have, upon completion, a portfolio of official documents (e.g., the criminal or child abuse and neglect record checks or transcripts) that can be used in future child-care job positions. After conducting the background records search, the applicant can show you the original documents, provide you with a copy of each, and then retain the official documents for his own job portfolio.

WAIVING THE INVESTIGATION

O ccasionally you may want to waive the investigation because you feel you know the applicant well enough. Because this decision may also have legal implications, think it through carefully to be sure you are not just trying to save time.

• • • • • • • • • • • • • •

Only waive a background check with applicants you have a great deal of information on from other highly reliable sources.

Consider how much other supporting information you have on a candidate. For example, you may elect to waive some or all of the background checks if the applicant has worked over an extended period of time for someone you know well. Or, you may also elect not to conduct a background search on someone who has been recommended by a friend or relative who has known him and his family for years.

To help you make this decision, take into consideration that what someone else might feel is adequate information about an applicant may not meet your standards. There are situations in which families have hired someone they thought a friend or relative knew well, only to later discover a pattern of serious problems. It is not worth giving up access to this valuable information to save a little bit of time or for mere convenience unless you have access to the information from another highly reliable source.

THE INVESTIGATIVE PROCESS

The major purpose of a background search is to provide you with identification and collaborative information. It will help ensure that the person you hire is who he professes to be. The "Job Application Form" (see Box 8.1) asks the applicant if he has ever had criminal or child abuse charges brought against him, for example. The background search, on the other hand, will provide collaborative information from the appropriate government agencies so that you can verify that the applicant is indeed responding honestly to those background questions posed on the last page of the application form.

Keep in mind that background searches, even those conducted by law enforcement agencies themselves, are not foolproof. The data you obtain is limited, for example, by laws that protect citizens who have been charged but not found guilty of crimes, who have served time for crimes and whose records have been expunged by the court, etc. Also, every state differs in the accessibility of criminal and sexual abuse records. Some states are more advanced than others in their record-keeping systems and their accessibility of information to the public. Some states are set up to provide information upon request; others are not. For example, some states allow the release of sexual abuse and neglect records upon a child caregiver applicant's request, but other states, unbelievably, do not allow this information to be released.

Gather whatever information is available and allowable in your state, while recognizing that you may encounter roadblocks. You will be rewarded for the time you devote to this process with the sense of relief you feel when you know you have done all you could to check out an applicant.

The rest of this chapter contains information and forms for conducting background record searches in seven areas:

1. criminal records

2. child abuse or neglect records

3. driving record and automobile insurance (to be requested when driving may be a part of the job)

4. academic transcripts

5. verification of training in emergency medical procedures for children

6. medical verification that the caregiver is not a carrier of an infectious or communicable disease, such as tuberculosis

7. preemployment drug screen

Also, you can request a copy of an applicant's military discharge papers if you wish to verify that he was honorably discharged.

The material has been set up so that searches can be conducted with a minimal amount of time and effort on everyone's part. However, because of the time and fees involved, only request background records from those applicants you are seriously interested in hiring. You can inform an applicant that after the reference checks are completed, you plan to officially offer him the position if the checks collaborate the information he provided. You can then get the process underway by giving the applicant the instruction sheets and forms. Background checks can take 2 to 4 weeks (and sometimes longer) for processing after the necessary forms have been submitted.

Criminal Record Background Checks On Child Caregivers

In conducting a criminal record background check, it is best to request information from the state rather than from a county or municipality. The benefit of a statewide search is that you will receive information on crimes committed by a nonjuvenile anywhere in the state and not just in a particular locality. In some states, juveniles are persons 16 years and younger, but in other states they are 18 years and younger.

To be thorough, request criminal records checks from all of the states that the applicant has resided in during the previous 5-year period. If an individual has worked in a nearby state, you may also want to request a search in that state as well. The "Job Application Form" (see Box 8.1) asks applicants to list all of their residential addresses for the past 5 years, so you can use this information to guide your search.

Unfortunately, there are no national databanks for criminals in general, nor for child abuse offenders more specifically. There is a need for these, and hopefully someday soon they will be in place to protect our children. Meanwhile, the criminal record check on the state level is the process to follow. If a particular state does not have a central repository for

criminal records, you can call the local or county courthouse where the individual resided and obtain information about conducting a background criminal record check in that locality.

In some states, the law allows the release of both closed criminal records and open criminal records on individuals (nonjuveniles) applying for caregiver positions for children and the elderly. Open records usually are records of convictions, pending charges, and suspended imposition of sentences during the term of probation. Closed records are usually records of arrest, where the arrest did not result in a conviction, or where the suspended imposition of sentence was completed and a judge ordered no conviction for record purposes. Closed records will also sometimes reflect the following situations: (1) The defendant was found not guilty; (2) the charges were not prosecuted or were dismissed; or (3) the arrest is over 30 days old and charges have not been filed. In other words, access to closed records will provide you with additional, valuable information not usually released to employers.

*The information pertaining to open and closed records varies from state to state. T*he information in this chapter is based on the criminal records process in Missouri.

According to federal law, it is acceptable to base an employment decision on an applicant's record of criminal *convictions*. In some states, you'll be able to procure, through a criminal record background check, information other than the applicant's record of criminal convictions, such as records of arrest. Before making a decision to disqualify an applicant based on anything other than a criminal conviction, I recommend that you seek competent legal counsel.

Box 12.1 provides applicants with instructions for requesting a criminal record check, and Box 12.2 provides a form that requests as much information as is allowable by law in your state.

Before being officially offered this position, you are required to have a statewide criminal record check conducted in all of the states in which you have resided in the past 5 years. Please follow these instructions to obtain this information. It generally takes about 2 to 4 weeks for this information to be processed after a request is submitted. Your prompt handling of this matter will be very much appreciated.

1. Contact your local police department, state police, or highway patrol, and obtain the name, address, and phone number of the state agency that houses the central terminal or repository for all criminal records for the entire state. Fill in this information at the top of the attached "Criminal Record Request Form for a Child Caregiver Job Applicant."

2. Call this state agency and explain that you are an applicant for a child-care position and are being required to undergo a criminal background record check.

Ask if they require you to use their official clearance form or if you can send them the attached, notarized form. If you use the attached form, ask if all the information requested on this form is necessary. If it is not, it is not necessary to fill it in. If their form is required, ask them to send it to you.

Also, ask what fee they charge for conducting the search and if a cashier's check or money order is required. Finally, please ask them how long it will take for them to process the request once they have received it from you.

3. Fill out their clearance form, following their instructions, or complete the attached "Criminal Record Request Form for A Child Caregiver Job Applicant." A separate form must be completed for *each* of the states you have resided in over the past 5 years. *Do not sign the form, however, until you are in the presence of the notary public.*

Have the records sent directly to us, if the state allows it. If not, do step 6.

4. Present the following *official documents* (photocopies are not acceptable) to a notary public and obtain notarization of the "Criminal Record Request Form for a Child Caregiver Job Applicant":

- a birth certificate
- a social security card

(Continued on following page)

• a valid motor vehicle operator's license issued by a state or a state ID
• naturalization papers (if applicable)

Note: All of the names need to match on these documents. If not, you will need to provide a marriage certificate, divorce decree, or an official court document granting a name change.

Notaries are located at many local banks and law offices and generally charge a minimal fee for their services.

5. Mail the notarized clearance form or the notarized "Criminal Record Request Form for a Child Caregiver Job Applicant," with the appropriate fee, to the state agency identified in step 1. Please give us a call to let us know the date on which you submitted this form and the amount of time it will take for the agency to process the request.

6. If the state will only release its findings to you, please present to us the official criminal record document sent to you, along with a copy of the document. We will retain the copy for our files and give you back the official document for your later use.

7. Please keep track of fees and the time you spend doing this search, so we can reimburse you. You will be paid $_____ per hour for your time.

Thank you for taking the time to provide us with this information.

BOX 12.2. *Criminal Record Request Form for a Child Caregiver Job Applicant*

....

_____

Name and Address of State's Central Repository for Criminal Records

_____

Phone Number

Date: _____

To Whom It May Concern:

Please accept this letter as my permission to release all criminal record information allowable by law (i.e., both open and closed records) to _____, my potential child-care employer, at the following address: _____

_____

I have presented official copies of the following documents to the notary public whose name and stamp appears on this document: birth certificate, social security card, valid motor vehicle operator's license or a state ID, and naturalization papers (if applicable). All of the names match on these documents. If not, I have provided an official marriage certificate, divorce decree, or court order granting a name change.

A processing fee of _____ is enclosed in the form of a (check appropriate box) ___ cashier's check, ___ money order, ___ personal check.

_____

Print Your Full Name (Include Jr., Sr., etc.)

_____

Signature **(To be Signed only in the Presence of the Notary)**

_____

Please Print Any Other Formerly Used Names Including your Maiden Name, Nicknames, All Aliases

_____

_____

Current Address

_____

_____

Previous Address (Please list *all* addresses you resided at in this state over the past 5 years and the dates). **If additional space is required, please use the reverse side of this form.)**

(Continued on following page)

(Continued on following page)

BOX 12.2. *Criminal Record Request Form for a Child Caregiver Job Applicant* (Continued)

● ●

_____   _____
Date of Birth   Place of Birth

_____   _____
Race   Sex

_____   _____
Driver's License Number   Issuing State of Driver's License

_____
Social Security Number

STATE OF _____

COUNTY OF _____

On this _____ day of _____ in the year _____ before me,
_____ (name of notary), a Notary Public in and
for said state, personally appeared _____
(name of individual), known to me to be the person who executed the within
CRIMINAL RECORD REQUEST FORM FOR A CHILD CAREGIVER JOB
APPLICANT, and acknowledged to me that s/he executed the same for the
purposes therein stated.

_____   (SEAL)
Notary Public in and for said County and State
My commission expires:

Child Abuse and Neglect Record Check

Most states have child abuse hotlines and state agencies that receive and investigate reports of suspected child abuse and neglect. Many of these states maintain a computerized registry or database of individuals who have, upon investigation, been found to be abusive or neglectful of children under their care. Keep in mind that this list generally does not contain the names of everyone who has been the focus of a formal report but rather only those with whom the abuse has been substantiated.

Each state has its own laws regarding the retention of records, the definition of abuse and neglect, and protocols for the release of names of perpetrators. It is sometimes difficult to access this information. Often, a way around such a problem is the following: The applicant can request records or an official statement that no records exist. It is likely that each state has provisions allowing perpetrators legal access to their child abuse or neglect records. Likewise, if there is *no record* on an individual, a person should be able to obtain an official statement of that fact from their state agency. In general, the state laws are changing very rapidly across the country, making it easier for job applicants to access this information. *Thus, with child abuse and neglect background checks, the goal for parents is to obtain an official statement that the job applicant does <u>not</u> have a record on file.*

Currently, some states will verify whether a particular individual is on their child abuse or neglect list, but others will not. Some states will allow the release of this information, however, for the purpose of a child-care job application background check. Other states will only release this information to child-care agencies and not to parents employing a caregiver in their own home.

You can require that your job applicant obtain verification from the state, if it is allowable, that he does *not* have a child abuse and neglect record on file. Copy the attached "Instructions for Caregiver Applicants on How to Request a Child Abuse and Neglect Record Check" (Box 12.3) and give it to your applicant along with a copy of the "Request Form for a Child Abuse and Neglect Background Investigation on a Child Caregiver Job Applicant" (Box 12.4). Just as with the criminal record check, require this record check for every state the applicant has resided in over the past 5 years. Again, if he has worked in a nearby state other than where he resides, you may also want to request a clearance from that state.

BOX 12.3. *Instructions for Caregiver Applicants on How to Request a Child Abuse and Neglect Record Check*

To be considered for this child-care position, you are required to receive an official statement from every state in which you have resided in the last 5 years that you do *not* have a child abuse and neglect record on file. Many states will provide this information. If the state will not release the information to you, please bring the situation to our attention. Please follow these instructions to request this official record check. We appreciate your time and *prompt handling* of this matter. Thank you.

1. Contact the child abuse and neglect state agency. You can call directory information for 800 numbers (1-800-555-1212) and obtain the 800 number for the child abuse hotline in the state, or you can obtain the phone number in the government offices section in your phone book. The child abuse and neglect central registry is often located in the state capitol.

2. When you call this state agency, ask to speak directly with the official handling child abuse background checks for child-care job applicants. Explain that you are being considered for a child-care job position and your potential employer requires that you receive an official statement that you do *not* have a child abuse and neglect record on file.

Explain that you can send them a written, *notarized* request for this official statement along with any required processing fee. If you use the attached form, review its contents with them to make sure that it contains all of the information they require. You do not have to provide any information on this form that is not explicitly requested *by them*. Some states will require the use of their own clearance form and a processing fee. The state may also require you to appear in person to obtain this clearance. If a fee is charged, ask if a cashier's check or money order is required, or if a personal check is acceptable.

Obtain the correct name and mailing address of the agency and the name of the official handling these requests. Fill this information in on the top of the attached "Request Form for a Child Abuse and Neglect Background Investigation on a Child Caregiver Job Applicant."

Finally, ask how long it will take to process your request once it is received.

3. Fill out either the attached "Request Form for a Child Abuse and Neglect Background Investigation on a Child Caregiver Job

(Continued on following page)

Applicant" or their clearance form, following their instructions. A separate form must be completed for *each* of the states you have resided in over the past 5 years. *Do not sign the form, however, until you are in the presence of the notary public.*

4. Present the following *official documents* (not photocopies): birth certificate, a social security card, a valid motor vehicle operator's license issued by the state or a state ID, and naturalization papers (if applicable) to a notary public and obtain notarization of the "Request Form for a Child Abuse and Neglect Background Investigation on a Child Caregiver Job Applicant." Notaries are located at many local banks and law offices and generally charge a minimal fee for their services. Note: All of the names need to match on your official documents. If not, you will need to provide a marriage certificate, divorce decree, or an official court document granting a name change.

5. Mail the notarized form, with the appropriate fee, to the attention of the official in the state agency identified in step 2. Please give us a call to let us know the date on which you submitted the form and the amount of time it will take for your request to be processed.

6. When you receive the response, please present the *official document* (not a photocopy) to us for our review as soon as possible, along with a copy for our records. We will then return the official document to you for your files.

7. Please keep track of the fees and the time you spend doing this search, so we can reimburse you. You will be paid $____ per hour for your time.

Again, thank you for your help with this clearance.

In general, this information is most typically released to the job applicant and not to the employer. The applicant can show the original document to you and then give you a copy. An official document is usually on official letterhead or is stamped, embossed, or has some other marking indicating that it is an official document.

If the applicant is unsuccessful in obtaining this clearance, indicating that the state does not release this information to anyone, including the job applicant, you can contact the child abuse and neglect state agency on your own. I suggest that you ask to speak directly to the official handling child abuse record checks for child-care job applicants and verify that the information given to you by your job applicant is accurate. For the sake of caution, verify that a record check is indeed not available in the state.

BOX 12.4. *Request Form for a Child Abuse and Neglect Background Investigation on a Child Caregiver Job Applicant*

●●

_____
Name and Address of State's Child Abuse and Neglect Central Repository for Perpetrator's Records

_____
Name and Phone Number of Official Handling Child Abuse Background Checks for Child-Care Job Applicants in this State

Date: _____

To Whom It May Concern:

Please accept this letter as my permission to release <u>all</u> child abuse and neglect record information allowable by law to _____ _____, my potential child-care employer, at the following address: _____ _____.

Or, more specifically, please provide to the designated employer a statement verifying that you do <u>not</u> have me on record as having been in violation of the child abuse or neglect laws of this state.

If you are unable to release this information to the designated employer, then please release this information to me at my current address, listed as follows: _____

_____

_____

A processing fee of _____ is enclosed in the form of a (check appropriate box) ___ cashier's check, ___ money order, ___ personal check.

I have presented official copies of the following documents to the notary public whose name and stamp appears on this document: birth certificate, social security card, valid motor vehicle operator's license or a state ID, and naturalization papers (if applicable). All of the names match on these documents. If not, I have presented an official marriage certificate, divorce decree, or court order granting a name change.

_____
Print Your Full Name (Include Jr., Sr., etc.)

_____
Signature **(To be Signed only in the Presence of the Notary)**

_____
Please Print Any Other Formerly Used Names, Including your Maiden Name, Nicknames, All Aliases

(Continued on following page)

_____

_____

Current Address

_____

_____

Previous Address (Please list *all* addresses you resided at in this state over the past 5 years and the dates). **If additional space is required, please use the reverse side of this form.)**

_____   _____
Date of Birth   Place of Birth

_____   _____
Race   Sex

_____   _____
Driver's License Number   Issuing State of Driver's License

_____
Social Security Number

STATE OF _____

COUNTY OF _____

On this _____ day of _____ in the year _____ before me, _____ (name of notary), a Notary Public in and for said state, personally appeared _____ (name of individual), known to me to be the person who executed the within REQUEST FORM FOR A CHILD ABUSE AND NEGLECT BACKGROUND INVESTIGATION ON A CHILD CAREGIVER JOB APPLICANT, and acknowledged to me that s/he executed the same for the purposes therein stated.

_____   (SEAL)
Notary Public in and for said County and State
My commission expires:

Driving Record and Automobile Insurance Background Check

DRIVING RECORD

If driving is part of the caregiver's job responsibilities, it is a good idea to require a background check on the applicant's driving record and verification of current automobile insurance. The driving record will verify whether the applicant possesses a valid driver's license, whether the license has ever been suspended or revoked, whether there are any restrictions on the license, any history of driving under the influence of alcohol (DUI), and the number of points against the license for traffic violations. All of this information can be helpful to you in determining if the applicant is a mature, safe, responsible driver. Obviously, a poor driving record or a history of driving under the influence of alcohol are very serious matters when one is considering having this individual transport a child. Furthermore, a DUI can signal an underlying problem with alcohol or drug abuse.

Because of privacy laws, the applicant must request the driving record himself. The applicant can call the local police department, state police, or highway patrol office and ask for the phone number and address of the state office that conducts the driving record checks. In many states, the office is located in the state capital.

The form "Instructions for Caregiver Applicants for Requesting the Driving Record Check" (Box 12.5) can be given to the job applicant. It instructs the caregiver on how to expediently order a driving record check.

BOX 12.5. *Instructions for Caregiver Applicant for Requesting the Driving Record Check*

Because transporting our child will be part of the job, you need to submit an official copy of your driving record to us. Please follow these instructions to obtain this information from the state. *Your prompt handling of this matter will be very much appreciated.*

I. Contact your local police department, state police, or highway patrol, and obtain the name, address, and phone number of the state office that conducts driving record checks in the state that issued your driver's license. Frequently, these offices are located in the state capital.

2. Contact this state office, and ask them for information on how to obtain an official copy of your driving record for a prospective employer. Ask them to send you their request form and information regarding their processing fee. Most states will require you to have the form witnessed or notarized along with verifying documents, such as an official birth certificate, social security number, valid driver's license, and state ID.

Ask them how much time it will take for them to send you their request form and then to process it upon its receipt back from you.

3. Submit the driving record request form with the appropriate processing fee.

4. Please contact us and let us know when you have completed step 3 and when you expect to receive their response.

5. When your official driving record arrives, please allow us to view the *official document* and provide us with a photocopy for our files.

6. Please keep track of the fees and the time you spend doing this search, so we can reimburse you. You will be paid $____ per hour for your time.

Thank you very much for taking time to do this.

RELATED MATTERS

In addition to checking the applicant's driving record during this part of the process, you can check the following matters related to automobile safety: (1) the caregiver's motor vehicle insurance, (2) the caregiver's vehicle, and (3) the caregiver's driving ability.

To determine if an applicant has motor vehicle insurance, simply request the applicant to have his insurance agent send you verification of automobile insurance coverage. Then review this information to make sure the insurance is current and adequate. Also take note of when the insurance expires, and request the caregiver to provide you with an update at the time of renewal.

If the caregiver is going to use his own vehicle to transport your child, you may want to conduct a visual inspection of the vehicle. You may also require that the car have passed a state inspection if that is required in your state. If not, the American Automobile Association (AAA) has diagnostic clinics in many localities that provide full diagnostic checks with a written report for a nominal fee. Obviously, if the car is in poor repair, you may determine that it is not suitable for your child's safe transportation.

Finally, consider how long the applicant has been driving. Some caregivers may be very inexperienced behind the wheel. Do not assume that just because someone owns a car, that person is a good or experienced driver. Although this can be a sensitive issue to explore with your caregiver, it is nonetheless an important one. Ask the applicant how many accidents they have been involved in during the past 5 years, and carefully review their driving record. You may also want to ask the applicant to transport you somewhere, for example to and from your child's preschool, so you can observe his driving firsthand before deciding whether you want him to transport your child.

If the caregiver will be using your car to transport your child, it is wise to have him listed as a driver on your car insurance policy. This step will help ensure coverage in the event of an accident.

When you hire the caregiver, call your insurance agent and make the arrangement. Generally, they will ask for the date of birth, driver's license number, and history of any accidents and then run a motor vehicle record check.

Although one's rate does not generally increase for this coverage, there are exceptions. A higher rate may be charged for caregivers who are young drivers or for those with a poor driving record.

Take the time to evaluate your caregiver's driving record and insurance status. A family I know recently discovered that their child caregiver of several years did not possess a valid driver's license or car insurance *after* she was in an accident transporting their son. They were utterly

shocked when they discovered the situation. You can spare yourself this kind of trauma by specifically checking the record before hiring your caregiver.

Academic Record Check

Box 12.6 gives the applicant instructions for requesting an academic transcript, and Box 12.7 provides a form that can be used to request that an official copy of a high school, college, or university academic transcript be sent to you. The transcript will list courses, grades, and degrees earned. Or, the applicant can use the form to request a copy of a G.E.D. certificate (high school equivalency) and test scores.

In my experience, good students make good caregivers and excellent students make excellent caregivers. A person's grade point average not only reflects general intelligence but also how hard-working, focused, and committed that person can be in accomplishing tasks. There is a lot of evidence that, in general, the higher the education, the better the child caregiver.

If you want a caregiver who has formal training in areas related to child care, such as child development, child psychology, or early childhood education, the transcript will verify that the applicant completed these courses and earned at least a passing grade.

Verification Of Coursework In Emergency Resuscitation Procedures For Children

Anyone caring for children should be trained in emergency resuscitation procedures for infants and young children. If the caregiver has not taken a course in the last 12 months, have him retrain. You may request that he take a refresher course (and you may elect to pay for the course) or view a training video on the topic. (For more information, see Chapter 16). Parents and caregivers alike need to review emergency resuscitation materials on a regular basis to be adequately prepared in the event of an emergency.

Courses are readily available. The American Red Cross, for example, offers a 5-hour "Infant/Child CPR" course in many communities for parents, grandparents, and child-care providers, which covers the prevention of and emergency response to life-threatening emergencies, such as choking, respiratory crises, and cardiac arrest. The American Red Cross course is very affordable (currently $26.00 in our community). To find out more about this course offering, call the American Red Cross or the

BOX 12.6. *Instructions for Caregiver Applicant for Requesting Academic Transcript*

You are required to submit to us your academic transcript from the institution awarding your highest earned degree. If you have multiple degrees or have completed additional coursework towards another degree, we are interested in reviewing these transcripts as well.

If you have an official copy (not a photocopy) of your G.E.D. certificate, it is not necessary to request one. Please just present the official G.E.D. certificate to us for our review along with a photocopy for our records. If you do not have an official copy of your G.E.D., request one by contacting the office that oversees and records G.E.D. certification in the state that awarded your G.E.D. Ask this office if they will accept the attached "Academic Transcripts Request Form" in lieu of a release of information form. If you do not know who to contact to obtain a copy of your G.E.D., call the American Council on Education at (202) 939-9490. This organization, run by college and university presidents, oversees G.E.D. programs in all states.

1. Check the appropriate box at the top of the attached "Academic Transcripts Request Form" indicating the type of institution issuing the transcript or G.E.D. certificate.

2. Call the institution and request information on what office to send your transcript request, the institution's address and phone number, their processing fee, and the amount of time it takes to receive the transcript. Also, ask what information you need to provide in your request. Review the "Academic Transcripts Request Form" with them to make sure it includes everything they require.

3. Fill in the institution's name, address, and phone number in the blank spaces at the top of the form, along with the name of the office in the institution that handles academic transcript requests. Complete the rest of the transcript request form, have it witnessed (if required), and prepare to mail it in with your payment.

On the outside envelope, write "Requires Prompt Attention: Transcript Request Enclosed."

4. Contact us to let us know that you have mailed your transcript request and when you expect a response.

5. When your transcript arrives, please show us the *official document* and provide us with a photocopy for our records. You will then have a copy of your official transcript for your own files.

6. Please keep track of the fees and the time you spend doing this search, so we can reimburse you. You will be paid $____ per hour for your time.

Thank you for providing this information to us.

BOX 12.7. *Academic Transcript Request Form*

··

Please check one: ___ high school, ___ college/university, or ___ grantor of G.E.D. certificate

Attention: Transcript or G.E.D. Request

_____
Name of Institution and Office Handling Transcript/G.E.D. Requests

_____
Address

_____
Phone Number

To Whom It May Concern:

    Please accept this letter as my permission to release a copy of my official academic transcript or verification of receipt of a G.E.D. to my prospective employer: _____

_____
(fill in name and address of prospective employer).

Years of Attendance: _____ Graduation Date: _____

Degree Earned: _____ Social Security #: _____

A personal check for your processing fee of $_____ is enclosed.

_____   _____
Print Your Full Name   Your Signature and Date

_____   _____
Print Your Maiden Name or Any   Witness and Date
Other Name Used

_____
Print Your Address and Phone Number

Your prompt handling of this request will be appreciated. Thank you.

YMCA, which offers similar courses. Or, call the American Heart Association, your local hospital, or your child's pediatrician for information on course offerings in your community.

This book's request form for verification of training in emergency medical procedures (Box 12.8) can be given to child-care applicants.

149

BOX 12.8. *Instructions for Providing Verification of Training in Emergency Medical Procedures for Children*

••

We would like you to provide official verification of any training (and retraining) that you may have received in emergency resuscitation procedures or CPR for infants and children. Please show us any documents or certifications verifying completion of coursework or training in this area.

Depending on how recent and extensive your training, we may require you to take additional training. In this event, we will pay for the course but not for your time attending the course. Or, we may ask you to view training videos on this topic. We will provide the videos but may expect you to view them on your own time.

Please let us know if you have any questions about this request.

The Infectious and Communicable Disease Medical Examination For Child Caregivers

To help ensure that your child does not contract a serious infectious disease, like tuberculosis, from his caregiver, you can require a medical examination for infectious and communicable diseases after you have made a job offer.

Under the Americans with Disabilities Act of 1990, an employer may condition a job offer on the satisfactory result of a post job offer medical examination or inquiry as long as such an examination is required of all employees who have been extended an offer.

150

One may disqualify an individual who would pose a direct threat to the health and safety of their child or family. Under federal law, HIV is not currently considered an infectious disease that necessarily constitutes a direct threat. Nonetheless, if you encounter this situation, it's advisable to consult with a competent attorney.

The instructions (Box 12.9) and accompanying form "Infectious and Communicable Diseases Medical Examination for Child Caregivers" (Box 12.10) can be given to your new caregiver. The caregiver can take this form to his own physician, or, you can require him to be examined by a physician of your choice.

If you select the physician, you will have greater control over the examination. You will be able to call the physician in advance, discuss your concerns and desire to hire a child caregiver who is not a carrier of serious infectious and communicable diseases, and determine whether he is willing and able to provide such an examination. Your own family physician or internist may take a more personal interest in providing this examination because it involves your child.

Because this examination is unlikely to be covered by the caregiver's health insurance, I recommend that parents pay for it. You can arrange for payment with the doctor's office at the time the appointment is made. Many doctor's offices will accept a credit card number by phone, or you can mail them a personal check.

Knowing that your child's caregiver is free of serious infectious and communicable diseases will be one less thing to worry about and is therefore well worth the cost. This examination will help prevent the costly medical expenses and serious health problems that you and your entire family could incur should your child contract a serious infectious and communicable disease.

BOX 12.9. *Instructions for Undergoing the Infectious and Communicable Diseases Medical Examination*

Before caring for our child, you must undergo an infectious and communicable disease medical examination to ensure that you are not a carrier of an infectious and communicable disease, like tuberculosis. *As soon as possible*, please make an appointment with your physician and have him/her complete the attached "Infectious and Communicable Diseases Medical Examination for Child Caregivers" form.

We will pay for this examination. If your doctor's office requires payment at the time of service, please ask the office to call us at _____(our phone number), at the time you set up the appointment, and we will arrange for payment in advance.

Please submit the completed examination form to us as soon as possible.

Thank you.

BOX 12.10. *Infectious and Communicable Diseases Medical Examination Form for Child Caregiver*

Patient's Full Name: _____

Date of Birth: _____

I, the undersigned physician, hereby certify that the above named individual is free of infectious and communicable diseases that could pose a direct threat to the health and safety of children under his/her care.

Physician's Name:_____
                               (Please Print)

Address: _____

Phone: _____

_____
Physician's Signature and Date

Preemployment Drug Screen

Under federal law, you can also ask a caregiver to undergo a drug test before extending an offer of employment. However, if you require this test for one employee, you need to be consistent with all employees. You should also offer to pay for the test (it costs in the range of $75.00). Some states may restrict your ability to ask an applicant to submit to a drug test. To check the laws in your state, call your state department of labor or a competent attorney.

Although I personally have not requested drug screens, you may want to invest in this for your own peace of mind.

152

SUMMARY

Critical information about a caregiver applicant can be obtained through well-conducted background record checks. If you are wondering, "Why bother?" remember that this person will be in the inner sanctuary of your home and could potentially rob you of the things you treasure the most: your privacy, your prized posessions, and your child's and family's sense of well-being and happiness.

The materials in this chapter are designed to make your background searches as efficient and trouble-free as possible. With the data in hand, you'll be better prepared to select the best candidate.

Calling the Applicant's References

"I would like to speak to someone who knows the applicant well, but I am afraid they will offer a biased portrayal because they are a friend or they will be afraid to speak to me for fear of being sued. Also, I'm not sure what are the most important questions to ask."

154

S*peaking directly to at least two individuals* <u>*who know the caregiver well*</u> *before you make the decision to hire is essential.* People who have actually worked with the applicant, preferably a former boss, are often the most informative. A caregiver may present a good impression during the interviews and on paper, provide glowing letters of recommendation, but still be a difficult person to work with or a poor employee. The best predictor of future behavior is past behavior. Speaking with someone who has directly observed and experienced this past behavior can be very helpful—provided you ask the right questions and receive spontaneous, honest replies. Using the "Form for Calling a Job Reference Provided by the Child-Care Applicant" (Box 13.1) can help you ask the right questions to solicit spontaneous, honest responses.

You will automatically have a list of job references to call if you use this book's "Job Application Form" (see Box 8.1). On this form, applicants are instructed to list at least three references who have known them well, preferably in the last several years, including at least two employment references and one person who has known them well for at least 5 years.

So often people make the false assumption that people serving as references won't be willing to share "the truth" about an applicant. *I have been amazed over time at just how much job references are willing to share.* Sometimes I have gotten off the phone, shaking my head in amazement, surprised that the applicant listed that person as a reference. *If you feel tempted to bypass this step in the hiring process, don't.*

It is well worth your time, and using the "Form for Calling a Job Reference provided by the Child-Care Applicant" will help make these phone calls go smoothly. In fact, the form's script makes it easy even for those I lightheartedly refer to as "phoneaphobics." You can photocopy this form or use this book's optional computer diskette (see Appendix A for ordering information) to customize the form to suit your needs.

・・・・・・・・・・・・・・

In my experience, it takes about 10 minutes, using the form's script, to call a reference.

When you call the reference, place the form in front of you and take notes in the space provided.

SPEAK TO KNOWLEDGEABLE REFERENCES

Speak to at least one person who has known the caregiver for at least 5 years. Such references will give you a better picture of how well your potential caregiver handles work and life in general over the long haul. You'll get a clearer idea of how she functions during stressful times (we all have those) as well as on a day-by-day basis. You'll likely get more valuable insight into the type of person the applicant truly is, what matters most to her in life, and how committed she is to children and to their care.

Also, speak to at least one reference who previously employed the applicant as a child caregiver. This type of reference will have the most information to offer regarding the applicant's child-care and work-related skills.

However, some excellent candidates, like an immigrant or a retired person who raised their own family, may not be able to provide such a job reference. They may not have worked in child care before but are nonetheless very capable. In these situations, speak to someone who has known them well over a period of time, such as a former employer, pastor, doctor, English language teacher, host family member, or long-term family friend.

In addition, sometimes job applicants are reluctant to ask their current employer to serve as a job reference because they don't want to jeopardize their current job in the event that they are not hired by you. Sometimes they may be willing to let you speak with a co-worker instead.

SPEAK DIRECTLY WITH THE REFERENCE

In general, speaking directly with a reference by phone or in a personal meeting is better than reading a written reference: You can follow through on comments to get the whole story, and you can determine if the reference is reliable.

When you speak with a reference, you can pick up subtle clues, such as a pause indicating a reluctance to share some information or a tone of voice that might convey a lack of enthusiasm about the applicant. These nonverbal clues are not available in a carefully polished letter of recommendation.

• • • • • • • • • • • • • •

When I suspect that there is something important not being said, I am able to say something like, "You seem somewhat reluctant to endorse this individual fully; is there something about her that is difficult to discuss but perhaps important for me to know?" Whenever I ask such a question, the respondent usually jumps in and shares something important.

Speaking directly with the reference also gives you the opportunity to evaluate the reference herself. Some people provide thoughtful, fair, well-balanced evaluations, but others may be incapable of providing this for one reason or another. It is important to evaluate the person providing the job reference because it will help you decide how much weight to give their evaluation. Some may be unwilling to take the time required to give a thoughtful response, others may have an ax to grind and thereby are unable to give an impartial evaluation, and still others may not have enough experience with the individual to provide the information you need. Box 13.1 includes questions to help you assess whether the person serving as a reference is capable of doing a good job.

If the applicant provides the names of individuals who turn out to be poor sources of information, you can always ask her for additional names, emphasizing that you want references who know her and her work well. If an applicant does not provide references who know her well, it is important to consider the possibility she may not want you to speak to anyone who knows her well.

Again, the form in Box 13.1 helps you assess the references by asking such questions as, "How long have you known _____ and in what capacity have you known him/her?" and "On a scale of 1 to 10, how well do you feel you know him/her, with 1 being very very little and 10 being very very well?"

• • • • • • • • • • • • • •

I once encountered a situation in which a job applicant gave references who did not know her child-care skills well enough. Fortunately, I just happened to meet someone who knew her well, had worked with her for 3 years, and told me that she had many interpersonal problems on the job. I was very glad to have this information.

ELICIT FULL RESPONSES

You are more likely to get full, honest responses from references if you let them know what the position is, ask questions to clarify general statements, express an open attitude toward the applicant, and inform the reference of their legal protection in giving a reference.

Tell the reference something about the position and your child at the outset of the call so that she will know that the job position the applicant is being considered for is a very important one.

. . . .

I try to convey what I believe: No job is more important than providing loving care to a child during their early, formative years.

Also, ask follow-up questions. Frequently, the person providing the reference will make general statements that require clarification. If you are not sure what the person is trying to communicate, ask her. For example, you may be told that the person sometimes arrived late for work. When you ask for clarification, you find out that it was never more than 5 minutes and it happened perhaps 3 or 4 times a month. With this kind of detailed information, you can decide for yourself how much weight to give it. When an evaluative judgment is made about an applicant, for example, "She is very assertive," I will typically follow this up with, "Can you give me an example of what you are referring to?" Behavioral examples will let *you* decide whether this information about the applicant is something positive or negative.

In addition, following the form in Box 13.1 will help prevent you from falling into a trap I have caught myself falling into more than once: leading the witness.

. . . .

I was so excited about hiring a particular person that I posed questions in such a way as to elicit only positive information. On such occasions, I found myself hanging up and only then realizing that there were important areas I did not address and that I had phrased questions in such a way that would have made it very hard for the person I was calling to do anything but agree with me. For example, I would say something like, "She seems terrific; did you enjoy having her work for you?" I might as well

have said, "Oh please, don't tell me anything bad. I really like this person and I don't want to be disappointed."

I was most apt to fall into this trap when I was forgetting that there are many wonderful, available people out there to care for young children. I falsely believed that if that particular applicant didn't work out, I would have no one.

If this happens to you, take a deep breath, remind yourself once again that there are many wonderful caregivers out there, and then place the call. Following the form in Box 13.1 will help you conduct an unbiased reference check and also elicit the unbiased responses you need, so that you hire someone who is going to work out best for you and your child in the long run.

Also inform the reference that the applicant signed an indemnification agreement on the "Job Application Form" (see Box 8.1). The indemnification agreement states, "I authorize the release of any or all information regarding my person, past or present employment, or any other aspect, whether personal or otherwise, and do hereby further release and agree to hold harmless any individual, company, organization, or entity from any and all liability or damage whatsoever that may develop from furnishing such information to my potential employer identified above at the top of this application form." Having the applicant sign this statement, although no guarantee, will provide the person serving as a reference with the legal protection they need to respond honestly to all of your questions.

Many state legislatures have enacted laws to protect former employers being asked to provide references from lawsuit. As of June, 1996, 10 states have enacted such laws, and several other states are considering such legislation. Talk to your attorney about the above indemnification agreement and laws in your own state so that you can obtain the information you need without placing the reference in jeopardy (Safer reference checks, 1996, p. 15).

Reference

Safer reference checks. (1996, June). <u>Bottom Line/Business,</u> p. 15.

BOX 13.1. *Form for Calling a Job Reference Provided by the Child-Care Applicant*

Applicant's Name: _____

Date: _____

Reference's Name: _____

Phone Number: _____

Reference's Relationship to Applicant: _____

1. Placing the call and introducing yourself to the reference:

"Hello, my name is _____. Your name was given to me by _____ who is applying for a child-care position in our home. S/he indicated that s/he worked with/for you between _____ and _____, and s/he listed you as an employment reference."

"If hired, s/he will be caring for our _____-year-old child. We want to hire someone who is loving, responsible, competent, mature, and committed to providing excellent care. Our child is very precious to us. We're interviewing a number of people for this position, and we want to select the best."

"I was wondering if you would be willing to speak to me about him/her and if this would be a good time for you to talk? I anticipate that this will require less than 10 minutes of your time." (Pause for a response)

If the reference seems reluctant, advise him/her that the applicant signed a release of information and indemnification agreement on the job application. You can read this agreement (see Box 8.1) to the reference and offer to mail a copy upon request. You can also offer to have the applicant call them first, if they haven't already, and confirm that they want the reference to speak openly with you.

(If the response is affirmative, proceed with the following.)

"As I ask you questions, I would like to take some notes on your responses. If I pause as we speak, it is because I am taking time to do this."

"Also, if I ask you any questions that you feel you cannot adequately answer for any reason whatsoever, please just let me know."

2. Assessing how well the reference knows the applicant:

a. *"How long have you known _____ and in what capacity have you known him/her?"*

(*Continued on following page*)

b. If this is a previous employer, boss, or coworker, you can ask:
   "_____ *indicated that s/he worked for/with you between the dates of _____ and _____. Is that accurate? What was his/her job title, and what were his/her responsibilities?*"

c. "*On a scale of 1 to 10, how well do you feel you know him/her, with 1 being very very little and 10 being very very well?*"

d. If an applicant does not feel s/he can adequately serve as a reference, you can ask the following:
   "*Is there someone else you know who might provide information on _____, whom you might recommend to us? Naturally, we will obtain _____'s permission first before contacting this person.*"

3. Eliciting information and asking questions:

I suggest that you begin with open-ended questions and then follow these up, as needed, with more specific questions. The following are some questions you might want to ask.
   Open-ended questions:

a. "*What can you tell me about _____?*"

b. "*What words or phrases would you use to describe him/her*
   (1) *as a child caregiver?*
   (2) *as an employee?*
   (3) *as a person?*"

c. "*How would you describe your relationship with him/her?*"

d. "*If given the opportunity, would you hire him/her to care for your own child or grandchild? If not, why not?*"

e. "*What are his/her strengths?*"

f. "*What are his/her weaknesses?*"

g. "*What do you like the most and what do you like the least about him/her?*"

h. "*How would you describe his/her relationship with his/her own children/grandchildren?*"

Specific Questions:

i. "*Is there anything about him/her that we've not covered so far that you feel I should know about?*"

j. "*I would now like to ask a series of questions that you can answer <u>yes</u> or <u>no</u> to. Do you have any knowledge about this applicant with regard to the following:*

(*Continued on following page*)

(1) *child mistreatment, abuse, or neglect, or just plain insensitivity towards a child?*
(2) *stealing, dishonesty, or criminal activities?*
(3) *current drug abuse or addiction?*
(4) *excessive absenteeism, showing up late, or not showing up at all for work for any reasons unrelated to any disability?*
(5) *being a difficult person to work with?*
(6) *being (*note: read the following slowly*) moody, unmotivated, inflexible, uncooperative, controlling, demanding, immature, irresponsible, etc.?*
(7) *having personal problems which interfere with her ability to function well at work?"*

k. *"Is s/he able to do the following:*
(1) *say* no *as well as respect another's* no*?*
(2) *remain patient and loving with a child when she is exhausted and exasperated?*
(3) *respect a family's privacy and not gossip?*
(4) *deal with conflict appropriately?*
(5) *remain positive and motivated?*
(6) *remain focused on the child's needs versus his/her own while caring for a child?"*

l. *"How intelligent do you think s/he is on a scale from 1 to 10, with 10 being extremely bright?"*

m. *"Do you know if s/he feels spanking is sometimes an ok way to discipline a child? If so, can you elaborate?"*

n. Review the "Required Qualifications for Child Caregivers" (see Box 6.1) and the "Personalized List of Important Caregiver Qualities" (see Box 6.3) to see if you want to inquire about any other qualities here.

4. Ending the call and expressing appreciation:

a. *"Is there anything else that I haven't asked about that you think is important or that you would like to add or clarify before we stop?"*

b. *"Thank you so much for your time and information. It will be very helpful to us in making a good decision. I would like to leave with you my name and phone number, in the event that more information comes to mind and you would like to contact me. My name is _____ and my phone number is _____. Again, thank you very much."*

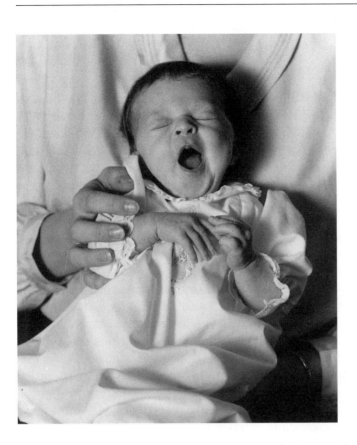

14

Orienting the Caregiver to Your Child and Your Home

"There is so much I would like the caregiver to know about our child and our home before I would feel comfortable leaving for work. Help. Where do I start? How can I do this without overwhelming either one of us?"

164

Taking time to orient a caregiver is a good investment. It will prevent problems and save considerable time in the long haul. An orientation allows time for your child and caregiver to get to know each other and for your caregiver to learn the new job before taking over. When the time comes for you to walk out the door to go to work, you, your child, and the caregiver will all feel a greater inner peace because the stage has been set for a smooth transition.

Introducing a new caregiver in the home does involve a period of adjustment and can be stressful for everyone, but you can make the change positive by taking your time, sharing information, and focusing on what's important: enjoying caring for your child. In fact, I am always delightfully surprised at how well things can go during the orientation of new caregivers. I keep expecting it to be more stressful. Still, it usually takes several months before everyone is settled into the new arrangement.

Being organized helps tremendously, though, and this chapter will help you make the transition go smoothly. It provides suggestions on orienting your child to the caregiver and giving the caregiver important information about your child, your home, and job responsibilities.

The orientation will be most productive if you focus on what is most important—the caregiver-child relationship—and introduce less important information at a later date. Remember, you will also be giving the caregiver written instructions, including the written "Child-Care Agreement Form" (see Box 9.1), to refer to as he learns the new job.

Taking your time to orient the caregiver and having realistic expectations at the beginning will help keep your caregiver's anxiety low. The more relaxed everyone is, the smoother the adjustment.

• • • • • • • • • • • • • •

I learned through experience what is most important to cover during orientation and how to focus on that. At first, however, I made the mistake of trying to provide too much information at once, and I overwhelmed our first caregiver. Over time I have learned that it works best to go slowly and do it over a period of days or weeks, rather than all at once.

Now, at the beginning, I tell the caregiver that I don't expect him to remember everything we discuss. There will be a lot of new information, and it will take time to assimilate everything. Repetition greatly enhances

learning, so I repeat important points. I point out that my repetition of instructions is not a reflection on his intelligence but rather an attempt to help him remember the most important facts.

To prevent the caregiver from feeling overwhelmed, I also give brief written instructions for some things, like how to operate the washing machine or the microwave. In that way, he can concentrate on retaining other, more important information.

Also, at the beginning, I may have the caregiver do fewer chores to give him time to adjust to the new situation. As his relationship with our child is more secure, I will introduce his other responsibilities. I explain that I will simplify the job in the beginning, gradually adding tasks when it seems appropriate, giving extra time to focus on the most important part of the job, that of establishing a positive, loving relationship with our child.

The transition will also go smoothly if you make it clear from the beginning that you are in charge. *When you hire a caregiver in your home, handle things in a professional manner and always keep in mind that this is a business relationship.* Just as you convey to your child that you are the boss, it is equally important to convey that same message to your caregiver. That doesn't mean that you can't develop a warm, caring relationship. It does mean, however, that things function best when you, the employer, are able to offer direction, guidance, feedback, and respectfully address matters that are not to your liking. Take a leadership role to ensure that your child receives the best possible care.

ORIENTING YOUR CHILD TO THE NEW CAREGIVER

One of the most important tasks at the outset of this new relationship is helping your child adjust to the new caregiver and helping the caregiver get to know your child. How difficult this adjustment will be for your child depends on a number of factors: your child's age and disposition, his attachment to you, and his previous experience and exposure to others. If previous social and caregiver contacts have been positive, your child will probably adjust well and fairly quickly.

. . . .

I have been amazed at how well my son has adjusted. He had to adjust to new part-time caregivers at 12, 18, and 27 months, and each time he did

very well. I had anticipated that it would be more problematic and was always delightfully surprised.

Taking special steps to help your child adjust to the new caregiver will certainly decrease the likelihood of difficulties. The following are strategies I have used that were particularly helpful.

Suggestions for Orienting Your Child to the New Caregiver

- Set a positive model by talking to your child enthusiastically about the caregiver coming.

....

When I talk with my son about a caregiver coming to care for him, I say it with excitement in my voice, conveying the message that this person is very special. I talk with him about some of the fun things they will do together (e.g., read books, go to the park, play with his blocks). My excitement is genuine. My son has loved his caregivers and has developed a very special relationship with each of them. They are his "friends."

- Allow your child and your new caregiver to go slowly to get to know each other. Do not force them on each other. Allow plenty of time for your child to be with the new caregiver in your presence before leaving. This can be arranged by asking the caregiver to come and spend time with you and your child, for several hours on several different occasions, before you have to leave for work. If you are unable to make such an arrangement during the week, you can ask if the caregiver is available to come on the weekend or for one or more hours in the morning before you leave for work.

  Children typically do best when they have had prior opportunities to observe their parents and caregiver interact comfortably. Paying your caregiver for his time during orientation is money well spent.

- Arrange for your former caregiver to be present while your child is getting to know the new caregiver. I only recommend taking

this step, however, if you have been pleased with him. I have made this arrangement with our caregivers, and it has worked very well. It allows the new caregiver to learn a typical day's routine, while we are at work, before taking over on his own.

You can also ask your former caregiver to pass along information and advice. A friend of mine asked her cherished caregiver who was leaving to prepare a list of child-care tips and insights on her children for the new caregiver.

- In the beginning, have the caregiver engage in activities that are fun and enjoyable for your child.

167

. . . .

Initially, for example, I do the difficult tasks, like diaper changing, if possible. This step keeps my son's relationship with the new caregiver on a positive note, and it also allows the caregiver time to observe how I handle my son when he is being uncooperative. The caregiver can observe me turning the difficult activity into a game, distracting my son, and thereby getting the job done with a minimum of fuss and tears. This information will be very helpful to the caregiver at a later point when he is handling him on his own.

- Share with the caregiver tips you have learned that help calm your child when he becomes upset.

. . . .

I tell my caregiver, for example, how my son calms down quickly and loves it when I pick him up and take him to the window to look out, pointing out what we see. Or, he likes it when I sing a song or hand him a favorite toy or his pacifier.

- Model tasks for the caregiver, showing established routines. Children love routine. It helps them feel secure. They will feel more comfortable if the caregiver follows a familiar routine at the beginning. Later, as they feel more comfortable with each other, they will establish their own way of doing things.

• • • • • • • • • • • • •

When time allows, I model such tasks as feeding and putting our son to sleep so that the caregiver can directly observe our routines.

As a parent, I have found that things go more smoothly when I follow a fairly predictable schedule for mealtimes, naps, outings, playtime, and bedtime. If you have an established daytime routine, share this schedule with the caregiver. It will help him organize his day, and the routine will be familiar and comforting for your child.

• At the beginning, offer the caregiver a lot of support, reassurance, and help. Let him know that it will take time for both him and your child to be comfortable and to establish a bond and a relationship on their own terms.

• • • • • • • • • • • • •

I want my son to have caring relationships with people outside of our family and I am very supportive of these relationships. The emotional bonds he establishes during these early, formative years will serve as the blueprint for his friendships and intimate relationships later in life.

Because these early bonds are so critical to my son's social and emotional development, I will gently intervene if I feel the caregiver is unknowingly doing something my child doesn't like or that I feel is negative. For example, if a caregiver were to say to my child, "You're a bad boy," I would intervene and model an alternative comment that is more appropriate such as, "Matthew, I don't want you to tear your book. Be gentle. Books are very special." I would then explain, "Jim, please don't tell Matthew that he is a bad boy. I want him to know that although his behavior might be unacceptable at times, <u>he</u> is not bad. If he is doing something you don't like, you can focus on his unacceptable <u>behavior</u>. In that way, he will learn what's right without receiving a message that he is bad."

Particularly at the beginning, you may need to train your caregiver to relate to your child in the manner that you desire. You need to step in and respectfully offer guidance, feedback, and correction, balancing all of this with lots of praise and positive feedback for what he is doing well. I have found that if I have done a good job of selecting an excellent caregiver, minimal or no effort on my part is required for such training.

PROVIDING THE CAREGIVER WITH IMPORTANT INFORMATION ABOUT YOUR CHILD, YOUR HOME, AND JOB RESPONSIBILITIES

Providing General Orientation

The "Orientation Checklist" in Box 14.1 includes important information that you will probably want to cover during orientation. This list is included in the book's optional computer diskette containing all the book's forms (see Appendix A for ordering information). To keep track of what information you have given him, make a checkmark next to each item that you cover and then place the list in his employment file.

169

Providing the Caregiver with Written Information About Your Child

The "Information About Our Child" form in Box 14.2 can be completed by you and given to your new caregiver during orientation. It elicits helpful tips and valuable information about your child. You will probably only use this form at the beginning with a new caregiver because this kind of information is typically shared verbally on an ongoing basis. This form can also be used with others watching your child, like grandparents and babysitters. All of your child's caregivers will appreciate having this kind of information in writing so that they can refer to it while building a relationship with your child.

This form is included in this book's optional computer diskette (see Appendix A for ordering information). Make two copies of the completed form: Give one to the caregiver, and place the other in the "Emergency Information" file located with his time sheets. This second copy will help you keep track of the information you have provided, and the caregiver can refer back to it as needed. You can then keep the original in the caregiver's employment file. It is helpful to keep the original so that you can make copies of it in the future for other caregivers.

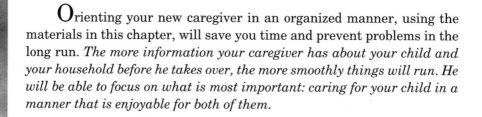

SUMMARY

Orienting your new caregiver in an organized manner, using the materials in this chapter, will save you time and prevent problems in the long run. *The more information your caregiver has about your child and your household before he takes over, the more smoothly things will run. He will be able to focus on what is most important: caring for your child in a manner that is enjoyable for both of them.*

BOX 14.1. *Orientation Checklist*

Important information to cover with your new caregiver during orientation:

- The completed "Information About Our Child Form" (Box 14.2)
- The location of child-related items: kitchen utensils used for milk and food preparation, food and snacks, bottles, nipples, pacifiers, surplus supplies of diapers, wipes, tissues, sun protection lotion, etc.
- The location of your child's clothes, linens, bath supplies
- The location of a copy of the "Child-Care Agreement Form" (see Box 9.1), ideally filed in the "Emergency Information" file, which is placed with the time sheets
- The chores you expect to have done on an ongoing basis, such as keeping the child's room and toys picked up, washing dishes after meals, keeping the kitchen clean, helping with laundry, meal preparation, and light housecleaning
- The location of household items, such as the broom and dust pan, cleaning supplies, toilet paper and plunger, scissors, tape, pens and paper, sewing kit, garbage bags and container
- Instructions on sorting and doing the laundry
- Instructions on how to operate the washer and dryer, dishwasher, microwave, answering machine, etc., with brief written instructions
- Emergency instructions: the completed "Emergency Information Sheet" (see Box 16.4)
  The location of the first aid kit, fuse boxes, fire extinguishers, and smoke detectors
  Instructions with written signs on how to turn off the electricity, furnace, and central air conditioner, and the main gas and water lines in the event of an emergency
- The location of your (1) "Emergency Information" file, ideally placed with the caregiver's time sheets, (2) "Emergency Information Sheets," ideally placed near each phone, with one copy for your caregiver's wallet, (3) "Consent Form for Emergency Medical Care" ideally filed with item 1, with one copy for the caregiver's wallet, and (4) "List of Important Phone Numbers," placed near each phone with one copy for the caregiver's wallet (see Boxes 16.1–16.4)
- Instructions for completing time sheets and their location (see Boxes 18.2–18.3)

BOX 14.2. *Information About Our Child Form*

• •

Date: _____

Our Child's Name: _____ Nicknames: _____

A brief description of our child's typical daily schedule:

A.M.

_____
_____
_____

P.M.

_____
_____
_____

Feeding:

Please feed our child the following liquids/foods (specify types and amounts), according to the following, typical feeding schedule:

_____
_____
_____

This is how our child lets us know s/he is hungry:

_____

Our child's favorite foods: _____

Healthy snacks you can feed our child: _____

Please do *not* feed our child the following liquids/foods:

_____
_____
_____

A brief description of our feeding routine (e.g., hold while feeding, burp after every 3 oz.'s, place in high chair, child feeds self) and strategies we use to encourage healthy eating (e.g., keep mealtime pleasant, please do not insist that our child eat if s/he is not interested, no sweets unless approved by us):

_____
_____
_____

Special feeding problems and how we respond when they occur:

_____
_____

(Continued on following page)

BOX 14.2. *Information About Our Child Form* (Continued)

Sleeping:

Our child's typical naptime/bedtime schedule (including length of sleep):

_____
_____

This is how our child lets us know s/he is tired:

_____

A brief description of our child's naptime/bedtime routine and strategies we use to promote healthy sleep, including special ways we put our child to sleep (such as rocking, listening to soft music, placing in the crib awake):

_____
_____
_____

Our child sleeps with the following (e.g., pacifier, blanket, toy):

_____

Our child's sleep position (e.g., on his/her back): _____

Special sleep problems and how we respond when they occur:

_____
_____

Diapering/Toileting Behavior:

Our child _____ is _____ is not (check) toilet trained.

Our child needs his/her diapers changed approximately every _____ (specify time).

This is how our child lets us know s/he needs to have his/her diaper changed or to go to the bathroom:

_____

Other special diapering/toileting instructions:

_____
_____

Bathing:

Our child's bath time schedule:

_____

(Continued on following page)

BOX 14.2. *Information About Our Child Form* (Continued)

Our suggestions for making it go smoothly:

_____
_____
_____

Additional comments:

_____
_____

Special Medical Problems or Disabilities:

Allergies:

_____

Food Sensitivities:

_____

(Note: Please take great care to prevent exposure to these.)

Our child has the following medical problems or disabilities:

_____
_____

This is how we respond to these special needs:

_____
_____

Our child is on the following medication (specify what it is for, where it is stored, possible side effects and how to respond should they occur, and dosage amount and specific instructions on how and when it is to be administered by the caregiver):

_____
_____
_____
_____
_____

Reminder: Please document the time, amount, and name of medication given on the form "A Report of Our Child's Day."

Emotional Well-Being:

This is how our child exhibits the following emotions and ways that we respond or comfort our child:

fear or anxiety: _____

shyness: _____

(Continued on following page)

BOX 14.2. *Information About Our Child Form* (Continued)

sadness: _____

anger or frustration: _____

aggression: _____

The following things/situations upset or frighten our child, and this is how we respond:

_____

_____

The following lists our child's *favorite* things and activities:

toys: _____

books: _____

songs or music: _____

arts/crafts activities: _____

videotapes or TV programs: _____

games: _____

activities: _____
        (Can include such things as sitting in his/her bouncy seat
        or going to the park.)

comfort items: _____
        (Can include such things as a special blanket or toy
        or a pacifier.)

Additional Comments:

_____

_____

_____

Maintaining a Positive Working Relationship with Your Caregiver

"Now that we've found someone wonderful, I want to make sure that she is happy so that she will stay with us for a long time. I also need help in knowing how to deal with the normal tensions that might arise. Do you have any suggestions?"

Handling the interviewing and orientation phases well, as discussed in previous chapters, will lay the foundation for an ongoing, mutually satisfying relationship. As an employer, being warm, genuinely caring, and kind, along with being organized, professional, and skilled in handling conflict, helps maintain a positive employer-employee relationship, as this chapter shows.

178

HOW TO BUILD A POSITIVE RELATIONSHIP

Recognize the Caregiver's Needs

Perhaps the most important thing you can do for the caregiver is to remain open, flexible, and willing to negotiate to meet *her* needs. *A good child-care arrangement exists when everyone's needs are considered and respected. Caring for children is at times a very demanding job. It is easy to forget or to minimize what it takes to provide good, attentive care for children. The caregiver will feel good about you and the job if she feels that her needs are also valued.* I encourage my caregivers to let me know if there is something they need. I try hard to do what I can, within reason, to accommodate their wishes. I have felt a great deal of joy in my relationship with our caregivers because they have always extended this courtesy back to me tenfold.

Value the Caregiver

Unfortunately, we live in a culture that devalues many of the occupations associated with caring for children, including child care. In my opinion, no job in life is more important than that of helping our young grow up to be healthy, capable, self-confident, and happy. The caregiver needs to know that you value what she does.

A positive relationship with a caregiver is based on deep respect and appreciation for her. Caring for children is not an easy nor a well-paying job. It requires maturity, responsibility, and love. What a good caregiver offers cannot be adequately compensated for financially, and I will often remind caregivers that I know what they offer is priceless. Taking time to express appreciation and saying "thanks" is very important.

Also, pay the caregiver as much as you can afford, even if that means paying more than the going rate. Low pay is one of the primary causes of the high turnover rate and low morale among child-care workers.

You can compensate the caregiver in ways other than money too. You can do something nice like purchase tickets for a special concert or play, give them a gift certificate redeemable at a favorite store or restaurant, or give them a bonus. These nice, unexpected compensations are always appreciated. I will sometimes surprise the caregiver with a treat if I want to remind her that I think she is terrific or if I want to thank her for doing something special for us, like providing tender, loving care to our child during an illness. Or, a simple note of thanks is also a meaningful gesture. One of my close friends marks her caregiver's birthday on the calendar and then gives her a card with a check and a note that says, "Please treat yourself to a birthday lunch on us." She includes enough money for two. She also gives a small gift on Valentine's Day, a special card on Mother's Day, and a large cash bonus at the end of the year.

Follow this basic rule of thumb: As an employer treat the employee as you would like to be treated.

Handle Conflict Constructively

As with any significant relationship, conflict is sometimes unavoidable. Misunderstandings, misperceptions, and problems can occur. What is important is *how* one handles it. The following are some tips for successfully handling conflict:

- *Address rather than ignore problems and, in general, the sooner the better.*

  It is best to nip a problem in the bud rather than allow it to develop into a bigger problem.

  The only exception to this rule is that some minor issues, which in the big scheme of things are not really that important, are best overlooked. A minor issue is one in which the child's well-being is not at stake but there is a difference of opinion about how things are done. For example, you prefer to bathe your child before dinner, but the caregiver prefers to bathe her after. Such differences in opinion are not necessarily problems.

  First decide if you have a "difference of opinion" or a "problem" that places your child at risk or creates tension. Then proceed accordingly. You can let some minor differences of opinion go. In other cases, you may acknowledge that they are minor but request an action anyway, saying, for example, "I realize this is just my individual quirk, but I'd prefer if you would bathe Becky

before dinner." *In trying to decide whether to say anything, take into account that if you ask yourself to ignore too many minor issues, you place yourself at risk for feeling angry and resentful down the road.* Remember, you are the boss. You get to have things handled the way *you* like. You are the one paying the salary.

- Take time, before you address any problem, to determine how to best bring the problem to the caregiver's attention.

    Acting with gentleness, showing respect, and giving the other the benefit of the doubt works best. Ask yourself, "How would I want someone to approach me with a concern like this one?" The following examples show some good ways to bring up problems.

    "I noticed that you put down on your time sheet that you worked 8 hours on September 4th. I could be mistaken, but I thought you only worked 4 hours that day because of a doctor's appointment?"

    "I've noticed lately that you haven't had time to give our daughter her daily bath. I know things can get very hectic, especially after naptime with the trip to the park and snack time. It's really important to me that she get a daytime bath because her early bedtime doesn't allow time for one in the evening. Can we talk about her daily schedule and see what changes can be made to fit this in without placing undue pressure on you?"

    "You've seemed more quiet than usual lately, and I've wondered if everything is going ok for you here? Is there something that is concerning you?"

    "Several times I have reminded you to pick up Natalie's toys at the end of each day, and I've noticed that it's not getting done. Is this because you have forgotten or haven't had time, or is there something bothering you about this situation?"

- After you have opened up the problem for discussion, listen carefully to the caregiver's concerns, paraphrasing them first before responding so that she knows that you have heard her.

    For example, you can say, *"Mary, what I hear you saying is that when I arrive home 15 minutes late, it makes things very difficult for you because your children are waiting for you to pick them up from school."*

    After conveying that you have heard her concerns, respond in a nondefensive manner with *I* statements. For example, you can say, *"I feel bad that my coming home late has caused you difficulties. This problem seems to come up most often on Tuesdays*

when I have the late meeting at work. I will see if the meeting can be scheduled 15 minutes earlier in an effort to prevent this problem in the future."

Or, if you are the one with the concern, you can respond to her possible defensiveness by remaining emotionally calm and nonreactive. *"Susan, I understand that you are not an early riser by nature and arriving on time for work is really difficult for you. I appreciate your efforts in this regard. It will make things go so much more smoothly for me at work, however, if you arrive on time because I am expected to be on time for the 9:00 o'clock sales meeting each morning."*

Express your concern, what you would like the other to do about it, and then respectfully "let go," trusting she will honor your wishes.

- Resolve any conflicts face-to-face and not through notes.

  One of my friends had a caregiver who left angry notes, and when she tried to discuss the problem with her, she would deny that she was angry. In such a situation, ask the caregiver to communicate in person rather than through notes.

HOW TO TERMINATE THE EMPLOYMENT OF AN UNSATISFACTORY CAREGIVER

If the caregiver does not respond well to your attempts to resolve conflict or correct unsatisfactory behavior, it may be in your best interest, in the long run, to find a new caregiver. An atmosphere of chronic conflict and unresolved tension is unpleasant for everyone, especially a child. It is very important to have a warm and caring atmosphere surrounding your child. It is best not to allow a negative atmosphere to exist for any extended period of time. Remember, there are excellent caregivers who will deal with conflict and constructive feedback in a healthy, mature manner.

My overall experience with caregivers has been very positive. The one exception taught me a valuable lesson: Take steps to terminate the employment of a caregiver much sooner if things are not working out after serious attempts have been made to rectify the problem. Nothing is worth having a cloud of tension in one's home.

If you do decide to terminate a caregiver's employment because you are dissatisfied, keep the following guidelines in mind:

- Handle the termination in a respectful, professional manner.

  Find a time and a place when you both can sit down and talk uninterrupted. It is best to do this at the end of the day or at the

end of the week because it will give the caregiver time to assimilate the upsetting news while off the job.

No matter what the circumstances are, a termination is usually upsetting for everyone. Be kind, yet firm.

- In most circumstances, the termination notice will not come as a shock.

  Whenever you are dissatisfied with the caregiver's performance, let her know you are dissatisfied and why. Give feedback describing what specific behaviors are unsatisfactory and how you would like them corrected. In this way, the caregiver will have received adequate warning and an opportunity to correct any unsatisfactory behaviors before being asked to leave.

  It is a good idea to document these feedback discussions by placing a note in the employee's file. If you are thinking about firing the employee and want these discussions to serve as warnings, write up the specific problems and behaviors you want them to change. Show the employee the written document, then give her a copy, and ask her to sign the sheet indicating that this information has been reviewed and discussed with her.

  In general, an abrupt termination, without warning, would only occur if the caregiver engaged in serious misconduct placing your child or family at serious risk. Employers reduce their risk of lawsuit when they give their employees a warning, whenever possible, before firing. Providing a warning is only fair, and gives the employee the opportunity to correct the problem.

- Give an employee as much advance notice as possible to allow her time to find a new job.

  Just as you would want a caregiver to let you know if she planned to leave, extend the same courtesy to her. If you feel uncomfortable having her care for your child after the termination notice, you can consider giving her severance pay to cover her expenses while looking for work. You can even arrange in advance to have a new caregiver already hired and ready to step into the job.

- Be knowledgeable about the legal risks involved in firing an employee.

  A termination notice that is handled well can decrease the risk of being sued. A brief, helpful article on this matter, written by an attorney and available in your local library, is "Tips for Handling Terminations" (Mickey, P. F., Jr., July 1994, Nation's Business, pp. 58, 60).

- To prepare for the termination meeting, write out what you want to tell the employee.

  The more prepared you are for this discussion, the less chance there will be for unexpected problems to erupt. For example, you might write:

"Heather, I came home early tonight so that I could sit down and talk with you. I am sorry to have to tell you that we have decided to terminate your employment in 2 weeks. Your last day of employment will be July 31st.

While on some level this might be shocking news for you, I know that on another level you have been aware that things just haven't been working out as we had hoped. On 3 different occasions over the last 3 months, I have asked you not to watch soap operas or talk to your friends on the phone while you are at work. I discovered you were watching TV again when I came home from work early on Tuesday. I have also expressed concern about your being impatient with Meredith, especially when she is fussy. You have also continued to arrive late 1 or 2 mornings each week. The fact that these problems kept reoccurring, despite our discussions, led us to reach this decision.

This decision was difficult because there were many other things that you did well while working for us. I especially appreciated the time you took to help toilet train Meredith and the warmth you showed her at the beginning when you seemed happier on the job. I noticed then how much she liked your reading to her. Mark has noticed that Meredith has lots of fun going for walks with you, and we both feel good about that. Your leaving will be sad for Meredith. We know that she is fond of you.

We are sorry things haven't worked out. Both Mark and I sincerely hope that you are happier in your next job, and we want the very best for you.

We want to make this transition of your leaving go as smoothly as possible, for you as well as for us. We would like you to continue to work the next 2 weeks, if that is agreeable to you. This will allow us time to find your replacement and give you some time to find another job. If you need time off for a job interview, we will rearrange your work schedule to accommodate that. This 2-week period will also give Meredith time to say goodbye to you. We plan to tell her a couple of days before you leave so that we can help her say goodbye to you too.

Is this plan agreeable to you? Why don't you take some time to think it over, and we can talk further on Monday, or, if you would like, you can give us a call over the weekend."

SUMMARY

Although almost all carefully selected caregivers work out well, you will not know for sure until the caregiver is on the job for awhile. The tips offered here, coupled with your own natural people skills, will help you keep conflict to a minimum. If you treat the caregiver as you would like to be treated, your efforts will be rewarded. Most employees thrive in an atmosphere of good will, sincere caring, and appreciation. They respect employers who offer constructive feedback on an ongoing basis and handle conflict calmly, with directness and nondefensiveness.

In most circumstances, an employee's job will not be abruptly terminated without adequate warning and an opportunity to improve job performance. The majority of employees will repay fair-minded employers by providing good child care and loyalty.

Reference

Mickey, P. F., Jr. (July 1994). Tips for handling terminations. Nation's Business, pp. 58, 60.

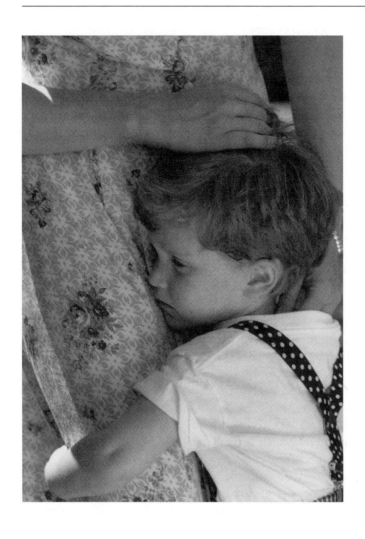

Ensuring That Proper Procedures are Followed in Handling Illness and Medical and Household Emergencies

185

"One of my biggest fears is that something will happen to my child while I am away. How can I help ensure that the caregiver will respond appropriately in the event of an emergency?"

This concern was certainly foremost in my mind when I returned to work after the birth of our son. Many of us worry that something catastrophic will happen, and the caregiver will not respond appropriately. This chapter contains a variety of different strategies and materials to help ensure that the caregiver receives the necessary guidance and training. Taking the preventative steps outlined in this chapter has allowed my husband and me to leave for work confident that our caregiver is prepared to handle just about any situation that might arise.

As you read this chapter, you might find yourself feeling overwhelmed with the amount of important information that needs to be conveyed. *One of the reasons I wrote this book was to help busy parents like you so you don't have to take time away from your child and your countless other responsibilities to compile all this information yourself.*

If you (1) use the materials and forms contained and mentioned in this chapter, (2) use the "Child-Care Agreement Form" in Box 9.1, and (3) require the caregiver to complete training in emergency resuscitation procedures for children (see Chapter 12), you will be preparing the caregiver for all kinds of medical and household emergencies. This preparation will involve little effort on your part. If you use this book's optional computer diskette containing all the book's forms (see Appendix A for ordering information), even less time on your part will be required. With your computer, you can adapt the forms contained in this chapter for your own use and print copies in the comfort of your own home or office.

Providing the caregiver with explicit instructions in advance will give *both* of you greater peace of mind. The caregiver will know how you want things handled, and you have the opportunity to outline your expectations. *It is best not to assume the caregiver will handle things in a manner that is congruent with your wishes unless your expectations have been clearly presented in writing and discussed in advance.*

There are a number of critical decisions to be made during any emergency or crisis. Offering instructions or guidelines gives the caregiver a base of information to rely upon during critical moments when it is more difficult to think clearly.

If you observe the caregiver doing something that you feel is unsafe, bring it to his attention immediately.

. . . .

For example, one day I walked into the nursery where our caregiver was diapering our 23-month-old son. He was lying on his changing table,

happily eating a holiday treat she had brought for him. I gently reminded her that it was dangerous for him to eat while in a supine position. She quickly realized that this situation was indeed unsafe and remedied the situation. She had been so wrapped up in the festivity of the holiday season, wanting to share something special with him, that she had overlooked the safety factor. Everyone makes mistakes, but we all have to stay on our toes with our little ones.

We all tend to make the mistake of believing that if we tell someone something once he will remember it. The caregiver will forget some information—we all do. Therefore, to ensure retention, present important information, such as emergency procedures, verbally as well as in writing and on a number of occasions over time.

Following are some of the strategies and materials I use with the caregiver to help ensure he is adequately trained.

REQUIRE COURSEWORK IN EMERGENCY INFANT AND CHILD RESUSCITATION TECHNIQUES

As mentioned in Chapter 12, we require our child caregiver to complete a recent course in Emergency Infant and Child Resuscitation techniques. These courses are offered to the public in most communities, and information can be obtained through your local chapter of the American Red Cross, American Heart Association, the YMCA, or local hospital. Courses typically cover the proper emergency response to and prevention of common childhood emergencies, such as poisoning, choking, drowning, and physical injury. You can request that the caregiver take a refresher course on an annual basis.

EXPOSE REPEATEDLY TO EMERGENCY INFORMATION

We supplement our coursework requirement with repeated exposure to emergency information. For example, you can rent a videotape on emergency medical procedures for children from a local library or video store and ask the caregiver to watch it during your child's nap time or bedtime. You can watch it too so that you also stay up-to-date on important information.

From time to time, I will spontaneously ask the caregiver how he might respond if a particular event like choking or loss of consciousness were to occur. Before I pose the question, however, I explain that I am going to take a few minutes to help him refresh his skills on how to respond to a particular emergency situation. I then pose a question like, "What would you do if you were feeding Jonathan and he suddenly choked on some food, turned blue, and stopped breathing?" After allowing him to respond and giving him feedback on his response, I review with him the correct steps to take and follow this review up by handing him a brief handout or pamphlet to review. I then file the material in our emergency information file, which is kept on hand beneath the caregiver's time sheets. From time to time, I ask the caregiver to review the materials in this file.

188

PROVIDE WRITTEN MATERIALS, REMINDERS, AND INSTRUCTIONS

Prepare an Emergency Information File for Your Home

Develop an emergency information file for the caregiver, and store it below his time sheets. This file ensures that the caregiver has quick access to emergency information should he want to refer to them in an emergency or just review them to keep the information fresh in his mind.

A comprehensive file contains the following:

1. **The materials listed on the "Childhood Emergencies, Health, and Safety Resource List" (Box 16.1).** Having these resources readily available in your home as part of your emergency information file will provide almost all you need to keep you and the caregiver well prepared for almost any situation that might arise.

2. **A copy of the "Child-Care Agreement Form" (see Box 9.1),** which contains instructions on what to do if illness or injury is suspected and what routines to follow to prevent infectious and communicable disease and common childhood emergencies.

3. **A copy of the completed "Information About Our Child Form" (see Box 14.3),** which includes such information as your child's food sensitivities or allergies, what foods not to give your child, and specific instructions on how to administer your child's medication.

4. **A "Consent Form for Emergency Medical Care" (Box 16.2),** which includes such information as your child's date of birth, allergies, special medical conditions, physician's name and phone number, and insurance information. The need for this form may arise because the care-

BOX 16.1. *Childhood Emergencies, Health, and Safety Resource List*

First-aid Chart

The American Academy of Pediatrics has an excellent 11″ x 17″ first-aid chart. It can be ordered by sending $2.95 and your request to Department of Publications, First-Aid Chart, American Academy of Pediatrics, 141 Northwest Point Boulevard, PO Box 747, Elk Grove Village, IL 60009-0747. "Side one gives instructions for common poisonings, fractures and sprains, burns and scalds, and head injuries. Side two concentrates on choking and cardiopulmonary resuscitation for infants and children" (American Academy of Pediatrics).

Books

Title: *A Sigh Of Relief: The First-Aid Handbook For Childhood Emergencies*
Author: Martin I. Green
Publishing Information: Bantam Books, New York, 1994, Revised Edition

Every family with children should have ready access to this excellent, 384-page reference book. It is easy to read, and the large illustrations are very useful. The four main sections are "Preventions: Reducing the Odds," "Be Prepared," "Common Childhood Illnesses & Disorders," and "Emergencies & Mishaps: First-Aid Procedures."

Title: *Caring For Your Baby And Young Child: Birth To Age 5*
Authors: Steven P. Shelov, M.D., F.A.A.P., Editor-In-Chief, Robert E. Hannemann, M.D., F.A.A.P., Associate Medical Editor
Publishing Information: Bantam Books, New York, 1991

This book has served as an excellent reference book on all aspects of child care in our household. It can be ordered through your local bookstore, or prepaid orders can be sent to the American Academy of Pediatrics, PO Box 747, 141 Northwest Point Blvd., Elk Grove Village, IL 60009-0747. Indicate the book's title and order number CB0001, and include payment for the cost of the book ($13.95/paperback; $19.95/hardcover) and shipping and handling ($2.95/paperback, $4.95/hardcover in the United States, and $4.95/paperback, $6.95/hardcover in Canada).

The following are a mere sampling of topics the book offers that I have suggested our caregivers read:

"Emergencies"   pages 447–464
An entire chapter is devoted to the prevention and treatment of common childhood emergencies, including burns, cardiopul-

(Continued on following page)

monary resuscitation (CPR) and mouth-to-mouth resuscitation, choking, electric shock, fractures/broken bones, head injury/concussion, and poisoning.

"Keeping Your Child Safe" pages 375–408

This chapter comprehensively covers topics related to childhood safety.

"Foods to Avoid to Prevent Choking" page 305

I made a list of these food items and posted it on our refrigerator so that everyone who cares for our son remains informed.

"Preventing Temper Tantrums" page 280

Title: *The American Academy of Pediatrics: Caring for Your School-Age Child*
Author: Edward L. Schor, M.D., F.A.A.P., Editor-in-Chief
Publisher: Bantam Books, New York, 1996
This 624-page book, similar to the previously named book but containing information on older children, is also a good reference source. It is available through your local bookstore or by calling the American Academy of Pediatrics at 800-433-9016.

BOX 16.2. *Consent Form for Emergency Medical Care*

••

Parent's Names: _____

Address: _____

Phone: _____

Child's Name: _____

Date of Birth: _____

Sex: _____

Name of Child's Physician: _____

Address: _____

Phone Numbers: _____ (Office) _____ (Exchange)

Medical Information:

Allergies: _____

Medical Problems: _____

Medications: _____

Insurance Information:

Insurance Company and Policy Number: _____

_____

Phone Number for Precertification: _____

   The undersigned, the parents of _____, do hereby expressly authorize qualified medical personnel, including emergency medical technicians, emergency room personnel, and physicians to provide any and all urgent medical care and treatment for our child. This authorization includes emergency procedures, surgery, and hospitalization if at the time of injury or illness, in my absence, a physician determines such intervention is urgent and necessary. The undersigned hereby expressly agree to pay all charges incurred on behalf of our child.

_____   _____

Mother's Signature   *Date*

_____ _____ _____

Mother's Place of Employment   *Business Phone*   *Home Phone*

_____   _____

Father's Signature   *Date*

_____ _____ _____

Father's Place of Employment   *Business Phone*   *Home Phone*

giver is unable to reach you and an immediate medical response is required or you are too far away to personally accompany your child. With this form, your child's emergency care will not be delayed. You can attach to the form the name of the hospital to which you would like your child taken if time is not a factor, along with directions on how to get there. In a dire emergency, an emergency medical service will generally transport a patient to the closest emergency room.

Provide Written Reminders

On the bottom of the form that our caregiver uses daily, "A Report on Our Child's Day" (see Box 17.1), I have written reminders for the caregiver to phone us right away (except in an emergency) if our child shows any signs of illness or injury and not to give any prescribed or over-the-counter medication without our written or explicit instruction by phone. *Using this form with these reminders helps ensure that you will be informed right away so that you, the parent, versus the caregiver, can decide what to do. You can then advise the caregiver on how to proceed.* The form also has a written reminder to "**Call 911 immediately in a medical emergency if you are unable to quickly remedy the situation using standard emergency medical procedures for infants and children.**"

I keep on our refrigerator a written list of foods that pose a risk for choking and should not be given to children below the age of 3. Posting this list is a small but important preventative step. In addition, the Child-Care Agreement Form" (see Box 9.1) instructs the caregiver not to introduce our child to any new foods or beverages without our explicit instruction. This rule is especially important in the first 3 years of life.

Stick-on notes are useful for calling attention to other concerns that come up.

. . . .

Whenever a safety concern comes to my attention, I write it on a stick-on note and place it for the caregiver to see. For example, I recently discovered that my son had learned to turn the lock on the inside of the bathroom door. I was concerned because he could easily lock himself in and the door would have to be removed to rescue him. I wrote a reminder identifying the potential problem and reminded everyone not to allow him to go into the bathroom by himself. Our caregiver had already been instructed in the child-care agreement not to allow him to be in a bathroom unattended, but this reminder helped reinforce that instruction.

Provide Written Instructions for Medication

If your child requires medication, instruct the caregiver both verbally and in writing how to administer the medication. Taking this step will help ensure that your child receives the proper medication and amount.

There is a section on the "Information About Our Child" form (see Box 14.3) where you can give detailed, written instructions on how and when to administer your child's medication.

Also, the form "A Report on Our Child's Day" (see Box 17.1) contains a column for "Medications Given and Amount" so that both you and the caregiver can keep track of when and how much medication has been administered.

193

Post Important Information Near Each Phone in Your Home

LIST OF IMPORTANT PHONE NUMBERS

Near each telephone in our home, I have a "List of Important Phone Numbers" (Box 16.3), to which the caregiver can quickly refer in the event of an emergency. This list includes our home address and home and work phone numbers (so the caregiver doesn't have to look them up in an emergency) and the numbers for the police, fire department, medical emergency services, poison information, our child's physician and phone numbers, and the name and phone number of a neighbor to call in the event of an emergency involving the house. There are also brief instructions on how to contact us at work in the event of an emergency. For example, I instruct them, "In emergency, tell answering service it is urgent."

To compile your list, you can use either the printed form in Box 16.3 or the optional computer diskette containing all the book's forms to design your own form.

EMERGENCY INFORMATION SHEET

Near each phone in the house, I have posted a 1-page "Emergency Information Sheet" (Box 16.4) that offers brief instructions on how to handle common emergencies involving (1) our child, (2) fire, (3) getting locked out of the house, and (4) our home (e.g., a gas leak or burst water pipes). Using this book's optional computer diskette (see Appendix A for ordering information), you can adapt this sample form to your particular needs, or you can photocopy the form at the end of the chapter.

Household emergencies can arise in your absence, and this information sheet will help ensure that the caregiver responds appropriately and

BOX 16.3. *List of Important Phone Numbers*

Important Phone Numbers

- Our Name and Address:
  _____
  _____
  _____

- Our Home Phone Number: _____

- Our Child's Name and Date of Birth:
  _____

- Police/Fire/Medical Emergency: **911** or _____

- Poison Information: _____

- Child's Doctor's Name: _____

  _____ (Office Phone)

  _____ (Exchange)
  (Please do not call doctor unless you have been unable to reach
  us and our child is acutely ill.)

- Mother's Work Number: _____
  (In emergency, say it is urgent)

- Father's Work Number: _____
  (In emergency, say it is urgent)

- Parents' Mobile Phone Numbers: _____

- Child Caregiver's Name: _____

  _____ (Home Phone)

- Neighbor's Name: _____

  _____ (Home Phone)
  (Call regarding emergencies involving the house if you have
  been unable to reach us.)

BOX 16.4. *Emergency Information Sheet*

· ·

FAMILY NAME: _____

ADDRESS: _____

PHONE NUMBER: _____

<u>Mother's Office:</u> _____ **(In emergency, please say the following:**

_____ **)**

<u>Father's Office:</u> _____ **(In emergency, please say the following:**

_____ **)**

In the Event of a Medical Emergency Involving our Child

Please follow the resuscitation procedures you have been trained to use. **Call 911 immediately if you are unable to quickly remedy the situation.**

In the event of a poisoning, please call the Poison Hotline at _____. There is syrup of ipecac (to induce vomiting) located _____. Always call the doctor or Poison Hotline <u>first</u> before giving syrup of ipecac.

Our child's doctor is _____ at _____ (office). If it is after office hours, call the exchange at _____. Our doctor hospitalizes at _____. *Please do not call the doctor unless you have been unable to reach us and need prompt medical advice.*

Our first-aid kit is located _____

Reminder: Our emergency information file and materials are located under your time sheets.

In the Event of a Fire

In the event of a fire, **please try to extinguish it immediately, or immediately call 911 if you are unable to quickly extinguish it on your own.**

Pan Fire on the Stove: Smother it with a lid and turn off the burner.

Trash Fire: Pour water on it.

Electrical Fire: Use fire extinguisher.

Fire extinguishers are located _____

Our home is equipped with smoke detectors. If one goes off, please check for a fire immediately.

If You Get Locked Out of Our Home

If you are unable to get back in, please do the following: _____

Our neighbor _____, who lives at _____ also has an extra key to our house. The phone number is _____.

In the Event of an Emergency Involving the House

For household emergencies, such as a burst water pipe, please try to rectify the situation if possible and then contact us at work. Located in the _____, there are signs indicating where to turn off the electricity, the main water line, main gas line, furnace, and central air conditioning in the event of an emergency. The fuse boxes are also clearly marked. If you're unable to reach us, please call _____ at _____.

Note: Copies of this document are posted near each phone in our home.

thereby averts even more serious problems. It will also serve as a useful reference for you and your family.

During orientation, I review this "Emergency Information Sheet" with the new caregiver and give him a personal copy to place in his wallet. This personal copy might come in handy during unforeseen situations, such as getting locked out of the house with your child, because it includes important phone numbers.

During orientation, I also show the caregiver the location of the fire extinguishers, fuse boxes, gas and water valves, and first-aid kit. This is a good way to ensure that all the important emergency information is communicated.

196

SUMMARY

In summary, you can be assured that you will have passed along all the important emergency information to the caregiver if you use the written materials and forms listed and contained in Boxes 16.1–16.4, the "Child-Care Agreement Form" (see Box 9.1), and the "Information About Our Child Form" (see Box 14.2). You will find that the time you devote to orienting the caregiver will be well worth the time spent.

It is a great relief to leave for work knowing that the caregiver has received all the necessary information and instruction on how to respond in the event of an illness or emergency. The forms will elicit from you all the important information to give the caregiver. They will save you considerable time and effort.

Reference

American Academy of Pediatrics. <u>Parent Resource Guide.</u> (Available from American Academy of Pediatrics, 141 Northwest Point Boulevard, PO Box 927, Elk Grove Village, IL 60009-0927. Send a self-addressed, stamped envelope to Dept. C-PRG at the address listed.)

Ensuring That Your Child Receives Consistently Excellent Care in Your Absence

198

"So many child-care arrangements merely warehouse children. I want to make sure that my child's needs are met and that she is well cared for throughout the day. I want her to thrive under the loving care of her caregiver. How can I ensure that this will happen?"

All the chapters in this book leading up to this one have set the stage for excellent child care. You have found and hired an excellent caregiver. In the child-care agreement and during orientation, you have spelled out what kind of care you expect. You have made many important decisions along the way that reflect what *you* think is most important for your child, and you have communicated these to the caregiver. You have learned ways to maintain a positive, mutually satisfying employer-employee relationship. Further, the caregiver has been trained in responding to childhood emergencies, illness, and injury so that you both have greater peace of mind. Your child and the caregiver are now beginning to bond, and they look forward to being together each day. Now, you want to ensure that the bonding continues and that your child receives this excellent care on an ongoing basis. This chapter will help you.

To ensure ongoing, consistently good care, <u>actively</u> oversee the caregiver's care and relationship with your child on a daily basis. Each day assess how things went that day and respond accordingly. Some days this will mean praising the caregiver for doing a wonderful job. On other days you might offer reassurance or suggestions, such as how to wash your child's hair in a way that doesn't elicit tears or how to get her to fall asleep more quickly. Or, you may encourage her to take your child outside more often to play or to feed her more healthy snacks. If you notice a problem and don't address it, you risk having the problem get worse. Also, the caregiver may wrongly assume that you do not consider it a problem.

OUR EXPERIENCE

I treat our child's caregivers as partners who are working together with us on a very important mission: successfully raising our child. Although my husband and I make all the final decisions, we are very open to our caregiver's ideas and suggestions. We all enjoy sharing anecdotes about our son and have many moments of laughter and shared concern. Most importantly, each caregiver has had great ideas on ways to care for our son.

. . . .

Just today, for example, Kristina accomplished something that I had been unable to do for an entire week: remove a well-worn Big Bird band-aid

from my son's thumb. Somehow, she convinced him that his little toy train car had a "boo boo" and needed the band-aid more than he did. I was delighted and amazed. And, I was so pleased our son's thumb was still intact underneath the band-aid. I was afraid his little thumb would shrivel up and fall off before I could convince him to give up his favorite pal, Big Bird. Kristina is a delightful 15-year-old caregiver who has helped us care for our son this summer.

I try to intersperse my feedback to my caregivers with a lot of warmth and praise. I believe on a very deep level that if I treat people with kindness and love, they are more unlikely to harm my child, me, or my family. Of course, there are always exceptions, but you are unlikely to hire a caregiver with a sociopathic personality disorder if you have evaluated her and her background thoroughly. It is important, however, to always keep an eye on how things are going. Trust your instincts and always be on the lookout for subtle signs of harm no matter how well things are going.

MONITORING YOUR CHILD'S CARE

General Guidelines

Many parents worry about how they will know if their child isn't being cared for properly or is being abused. My belief is that you are likely to notice that something is amiss if you stay observant and monitor how your child and the caregiver are doing together. In most circumstances, parents who are sensitive and in tune with their child will know when something is upsetting their child, no matter the age. When a child is very young and preverbal, you may not know what is upsetting her, but you will pick up nonverbal cues that she is distressed. It is similar to picking up nonverbal cues when your child is sick. The symptoms will be different, however, in that they will be emotional (e.g., clinging behavior, a sad or fearful expression, crying, listlessness, turning away, no eye contact) rather than physical ones.

When your child gets a little older, between the ages of 3 to 5, you can begin to talk to her about physical, emotional, and sexual abuse. You can convey to her that someone harming her will not be tolerated, and that it is imperative that she seek immediate help from you or from another adult. You can tell her that it is important to ask for help even if the perpetrator makes her feel like *she* has been "bad" or threatens to hurt her or someone she loves if she tells.

It is important for parents to spend some time at home on a regular basis when the caregiver is there. You can have the caregiver arrive a half hour before you leave for work each day or remain a half hour after you arrive home or have her there for a couple of hours each day while one parent is there. For example, we have a caregiver spend a few hours each day while I'm home. During this time, our son will share time with both of us while I am getting ready for work and she is preparing lunch.

Watching your child and the caregiver interact over time will provide you with invaluable information about their relationship together. When I see my son laughing and willingly interacting with a caregiver in my presence, I feel confident that this behavior continues when I am not there. I also see his face light up when she arrives or when I mention her name in the evening. By $2\frac{1}{2}$, our son could clearly let us know verbally as well as nonverbally if he didn't like a particular caregiver and why.

It is also a good idea to drop in unexpectedly from time to time to see how things are going. When you walk in and find the caregiver reading a book to your child or sharing a pleasant lunch with her, you will receive the reassurance you need that all is well. Our son and his caregivers play outside and in the neighborhood park on a regular basis. The other moms in our mother-child neighborhood play group often comment about seeing our son during the day with his caregivers. If I ever wanted feedback on any of our caregivers, I know they would give me their honest impressions.

Most importantly, trust your instincts when you suspect that something is not right. If either you, your child, or the caregiver don't seem to enjoy each other's company or are uncomfortable after a suitable period of time, it can be an important indication that something may be amiss. Or, if a once-good child-care arrangement is no longer satisfying for everyone, this too may be a sign that a change is needed. You and your child's relationship with the caregiver, and her relationship with you, should be relaxed, comfortable, satisfying, and certainly not tense. Even if your child seems happy with the caregiver but you are not, it still might be time for a change. Kids are very sensitive to an emotionally charged situation and parental discomfort. A child's early life is too short and too important to have it spent in a tense or unhappy child-care arrangement. If things aren't right, don't be afraid to take the steps to find a new caregiver.

Specific Tips

Here is a list of other suggestions to help ensure that the quality of care your child receives is maintained at a high level.

- Take a little time each day to talk to the caregiver in person.

To monitor your child's care, show personal interest in how things are going in your absence. Ask about the day's activities, highlights, or difficulties, as well as how things went overall. Inquire not only about your child but also about the caregiver. Show interest and concern for both of them.

Although this conversation may only last a few minutes, it gives you both a chance to discuss important matters. During this time, for example, I might explain that we started praising our son every time he lets us know he has to go the to the bathroom and ask her to do likewise. Or, I might tell her about a problem we are encountering with him and how we are handling it.

This brief talk will also give you a chance to give her constructive feedback on her performance. For example, I might ask our caregiver to try to spend more time reading to our son, to work with him on learning to pick up and put away his toys at the end of the day, or to remember to hang up the wet towels after his bath. This is also the time to mention something the caregiver might be doing that is not in accordance with the child-care agreement. For example, she might be forgetting to put on your child's sunscreen or leaving the back door unlocked.

I have discovered that to keep things running smoothly, it is often necessary to make many comments about many different matters, especially at the beginning, over the course of the week or the month. You can give yourself the title of "Quality Assurance Expert" and remind yourself that this is an important part of your job as a parent overseeing your child's care. If you are pleasant and warm, your feedback will be generally well-received. If it is not, you can begin by assessing the manner in which you offer the feedback (see Chapter 15). On the other hand, poor reception of feedback on the caregiver's part may reflect *her* difficulty with accepting constructive feedback.

Some caregivers spontaneously share a lot of information about the day while others do not. I have discovered that with some I may have to ask pointed questions, such as "Did he cry or get upset about anything today?" or "How did you spend your time together this afternoon?" This sharing of information on a daily basis will help you feel a part of your child's day, even in your absence. The caregiver and child will both appreciate your interest and concern.

And, last but not least, this daily touching base with the caregiver provides you with the opportunity to offer praise and express appreciation for the wonderful job she is doing for you and your family.

- Ask your caregiver to fill out the form "A Report On Our Child's Day" on a daily basis.

  This form (Box 17.1) allows you to monitor your child's care in your absence. At a glance, you will learn what your child had to eat and drink, her number of diaper changes, the number and length of naps, medication schedule, and whether she had any periods of fussiness. The form is available in this book's optional computer diskette (see Appendix A for ordering information) and can be adapted, if needed, to better fit your particular needs.

  At different times in your child's development, some of the columns of information will be more important than others. For example, when our son was very little and I was still breast-feeding, it was important for me to know exactly how many ounces of expressed milk he was getting throughout the day. Later, his fluid intake was less of a concern because it was obvious that he was drinking the appropriate amount each day. At that point, I told the caregiver it was no longer necessary to keep a record of that.

  I like this form because it allows me to assess how things went during the day and to make sure that my son's basic needs are being met. It also helps the transition at the end of the day go more smoothly. The caregiver can pass along in person only the most important information. The rest of the information is in writing on the form for our later review.

  The form also allows the caregiver to give us feedback. On the back of the form, the caregiver can jot down notes on anything she wants to share or remember to discuss with us.

- Encourage the caregiver to maintain a schedule so that your child's day is fairly predictable and there is time set aside for all of the important activities.

  This schedule, while being fairly predictable, can also be quite flexible. There are certain activities that I feel are important, and a schedule helps ensure that time is allotted for each of them. Such activities might include regular meals, naps, baths, walks and play outside, story time, and creative activities.

  If left on their own, many children will curl up in front of the television and not engage in active, physical play, games, listening to music, or reading. I want my child to be intellectually, socially, and physically challenged every day so that he will grow up to be a well-rounded, well-adjusted child. It is important that the caregiver be focused on and actively involved with your child and her activities, especially during the preschool years.

BOX 17.1. *A Report on Our Child's Day*

Date & Day: Time:	Bottle(s) Oz.'s Given	Food Amt. & Kind	Diaper Change (#1 and/or #2)*	Child Fussy Cause?	Sleep	Medication Given and Amount
7:00 A.M.						
8:00 A.M.						
9:00 A.M.						
10:00 A.M.						
11:00 A.M.						
12:00 Noon						
1:00 P.M.						
2:00 P.M.						
3:00 P.M.						
4:00 P.M.						
5:00 P.M.						
6:00 P.M.						

* Please note if our child has diarrhea.

Call 911 immediately in a medical emergency if you are unable to quickly remedy the situation.
Please phone us right away (except in an emergency) if our child shows any signs of illness or serious injury so that we can advise you on how to proceed.
Please do not give our child any prescribed or over-the-counter medication without written instruction or explicit in-structions from us or the physician over the phone.
We hope every day with our child is enjoyable for you!
Please write daily comments on the back of this form.

204

- Finally, keep the caregiver informed of your child's stages of development and special needs associated with each stage.

I have found a very easy way to accomplish this. I subscribe to an excellent monthly newsletter titled *Growing Child*. This 25-year-old publication, authored by professionals, arrives with timely information about your child's particular stage of development. It is available up to a child's sixth birthday.

Each issue discusses the developmental needs and concerns of children at the same age in months your child is about to become when the newsletter arrives, along with strategies, activities, and methods parents can use to facilitate growth and development. After I read each issue, I pass it along to each caregiver with the best articles highlighted. Each issue is typically 4 to 6 pages long so that one can read the entire issue in a brief period of time.

To order, call 1-800-927-7289, or write *Growing Child*, P.O. Box 1100, 22 North Second Street, Lafayette, IN 47902. You receive 12 issues each year. Trial membership for the first year is $15.00. Each year thereafter is $20.00.

Another way to receive excellent, parent-friendly written materials on child development is to participate in the free and voluntary Parents As Teachers program, now available in many communities. The program's handouts cover a range of issues and developmental stages, are brief and to the point, and can be shared with your child's caregiver.

My son has participated in this program since birth and has benefited from many of the program's offerings, especially the home visits by a Parents As Teachers certified parent educator. This program, offered in conjunction with local schools, provides information, support, and guidance to parents of children from birth to age 5. It was established to close the gap in educational services to the very young, a time when learning takes place at an explosive rate.

To find out if a Parents As Teachers program is available in your community, check your local phone directory, call your local school district, or contact the national center at the following address:

Parents As Teachers National Center, Inc.
10176 Corporate Square Drive, Suite 230
St. Louis, MO 63132
(314) 432-4330
FAX (314) 432-8963
e-mail: patnc@patnc.org
Web site: http://www.patnc.org

SUMMARY

Your job is not over once you have hired an excellent caregiver. To ensure that things continue to go well, oversee and monitor the situation. By showing genuine interest in how things are going on a day-by-day basis, offering assistance, praise, and feedback, you will help ensure that your child continues to thrive during this critical, early stage in life.

18

An Easy System for Keeping Track of the Hours Worked by the Caregiver and for Paying the Salary and Taxes

"The idea of having to pay taxes and handle the other business aspects of employing a child caregiver seems overwhelming to me. I'm so busy now I can't imagine when I would have time to figure this all out. I wouldn't know where to start."

Many parents feel needlessly intimidated by the prospect of scheduling, paying the salary, and filing the taxes for an in-home child caregiver. Once again, this chapter has been written with you, a busy parent, in mind. I have developed a system and forms that have worked very well for us. This step-by-step approach will help you cut through a lot of red tape and accomplish these tasks with a minimum of fuss. This chapter contains information you will need to arrange the work schedule and pay the salary and taxes for your in-home caregiver.

You will need, however, to obtain some information directly from your state and refer to updated versions of the governmental publications for accurate information. Requirements for state taxes, tax credits or deductions, and unemployment insurance vary from state to state, and the rules and regulations regarding federal employment taxes may change.

Also, remember that I am not a tax professional and the intent of this book is not to provide tax advice. A call to a competent tax professional will help you stay abreast of recent changes in the tax laws.

HOW TO USE THIS CHAPTER

The way to use this chapter is step by step, not all at once. Read the checklist in Box 18.1, "Employer's Checklist for Keeping Track of the Caregiver's Schedule and Payment of Salary and Taxes," for a quick overview of all the information in the chapter, and then work through the chapter one section at a time.

The checklist in Box 18.1 breaks down the various steps into tasks to complete at various times—before you hire, immediately after you hire, and when you pay the employee—with tasks listed by different deadline dates for filing taxes throughout the year. *If you feel overwhelmed, a review of Box 18.1 will assure you that (1) not every task applies to you, (2) not every task needs to be accomplished at once, and (3) that you can tackle these tasks at a reasonable pace.* This chapter will help you determine which tasks apply to you.

To use the chapter in an organized, helpful manner, follow one of these methods for working through the information: ·

1. Place a copy of Box 18.1 beside the book as you read through the chapter, and fill in the form as you read, checking the appropriate "applies to us" column.

BOX 18.1. *Employer's Checklist for Keeping Track of the Caregiver's Schedule and Payment of Salary and Taxes*

. . . .

Reminder: Tax laws change. Refer to *updated* versions of governmental tax publications or speak to a competent tax professional to ensure that you are following up-to-date tax requirements.

	Applies to Us	Task Completed

Before You Hire Any Employee
- Order *Handbook for Employers: Instructions for Completing Form I-9* by calling 1-800-870-3676 or by fax (202) 633-4708 (see Box 2.1), and review. _____ _____
- Order the free IRS *Household Employer's Tax Guide* (Publication 926) by calling 1-800-TAX-FORM (or 829-3676). _____ _____

Immediately After Hiring
- Complete Form I-9 (see Box 2.1). _____ _____
- Apply for an Employer's Identification Number (EIN), if you don't have one already. _____ _____
- View employee's Social Security card, and keep a record of his/her name and number, as it appears on the card. _____ _____
- Keep a record of the employee's address. _____ _____
- Make copies of time sheets (see Box 18.2 or 18.3). _____ _____
- Order copies of Forms W-2 or W-3 by calling 1-800-TAX-FORM (or 829-3676). _____ _____
- Contact your State Unemployment Tax Agency and ask about (1) what unemployment tax forms to file, how to calculate the tax, and deadlines for filing and (2) whether you are required to withhold or pay any other state employment taxes or carry worker's compensation insurance for the employee. _____ _____
- Beginning in 1998, if you owe household employment taxes that are not covered by your current wage withholdings, you must pay these quarterly or increase your wage withholding. _____ _____

At The Time you Pay the Employee
- Withhold the employee's share of Social Security and Medicare taxes from his/her paycheck. _____ _____
- Withhold federal income tax from the employee's paycheck if (1) s/he requests this and completes Form W-4 *and* (2) you agree to withhold. _____ _____

(*Continued on following page*)

BOX 18.1. *Employer's Checklist for Keeping Track of the Caregiver's Schedule and Payment of Salary and Taxes* (Continued)

	Applies to Us	Task Completed
By January 31		
• Complete Form W-2 or W-3 and give the employee his/her copies.	_____	_____
• Business and farm employers only: File Form 940 or 940-EZ and pay the FUTA Tax.	_____	_____
By February 7		
• Inform the employee about Earned Income Credit (EIC) if (1) you have not given him/her Form W-2 (with this notification printed on the back of the employee's Copy C) *and* (2) you have agreed to withhold federal income tax from his/her wages but the income tax withholding tables show that no tax should be withheld.	_____	_____
By February 28		
• Submit the completed W-2 or W-3 to the Social Security Administration.	_____	_____
By April 15		
• Before 1998: File Schedule H (Form 1040) with your annual federal income tax return and pay the Social Security and Medicare taxes and the FUTA.	_____	_____
• After 1998: File Schedule H (Form 1040) with your annual federal income tax return.	_____	_____
• Take a federal income tax credit for up to 30% of your child-care expenses for wages and your share of the paid federal and state employment taxes on Form 1040.	_____	_____
• Take the state income tax credit or deduction for child-care expenses.	_____	_____
By April 15, June 15, September 15, and January 15		
• Beginning in 1998, pay the employee's Social Security and Medicare taxes by filing Form 1040 ES if your withholding does not cover these taxes.	_____	_____
• Business and farm employers only: Pay the employee's Social Security and Medicare taxes along with your federal quarterly employment tax deposits for your business or farm employees.	_____	_____

(Continued on following page)

BOX 18.1. *Employer's Checklist for Keeping Track of the Caregiver's Schedule and Payment of Salary and Taxes* (Continued)

	Applies to Us	Task Completed
By April 15, June 15, September 15, and January 15–cont'd		
• File state unemployment tax forms. (Verify these dates with your state unemployment tax agency.)	_____	_____
Miscellaneous		
• Pay any other required state employment taxes by _____ (deadline date).	_____	_____
• Apply for worker's compensation insurance for the employee, if required by your state, by _____ (deadline date).	_____	_____
• Keep copies of all submitted federal and state tax forms and the supporting documentation.	_____	_____

2. As you read through the chapter, check off the tasks that apply directly to you in the task boxes following each section.

THE SYSTEM

Meet *Federal Guidelines as an Employer*

KNOW THE FEDERAL REQUIREMENTS

For Employment Eligibility.   The Immigration Reform and Control Act of 1986 was designed to ensure that only individuals who are legally authorized to work are employed. To understand the requirements, review Box 2.1, "Employment Eligibility Verification Requirements" and order and look over the *Handbook for Employers: Instructions for Completing Form I-9.*

....

TASKS

Order the Handbook for Employers: Instructions for Completing Form 1-9 *by calling 1-800-870-3676 or by fax (202) 633-4708 (see Box 2.1) and review.*

When: Before you hire any employee
_____ Applies to us
_____ Task completed

Complete Form 1-9 (see Box 2.1).

When: Immediately after hiring
_____ Applies to us
_____ Task completed

For Paying Social Security and Medicare Taxes.   The Internal Revenue Service puts out the *Household Employer's Tax Guide* (Publication 926), an easy-to-read booklet that reviews everything you need to know to comply with federal tax laws. You can order a free copy of this booklet, which was revised in November of 1995, by calling 1-800-TAX-FORM (or 829-3676). *Review this booklet for recent updates, additional information, and exceptions to the information provided in this chapter.* The information in this chapter merely summarizes information contained in this important document, which was written specifically for wages paid in 1996. Because this document is periodically revised, make sure you read the latest revision.

••

TASK

Order the free IRS Household Employer's Tax Guide (Publication 926) by calling 1-800-TAX-FORM (or 829-3676) and review.

When: Before you hire any employee

_____ Applies to us

_____ Task completed

OBTAIN AN EMPLOYER'S IDENTIFICATION NUMBER (EIN)

For federal tax purposes, apply for an EIN, if you don't have one already. If you have had business or household employees in the past, you will already have an EIN, and you can use that number on your federal employment tax forms. An EIN is also sometimes referred to as a Taxpayer Identification Number (TIN).

To obtain your EIN, file IRS Form SS-4, "Application for Employer Identification Number." To obtain this form, you can go to an area IRS Service Center or call 1-800-TAX-FORM (or 829-3676). Submit this completed form to your area IRS Service Center.

Form SS-4 will tell you how to get an EIN immediately by telephone or fax or how to apply for one by mail, which requires about 4 weeks.

••

TASK

Apply for an Employer's Identification Number (EIN), if you don't have one already.

When: Immediately after hiring

_____ Applies to us

_____ Task completed

Make Arrangements with Employees

REQUEST TO SEE THE EMPLOYEE'S SOCIAL SECURITY CARD

You are required to keep a record of the household employee's name and Social Security number, exactly as it appears on his Social Security card. This information must be requested no later than the first day on which you pay him. This rule applies if you pay the employee Social Security and Medicare wages or if you agree to withhold federal income tax from his wages. You are also required to keep a record of the employee's address.

All of this information is requested on the "Job Application Form for an In-Home Child Caregiver" (see Box 8.1). At the time of hiring, all you need to do is ask your new employee to show you his Social Security card so that you can verify that the information provided on the application form matches the card.

The employee can apply for a new Social Security number if he does not possess one, or he can apply for a new Social Security card if he lost his original card or if his name is incorrectly shown on his card. To apply for a Social Security number or a new card, one must submit Form SS-5, "Application for a Social Security Card." This form can be obtained from any Social Security Administration office or by calling 1-800-772-1213.

· ·

TASKS

View employee's Social Security card, and keep a record of his/her name and number, as it appears on the card.

When: Immediately after hiring

_____ Applies to us

_____ Task completed

Keep a record of the employee's address.

When: Immediately after hiring

_____ Applies to us

_____ Task completed

USE AN ORGANIZED SCHEDULING SYSTEM

Most families have a fixed schedule, and the caregiver's hours will be determined at the outset. You can fill in the hours you expect the caregiver

to work on a regular basis on the "Child-Care Agreement Form" (see Box 9.1). However, if your schedule changes from week to week, or you employ more than one caregiver, here is a simple scheduling method that works well.

Give the caregiver a written list of the upcoming child-care hours. Then fill in the initial of the caregiver's first name on the calendar, next to the hours that you have asked him to work. For example, you might write, *1:00–5:30 P.M. – M*. When he confirms that he can work, indicate his confirmation by circling his initial. If he can't work at that time, place a slash through his initial to indicate that he has been asked but was unavailable. Then ask another one of the caregivers to work, and place their initial next to those hours on the calendar.

This simple system works especially well during those weeks when your schedule is complicated and you need to schedule several different caregivers and babysitters. This system will allow you to keep an organized, uncluttered calendar and work schedule.

Have Caregivers Fill Out Time Sheets

Cash Arrangements.   If you pay the caregiver by cash or check, use the "Monthly Time Sheet and Pay Form" in Box 18.2. Keep the time sheet in one location, and have the caregiver fill it out on a daily basis. It has space to record the dates, work shifts, and total hours worked. The caregiver can turn in this form at the end of each month so that you can prepare his paycheck. It has instructions on how to compute and withhold the employee's portion of Social Security and Medicare taxes.

This form also has space to document the payment of the monthly salary along with any other withholdings. I recommend that you keep this completed form on file as part of the legally required, written record of the employee's work hours, salary paid, and taxes withheld.

The form is also in this book's optional computer diskette (see Appendix A for ordering information), and if you have a computer and printer, you can print extra copies and have them on hand.

Barter Arrangements.   Rather than pay the caregiver a salary, you may elect to enter into a barter arrangement. For example, you may give a student a place to live in your home in exchange for a set number of hours per week of child-care, household, or yard-care services. The Internal Revenue Service considers the monetary value of the barter as income, and both of you will be obliged to pay taxes on this amount. Speak with your accountant about how to meet your tax obligations with this type of arrangement.

One way to determine the value of the barter is to research the going rate for a comparable room or space in a home in your area. You can

BOX 18.2. *Monthly Time Sheet and Pay Form*

Employee's Name: _____ SS#: ____-___-____

Month: _____ Employee's Address: _____

Please complete this form daily and return to us on your last workday of each month.

Date	Time	Hours	Date	Time	Hours
Example:					
1/27/97	8:30–5:45	8.25			

Total Number of Hours Worked This Month: _____

_____ **Total Monthly Cash Wages** (Total Monthly Hours (_____)
x Per Hour Wage ($_____)

Note: You are required to withhold and pay Social Security and Medicare taxes if you pay $1,000 or more to any one household employee in this calendar year. Currently, these taxes are 15.3% of cash wages. The employee's share is 7.65%, and your share is a matching 7.65%. You can elect to pay the employee's share yourself and not withhold it. You, the employer, will be responsible for paying your portion of this tax, along with the employee's portion, by April 15 of the following calendar year. Please see IRS Publication 926, *Household Employer's Tax Guide*, for further information and exceptions regarding this and other state and federal requirements.

−_____ **Social Security Tax Withheld** (Fill in *0* if none withheld.)
(Multiply the Total Monthly Cash Wages by 6.2%*, and **subtract** this amount, the employee's share, from his/her check.)

−_____ **Medicare Tax Withheld** (Fill in *0* if none withheld.)
(Multiply the Total Monthly Cash Wages by 1.45%*, and **subtract** this amount, the employee's share, from his/her paycheck.)

* Note: This percentile may change over time.

−_____ **Other Amounts Withheld** (Describe: _____)

_____ **TOTAL AMOUNT PAID** (Total Monthly Cash Wages Minus Total Amounts Withheld)

obtain this information by cutting out newspaper ads for rooms for rent in area homes or obtaining ads from area bulletin boards that list rental fees. Keep these ads on file in the event you are later requested to provide this documentation to the IRS. Again, speak with your accountant.

If you make a barter arrangement, use the form "Weekly Hours for Child-Care Barter Arrangement" in Box 18.3 to keep track of the work hours and services provided by the caregiver. In these arrangements, it is not uncommon for the caregiver to work somewhat over or under the set number of required hours in a given week. This form allows you to keep track of these extra hours at the end of each week, as well as on an ongoing basis.

The form is also available in this book's optional computer diskette (see Appendix A for ordering information), and extra copies can be made and kept on hand.

217

TASK

Make copies of time sheets (see Box 18.2 or 18.3).

When: Immediately after hiring

_____ Applies to us

_____ Task completed

Comply with Federal Tax Guidelines

PAYING SOCIAL SECURITY AND MEDICARE TAXES

Determine If You Are Required to Pay. You are required to pay Social Security and Medicare taxes if you pay cash wages of $1,000 or more per year to any one household employee, unless the employee is your partner, your child under age 21, your parent, or any employee under the age of 18 whose household work is not his principal occupation. For example, if the employee is a student under the age of 18, you are not required to pay the Social Security and Medicare taxes.

A child caregiver or household worker is considered *your employee* by the IRS "if you can control not only what work is done, but how it is done" (Department of the Treasury, 1995, p. 2). If the worker alone controls how things are done, he is not considered the employee; he is considered to be self-employed, and you are not required to pay federal taxes on his wages. Obviously, a child caregiver as defined by this book is considered your employee.

BOX 18.3. *Weekly Hours for Child-Care Barter Arrangement*

Day	Date	Time	Hours	Child Care	House Chores	Yard Chores	Description (Please fill out daily & give completed form to us at the end of each week.)
Monday							
Tuesday							
Wednesday							
Thursday							
Friday							
Saturday							
Sunday							
Total Hours							

Example:

(circle) +/– _____ Extra hours worked (+) or owed (–), carried forward from past week(s)   –2.5

+ _____ Hours worked this week   22.0

_____ **Total hours worked**   **19.5**

– _____ Hours expected to work this week   20.0

(circle) +/– _____ Extra hours worked (+) or owed (–), to carry forward to next week   –.5

In exchange for a place to live in our home, you will be expected to give us _____ hours of work per week.

Pay the Taxes.   By April 15 of the following year, you are required to file Schedule H (Form 1040), "Household Employment Taxes," with your annual federal income tax return (Form 1040 or 1040A). At that time, you are required to submit the tax payment of 15.3% of the employee's cash wages for the preceding year. Half of this 15.3% is the employee's share (6.2% for Social Security tax and 1.45% for Medicare tax). The remaining half is the employer's share.

TASK

File Schedule H (Form 1040) with your annual federal income tax return, and pay the Social Security and Medicare taxes and the Federal Unemployment Tax (FUTA).

When: By April 15

_____ Applies to us

_____ Task completed

Beginning in 1998, you must either pay quarterly estimated tax payments (file Form 1040 ES, "Individual Quarterly Estimated Tax Form") or increase your own withholding to meet this federal tax obligation for Social Security and Medicare taxes. Always review the most recently revised IRS household employer's tax guide to stay on top of such changes in the tax law or speak with a tax professional.

TASK

File Form 1040 ES, and pay the employee's quarterly estimated Social Security and Medicare taxes, if your wage withholding does not cover these taxes.

When: (After 1998) By April 15, June 15, September 15, and January 15 (or the following workday if the 15th falls on a weekend or holiday).

_____ Applies to us

_____ Task completed

Choose from the following options for paying these taxes.

Pay the Employee's Share: It is permissible to pay the employee's 7.6% portion of these taxes by paying the entire 15.3% yourself on April 15 (rather than collecting his half by withholding these taxes from his paychecks throughout the year). Many household employees see it as a bonus if you, the employer, pay their portion of these federal taxes. I have elected to do so for two reasons: (1) It is a fairly inexpensive way to make my job offer more attractive because it increases the amount that the employee makes by 7.6%, and (2) it is easier for me when I prepare paychecks. I don't have to spend time calculating the withholding taxes.

If you elect to pay the caregiver's share of the Social Security and Medicare taxes, you must nonetheless include his share amount in his employee wages for income tax purposes on Form W-2 or W-3. The year-end instructions on these tax forms clearly explain how to properly report these taxes.

If you submit Schedule H (Form 1040) on April 15 in any year, you will automatically receive the necessary federal employment tax forms in January for the following year.

Withhold If You Do Not Pay the Employee's Share: If you choose *not* to pay his share, you must withhold his portion of these taxes from *each* paycheck. The time sheet contained in Box 18.2 provides instructions on how to withhold these Social Security and Medicare taxes.

TASK

Withhold the employee's share of Social Security and Medicare taxes from his/her paycheck.

When: At the time you pay the employee

_____ Applies to us

_____ Task completed

Make Payments with Those for Other Business or Farm Employees: If you own your own business or a farm operated for profit, you may elect to pay the household employee's Social Security and Medicare taxes along with your other federal quarterly employment tax deposits for your business or farm employees. That is, you can include the household employee's Social Security, Medicare, and withheld federal income taxes on either Form 941, "Employer's Quarterly Federal Tax Return," or Form 943, "Employer's Annual Tax Return for Agricultural Employees." If you elect not to take this option, then follow the guidelines for household employers who do not own their own business or farm operated for profit.

TASK

Pay the employee's Social Security and Medicare taxes along with your other federal quarterly employment tax deposits for your business or farm employees.

When: April 15, June 15, September 15, and January 15 (or the following workday if the 15th falls on a weekend or holiday)

_____ Applies to us

_____ Task completed

FILING FEDERAL FORM W-2 BY THE JANUARY 31 DEADLINE

You are required to file a Form W-2, "Wage and Tax Statement," for each of the household employees to whom you pay Social Security and Medicare wages or wages from which you withheld federal income tax. You must give Copies B, C, and 2 to the employee by January 31, and Copy A must be mailed to the Social Security Administration by the February 28 deadline.

If you have more than one employee requiring a Form W-2, you are required to submit Form W-3, "Transmittal of Wage and Tax Statements," to the Social Security Administration, in place of Form W-2.

Copies of Forms W-2 and W-3 can be obtained by calling 1-800-TAX-FORM (or 829-3676).

TASKS

Order copies of Forms W-2 or W-3.

When: After hiring the employee and no later than January 1 to allow time to complete before January 31.

_____ Applies to us

_____ Task completed

Complete Form W-2 or W-3 and give the employee his/her copies.

When: By January 31

_____ Applies to us

_____ Task completed

Submit the completed W-2 or W-3 to the Social Security Administration.

When: By February 28

_____ Applies to us

_____ Task completed

WITHHOLDING FEDERAL INCOME TAX

You are *not* required to withhold federal income tax unless your household employee specifically requests that you do so and you *agree*. I have always elected not to withhold federal income tax because I have wanted to avoid the hassle. Any time you have to withhold from a paycheck, it involves additional, time-consuming calculations. On the other hand, if an employee requested me to do it because it was important to them, I would agree to do so.

If you agree to withhold, the employee must complete and submit to you Form W-4, "Employee's Withholding Allowance Certificate."

For further information, refer to pp. 5-7 in IRS Publication 926, *Household Employer's Tax Guide* (revised November 1995). Again, you can obtain this document by calling 1-800-TAX-FORM (or 829-3676).

TASK

Withhold federal income tax from the employee's paycheck if (1) s/he requests it and completes Form W-4 and (2) you agree to withhold.

When: At the time you pay the employee

_____ Applies to us

_____ Task completed

Paying Federal Unemployment Tax (FUTA)

The *Household Employer's Tax Guide* (IRS Publication 926) also provides information on paying the FUTA. The FUTA is *not* withheld from the employee's paycheck. You, the employer, are responsible for the entire portion.

You are required to pay the FUTA if you pay your household employee $1,000 or more in any calendar *quarter*. A calendar quarter is defined by the IRS as January through March, April through June, July through September, or October through December.

You are not required to pay the FUTA if the caregiver is your partner, your child under the age of 21, or your parent.

The FUTA is 6.2% of the first $7,000 of wages per year. It can be reduced, however, to 0.8% if you pay all the required state unemployment taxes by April 15 of the following year. A credit of 5.4% is generally given for the payment of these state taxes, reducing your federal unemployment tax requirement to 0.8%.

To pay the FUTA, submit Schedule H (Form 1040) with your annual federal income tax return on April 15.

If you are a business or farm employer, you will pay the FUTA when you submit Form 940, "Employer's Annual Federal Unemployment Tax Return," or the shorter Form 940-EZ, with the IRS by January 31 of the following year. These forms can be obtained by calling 1-800-TAX-FORM (or 829-3676).

TASKS

Pay the FUTA along with Schedule H (Form 1040).

When: April 15

_____ Applies to us

_____ Task completed

If you are a business or farm employer, pay the FUTA on Form 940 or 940-EZ.

When: January 31

_____ Applies to us

_____ Task completed

NOTIFYING THE EMPLOYEE ABOUT EARNED INCOME CREDIT (EIC)

You are required to notify the employee about possible EIC under two conditions: (1) You have not given the employee Copy C of Form W-2 *and* (2) you have agreed to withhold federal income tax from the employee's wages but the income tax withholding tables show that no tax should be withheld. The EIC either reduces the tax of eligible workers "or allows them to receive a payment from the IRS if they do not owe tax" (Department of the Treasury, 1995, p. 6). If the employee is eligible to take EIC on his federal income tax return, he must complete the necessary paperwork first and submit it to you, and "you may have to make advance payments of part of your household employee's EIC along with the employee's wages" (Department of the Treasury, 1995, p. 6).

However, you do not have to concern yourself with this issue if you give the employee his copy (Copy C) of Form W-2 by January 31. The EIC notification is printed on the backside of this form.

••

TASK

*Inform the employee about Earned Income Credit (EIC) if (1) you
have not given him/her Form W-2 (with this notification printed on
the back of the employee's Copy C) <u>and</u> (2) you have agreed to
withhold federal income tax from his/her wages but the income tax
withholding tables show that no tax should be withheld.*

When: By February 7

_____ Applies to us

_____ Task completed

225

Complying with State Requirements

For information on what, if any, state unemployment taxes you are
required to pay, contact your state unemployment tax agency. You can obtain the phone number and address of your state's agency by looking at
the list of state unemployment tax agencies in the back of IRS Publication
926, *Household Employer's Tax Guide*. When you call, ask them to instruct you on what unemployment tax forms you are required to file, how
to calculate your tax payment, and the deadlines for filing. Also ask them
to mail you the required forms.

In addition, when you contact your state agency, ask whether you
are required to withhold or pay any other state employment taxes or carry
workers' compensation insurance for the employee.

TASKS

Contact your State Unemployment Tax Agency, and ask about (1) what unemployment tax forms to file, how to calculate the tax, and deadlines for filing and (2) whether you are required to withhold or pay any other state employment taxes or carry worker's compensation insurance for your household employee.

When: Immediately after hiring

_____ Applies to us

_____ Task completed

File state unemployment tax forms.

When: _____ (fill in deadline date)

_____ Applies to us

_____ Task completed

Pay any other required state employment taxes.

When: _____ (fill in deadline date)

_____ Applies to us

_____ Task completed

Apply for worker's compensation insurance for the employee, if required by your state.

When: _____ (fill in deadline date)

_____ Applies to us

_____ Task completed

Keeping Copies of Tax Forms and Tax Records

Keep copies of all submitted federal and state tax forms along with the supporting documentation.

Taking the Federal Income Tax Credit for Your Child-Care Expenses

You are allowed to take an income tax credit on Form 1040 for up to 30% of your child-care expenses (of the first $2,400 for one child and the first $4,800 for two or more children) for the caregiver's wages and your share of the paid federal and state employment taxes. The size of this tax credit, however, varies with the income of the family. Lower income families get the full 30% credit, while families with an adjusted gross income of $28,000 or more get 20% of their expenses up to the limit. This translates into a limit of $480 for one child and $960 for two or more children. This credit applies if your child is under the age of 13 or if your dependent is not capable of self care and you hire a caregiver so that you can work.

For additional information, call 1-800-TAX-FORM (or 829-3676). Request a copy of Publication 503, *Child and Dependent Care Expenses*.

TASK

Take a federal income tax credit for up to 30% of your child-care expenses for wages and your share of the paid federal and state employment taxes on Form 1040.

When: April 15

_____ Applies to us

_____ Task completed

Taking State Income Tax Credits or Deductions for Your Child-Care Expenses

Approximately half of the states offer either a tax credit or deduction for child-care expenses. To find out what is available in your state, contact your state tax office (their phone number is located in the government listings section of your phone book) or speak with a tax professional.

TASK

Take the state income tax credit or deduction for child-care expenses.

When: April 15

_____ Applies to us

_____ Task completed

SUMMARY

D̲o not let the paperwork and legal and tax requirements connected with hiring your own caregiver deter you from providing excellent in-home care for your child. As this chapter conveys, these requirements can be broken down into easy-to-accomplish tasks (see Box 18.1). Once you have this system in place, tailored to meet the requirements that apply to you, it is simply a matter of following it year after year.

Reference

Department of the Treasury. (Revised November 1995). <u>Household employer's tax guide: For wages paid in 1996</u> (IRS Publication 926). Washington, DC: U.S. Government Printing Office. (Cat. No. 64286A).

APPENDIX A. *Ordering Form for the Computer Diskette and Additional Copies of This Book*

☎ Call Toll-Free Anytime to Order with Credit Card: 1-888-601-CARE (2273)
St. Louis, MO area residents call: 314-862-6636
(Please have credit card information on hand when you call.)

FAX Fax Credit Card Orders Anytime to: 1-314-725-6350
✉ Send orders with checks or money orders to Family CareWare, Inc.
(Please fax or mail both pages of this order form.)

Family CareWare, Inc., Order Form
Dept. B, P.O. Box 50257, St. Louis, MO 63105-5257

Name (please print) _____

Address _____
UPS is unable to deliver to a box number.

City _____State _____ ZIP _____

Daytime Phone (___)_____ Evening Phone (___)_____
We will only call if we have a question about this order form.

Ship to: (if different)

Name (Please print) _____

Address _____
UPS is unable to deliver to a box number.

City _____ State _____ ZIP _____

Gift Message: _____

Method of Payment
(Please make check or money order payable to Family CareWare, Inc.)

☐ Check   ☐ Money Order
☐ VISA   ☐ MasterCard   ☐ AmEx   ☐ Discover

Card Number:

☐☐☐☐/☐☐☐☐/☐☐☐☐/☐☐☐☐

Expires ☐☐☐☐

Signature_____
Required for all charges   Date

(Continued on the following page)

229

	QTY.	TOTAL
COMPUTER DISKETTE—*IN-HOME CHILD CARE:* *A Step-by-Step Guide to Quality, Affordable Care* @ $9.95 (U.S.), $13.95 (Canada) **Please see the following page for important information about this diskette.** Specify: ____ PC version ____ MAC version	____	_____
BOOK—*IN-HOME CHILD CARE:* *A Step-by-Step Guide to Quality, Affordable Care* @ $24.95 (U.S.), $34.95 (Canada)	____	_____
BOOK-DISKETTE Discount Package Special— save $5.00 (If purchased together) @ $29.90 (U.S.), $43.90 (Canada) Specify: ____ PC version ____ MAC version	____	_____
SUBTOTAL		_____
MO Residents Add 6.475% **Sales Tax**		_____
Shipping and Handling (See costs below.)		_____
TOTAL		_____

Shipping and Handling Costs: $1.50 per diskette (First Class Mail); $5.00 per book or for Book-Diskette Package Special (UPS Ground Service)

THANK YOU FOR YOUR ORDER.

☐ (Check) I want to be included on Family CareWare, Inc.'s, mailing list.

☐ (Check) I give my permission for Family CareWare, Inc., to give my contact information to other trusted vendors of child-related items. My children are the following ages: _____

Return Policy

Defective computer diskettes, while extremely rare, will be exchanged at no cost. Please return the damaged one and we will send you a new one. Family CareWare, Inc., offers a full money-back guarantee (less shipping and handling and a re-stocking fee of 15% of the cost of the returned item, plus any tax, which will be credited to your account or deducted from your refund) on *unopened* computer diskettes and *unblemished* books, if purchased directly from Family CareWare, Inc., and returned within 30 days with a copy of the Family CareWare, Inc., receipt or your canceled check.

(Continued on the following page)

230

Important Information About Computer Diskette

This book's computer diskette will allow you to copy and modify all of the over 40 forms contained in this book (see List of Boxes and Appendices A and B). *This diskette is not intended to be used without this book, which contains important information about the forms, as well as the diskette's instructions (see Appendix B).* If you use this diskette without this book, you do so at your own risk.

- The IBM-compatible (PC) version requires the following:
  Media: 3.5″ HD diskette
  Word Processing Programs: WordPerfect 5.1 or higher for DOS; WordPerfect 5.2 or higher for Windows 3.x or Windows 95; Microsoft Word 2.0 or higher for Windows 3.x or Windows 95; Microsoft Works 2.0 or higher for Windows 3.x or Windows 95; or Rich Text Format (RTF)
- The MAC version requires the following:
  Media: 3.5″ HD diskette
  Word Processing Programs: WordPerfect 3.0 or higher; Microsoft Word 4.0 or higher; ClarisWorks 1.0 or higher; or Rich Text Format (RTF)

Regretfully, we are *unable* to offer technical support. If you encounter difficulties, consult your word processing or operating system manual. Defective disks, while extremely rare, will be exchanged free of charge.

General Instructions

For your convenience, the diskettes contain editable versions of each of the forms printed in the book in a variety of popular word processing formats.

When using the diskette-based forms, I recommend that you save your edited and customized copies on the hard drive of your computer, rather than on the diskette. This allows you to keep the diskette as a clean master copy for the next time you need it.

The **IBM-compatible (PC)** diskette contains copies of the forms in the following formats:

- WordPerfect 5.1 or higher for DOS
- WordPerfect 5.2 or higher for Windows 3.x or Windows 95
- Microsoft Word 2.0 or higher for Windows 3.x or Windows 95
- Microsoft Works 2.0 or higher for Windows 3.x or Windows 95
- Rich Text Format (RTF)

Other word processing programs should be able to read and convert at least one of these formats. Try the WordPerfect 5.1 for DOS version first; this is the *de facto* standard for word processing conversions.

The **Macintosh** diskette requires System 6.x to 7.5.x, and contains copies of the forms in the following formats:

- WordPerfect 3.0 or higher
- Microsoft Word 4.0 or higher
- ClarisWorks 1.0 or higher
- Rich Text Format (RTF)

Using the IBM-compatible (PC) Diskette

The IBM-compatible (PC) diskette has five directories or "folders," corresponding to each of the five included word processing formats:

Directory	Word Processing Program
WPDOS	WordPerfect 5.1 for DOS (*.WP)
WPWIN	WordPerfect 5.2 or higher for Windows 3.x or Windows 95 (*.WP)
WINDOC	Microsoft Word 2.0 or higher for Windows 3.x or Windows 95 (*.DOC)
MSWORKS	Microsoft Works 2.0 or higher for Windows 3.x or Windows 95 (*.WPS)
RTF	Rich Text Format (*.RTF)

(Continued on following page)

APPENDIX B. *Instructions for the Computer Diskette* (Continued)

1. Insert the diskette into your floppy disk drive (A: or B:).
2. Start your word processing program.
3. Use your program's "File Open" command (for Windows programs, choose the "File" menu, then choose "Open"; with WordPerfect 5.1, press the F5 key).
4. Select your floppy disk drive.
5. Select the directory corresponding to your word processing program, according to the previous list.
6. Open the file you wish to edit or print. The files are named according to the box or appendix numbers for the forms in the book: For instance, the Microsoft Word version of the form in Box 9.1 is found in the WINDOC directory as file 9_1.DOC, and the WordPerfect 5.1 version is found in the WPDOS directory as 9_1.WP.
7. If you are using a word processing program other than WordPerfect, Microsoft Word, or Microsoft Works, it may ask you to confirm a translation. Select "Yes" or "OK."
8. As soon as the file is open, save the document on your hard drive. To do this, select the "Save As" option under the "File" menu at the top of your screen. Make sure you select an appropriate directory on your hard drive (such as DOCS, FILES, or MYFILES—wherever you keep most of your word processing documents) as your destination.
   You can now edit or print the file's text. Be sure to save your work frequently.

For RTF Files
   The procedure is essentially the same, except that when you open the file, you may need to use either an import function or the "Open" command under your "File" menu at the top of your screen after you have started your word processing program.

(Continued on following page)

Using the Macintosh Diskette

The Macintosh diskette has four folders, corresponding to each of the four included word processing formats:

Folder	Word Processing Format
WordPerfect	WordPerfect 3.0 or higher
Microsoft Word	Microsoft Word 4.0 or higher
ClarisWorks	ClarisWorks 1.0 or higher
RTF	Rich Text Format

Each folder contains all the forms in the book, identified by their box or appendix names—for example, Box 9.1.

1. Begin by starting your computer.
2. After startup is complete, put the diskette into the diskette drive and wait for the diskette icon to appear.
3. Double-click the diskette icon (two quick clicks in close succession).
4. Double-click the folder icon corresponding to your word processing software. If you use a word processing program not included on the diskette, select the RTF folder (see instructions for RTF files).
5. Copy the file that you want to work with by clicking and dragging the file to a folder of your choice on your primary hard drive (most users have only one).
6. Double-click on the file on your hard drive that you wish to edit or print. This should start your word processing software. Your word processing program may ask you to confirm a translation.

You may now edit or print the text. Be sure to save your work frequently. When you are ready to print, you may wish to delete the first page of each form containing the copyright and disclaimer information.

For RTF Files

The procedure is essentially the same, except that when you open the file, you may need to use either an import function or the "Open" command under your "File" menu at the top of your screen after you have started your word processing program.

Index

Abuse. *See also* Child sexual abuse
  discussing with child, 199
Academic record check, 146
  Academic Transcript Request Form (sample), 148
  Instructions for Caregiver Applicant for Requesting Academic Transcript (sample), 147
Academic Transcript Request Form (sample), 148
Adjustment, of child to new caregiver, 165–168
Advantages, of in-home child care, 11. *See also* Benefits, of in-home child care
  emotionally healthy care secured, 3–6
  high quality care ensured, 2–3
  parental needs met, 8–12
  physically healthy care provided, 6–8
Advertising, of child-care position, 35–47
  sample job announcements and ads, 36–40
  sample letters announcing child-care opening, 40–47
Affordability, of in-home child care, 49–57, xxi. *See also* Costs, of in-home child care
  and cost/benefit comparison, 50–53
  and lowering costs strategies, 54–56
Agencies
  au pair, 32, 33
  hiring, for background searches, 129
American Heart Association, and courses offered in emergency resuscitation procedures for children, 149, 187

American Lung Association, and advertising for nonsmoking caregiver, 36n
American Red Cross, "Infant/Child CPR" course of, 146–149
Americans with Disabilities Act of 1990, and medical examination for caregivers, 150
APA Monitor, National Institute of Child Health and Human Development child care study in, 2–3
Appeal, of child-care position to applicants, 59–61
Appendixes
  A, 229
  B, 235
Applicants for in-home child care. *See also* Caregiver(s); Job application form(s)
  and background investigation process, 128–129
  career, 16
  Criminal Record Request Form for a Child Caregiver Job Applicant, 135–136
  effect of job interview on, 116
  federal and state laws concerning hiring of, 16n
  first phone contact with, 71–77
  identifying pools of, in community, 15–34, xxii
  images of ideal, 17
  initial phone call form for, 73–76
  Instructions for Caregiver Applicants on How to Request Criminal Record Check form (sample), 133–134
  investigating background of, 127–152
  making child-care position appealing to, 59–61

Applicants for in-home child care *(Continued)*
  men as, 17–19
  noncareer, 16
  nonverbal messages from, 72–77
  obtaining employer references, 117
  phone contact and immigrant applicants,
    77
  references of, 153–161
  students as, 19–22
"Application for a Social Security Card"
    (Form SS-5), 214
"Application for Employer Identification
    Number" (IRS Form SS-4), 213
Application form(s). *See* Job application
    form(s)
Appreciation, expressing to caregiver, 61,
    178–179
Arnold, C., 6
Atkins, Andrea, 51
Attorney. *See also* Laws and regulations
  and laws regarding employment, 119n
At will employment relationship, 119
Au pairs
  advantages as caregivers, 31
  considerations in using as caregivers, 32
  locating for child care, 32, 33
Automobile. *See* Car
Automobile insurance background check. *See*
    Driving record and automobile insurance
    background check
Availability, of in-home child care, xxi
Azar, B., 2, 53

Background investigation. *See also* Screening
    process
  academic record check, 146
  Academic Transcript Request Form (sam-
    ple), 148
  of applicants, 127–152
  applicant's help with, 128–129
  areas of, 130–131
  child abuse and neglect record check,
    137–140
  considerations for waiving, 129–130
  criminal record background check, 131–132
  Criminal Record Request Form for a Child
    Caregiver Job Applicant (sample),
    135–136
  driving record and automobile insurance
    background check, 143–146
  and emergency resuscitation procedures for
    children, 146–149, 187
  employer conducting of, 128–129
  Form for Calling a Job Reference Provided
    by the Child-Care Applicant, 159–161
  and hiring caregivers, xxx–xxxi

infectious and communicable disease medi-
    cal examination for caregivers, 150
Infectious and Communicable Diseases
    Medical Examination Form for Child
    Caregiver, 151
Instructions for Caregiver Applicant for Re-
    questing Academic Transcript (sample),
    147
Instructions for Caregiver Applicant for Re-
    questing the Driving Record Check, 144
Instructions for Caregiver Applicants on
    How to Request a Child Abuse and Ne-
    glect Record Check form (sample),
    138–139
Instructions for Caregiver Applicants on
    How to Request Criminal Record Check
    form (sample), 133–134
Instructions for Providing Verification of
    Training in Emergency Medical Proce-
    dures for Children, 149
Instructions for Undergoing the Infectious
    and Communicable Diseases Medical Ex-
    amination, 151
  limitations on, 130
  preemployment drug screen, 152
  purpose of, 130
  references, checking, 153–161
  Request Form for a Child Abuse and Ne-
    glect Background Investigation on a
    Child Caregiver Job Applicant, 141–142
  time of, 131
Barter arrangements, for child care, 215–217
  sample job announcement for live-in child
    caregiver, 39
  value of, 215–217
  "Weekly Hours for Child-Care Barter Ar-
    rangement," 218
Benefits, of in-home child care. *See also*
    Costs, of in-home child care
  child care applicants and appeal of special,
    61
  comparison with costs, 50–53
  estimating, 52–53
Bond, child and caregiver, 4–5
Book, ordering form for, 229–231
Boxes, list of, xv–xvii
Bulletin boards, student, using to reach col-
    lege applicants, 21
Business relationship, between employer and
    caregiver, 165

Car
  caregiver's usage of employer's, 145
  inspection of caregiver's, 145
Caregiver(s). *See also* Applicants for in-home
    child care; Child-care agreement form;
    Emergencies, medical and household;

Caregiver(s) *(Continued)*
    Live-in child caregiver; Non–live-in child
        caregiver
    and "A Report On Our Child's Day" form,
        202, 203
    au pairs as, 31–32
    background checks and, xxx–xxxi
    career, 16
    and child-care agreement form, 92
    and child illness, 7
    child of, and child care situation, 25–26
    college and graduate students as, 19–22
    current pay range of, 51
    with disabilities, 64n
    and emergency infant and child resuscita-
        tion techniques courses, 146–149, 187
    and employment eligibility verification re-
        quirements, 29, 30
    ensuring good selection of, 3
    exposing repeatedly to emergency informa-
        tion, 187–188
    federal and state laws concerning hiring of,
        16n
    formation of loving, emotional bond with,
        4–5
    former caregiver's role in orienting new,
        166–167
    free room for, 55
    getting feedback concerning care of, 200
    housecleaners as, 27
    identifying pools of potential applicants in
        community, 15–34, xxii
    images of ideal, 17
    immigrants as, 27–31
    keeping informed of child's developmental
        stages, 204
    keeping track of schedule of and paying
        salary and taxes of, 207–228
    laws and regulations regarding, xxxi–xxxii
        (*See also* Laws and regulations)
    and maintaining child's schedule, 202
    maintaining positive working relationship
        with, 177–184
    men as, 17–19
    monitoring care of, 197–205
    vs. nanny, xxiv
    negotiating child-care agreement with,
        93–94
    noncareer, 16
    offering meals to, 55
    orienting child to new, 165–168
    orienting to employer's child and home,
        163–175
    and parental scheduling flexibility, 8
    part-time vs. full-time, xxviii–xxix
    and performance of chores, 10

    personalized list of important qualities of,
        68
    preparing for medical and household emer-
        gencies, 186
    professional child, 32–34
    qualities of, 63–69
    qualities questionnaire, 66–67
    and quality of nonmaternal care, 2
    and reception to feedback, 201
    recognizing needs of, 178
    relatives, friends, and neighbors as, 24–25
    required qualifications for, 65
    retirees as, 22–24
    securing low turnover and high consistency
        of, 4
    spending time with, 200
    stay-at-home parents as, 25–26
    teens as, 55
    terminating employment of unsatisfactory,
        181–183
    training to relate to child, 168
    valuing, 178–181
Cash arrangements, for child care, 215. *See
    also* Salary
Monthly Time Sheet and Pay Form, 216
Child. *See also* Child care
    caregiver qualifications required in relation
        to, 65
    of caregivers, and child care situation,
        25–26
    caregiver's maintenance of schedule for,
        202
    caring for young, xxvii–xxix
    conveying message of new caregiver to, 166
    data on quality caregiving of, 53
    developmental stages of, informing care-
        giver of, 204
    eating schedule of, and in-home care, 8
    exposure to groups of children, 6
    and formation of loving, emotional bond
        with caregiver, 4–5
    and home advantage, 5–6
    Information About Our Child Form (sam-
        ple), 172–175
    nonverbal cues for distress, 199
    one-on-one care for, xxvii
    one-on-one care for infants, 2
    orienting to new caregiver, 165–168
    parental control over care for, 2
    preschool and, 56
    presence during job interview, 117
    and routine in caregiver orientation,
        167–168
    sleeping schedule of, and in-home care, 8
    social development and, xxvi–xxvii
    talking about abuse to, 199
    training caregiver to relate to, 168

Child abuse and neglect record check,
137–140
Instructions for Caregiver Applicants on
How to Request a Child Abuse and Neglect Record Check form, 138–139
Request Form for a Child Abuse and Neglect Background Investigation on a
Child Caregiver Job Applicant, 141–142
and state laws, 137
state sources for, 137
Child-adult ratios, and quality of child care,
2–3, 53
Child and Dependent Care Expenses (Publication 503), 227
Child care. *See also* Caregiver(s); In-home
child care
advertising of position, methods and materials for, 35–47
defined by National Institute of Child
Health and Human Development study, 2
ensuring excellent, 197–205
guidelines for monitoring, 199–200
one-on-one care, 2–3, 4–5, xxvii
overseeing, 198
personal experience in, 198–199
preparing in advance for, xxx
recognizing and meeting demands of,
xxvii–xxix
specific tips for monitoring, 200–204
swapping with neighbor, 56
Child-care agreement form, 91–109, xxii
addendum for live-in caregivers, 106–109
advantages of using, 92
as basis for legal agreement, 93
considerations for modifying, 92–93
in emergency information file, 188
example of, 95–109
negotiating with caregiver, 93–94
Child-care centers. *See also* Day care
quality of care in, 2
Child caregiver. *See* Caregiver(s)
Child Caregiver Qualities Questionnaire,
66–67
Child Care in the Home Job Interview Form
(sample), 117, 120–126
Childhood Emergencies, Health, and Safety
Resource List (sample), 188, 189–190
Child sexual abuse, safeguarding against, 18
Chinese caregivers, using (personal story),
28–29
Chores
during caregiver's orientation period, 165
performance of, and caregiver, 10
Church, and letter announcing child-care
opening (sample), 44
Closed criminal records, 132
College students. *See* Students

Collet, J., 7
Community, and pools of potential in-home
child care applicants, 15–34, xxii
Commuting, to day care, 10, 52–53
Compensation. *See also* Salary
in addition to pay, 179
Computer diskette
instructions for, 232–234
ordering form for, 229–231
Conflict, handling in employer/caregiver relationship, 179–181
Consent form, for emergency medical care,
188–192
sample form, 191
Consistency in child care, and importance to
child, 4
Contacts, university, using to reach college
applicants, 22
Convenience, for parents, of in-home care, 10
Conversation, with caregiver, and monitoring
child's care, 200–201
Costs, of in-home child care. *See also* Affordability, of in-home child care
calculating, 50–52
comparison with benefits, 50–53
strategies to lower, 54–56
Criminal record background check
Criminal Record Request Form for a Child
Caregiver Job Applicant (sample),
135–136
Instructions for Caregiver Applicants on
How to Request Criminal Record Check
form (sample), 133–134
state laws regarding, 132
statewide search in, 131
Criminal Record Request Form for a Child
Caregiver Job Applicant (sample),
135–136

Day care
calculating costs of, 51
caregiver turnover in, 4
and child/family needs, 8–9
and child's eating and sleeping schedule, 8
and consistency of caregivers, 4
emotionally bonding in, 4
fees for, 10
and home advantage, 5–6
vs. in-home child care costs, 50
and nonstandard parental working hours, 9
organized/family-centered, and in-home
child care, xix
quality of care in, xxvii
and spread of infectious/communicable diseases, 6–7
time spent commuting to, 10, 52–53

Department chairpersons (university)
  letter for, announcing child-care opening
    (sample), 46
  using to reach college applicants, 22
Developmental stages of child, keeping caregiver informed of, 204
Disabilities, caregiver with, 64n
Discrimination laws. *See also* Laws and regulations
  and caregivers, xxxi–xxxii
Diseases
  exposure to, in day care, 6
  family exposure to, 7
  reduction of, and in-home child care, 6–7
Documents, obtaining for background investigation, 129
Driving record and automobile insurance
    background check, 143–146
  caregiver's driving ability, 145
  caregiver's usage of employer's car, 145
  driving record check, 143–144
  inspection of caregiver's vehicle, 145
  Instructions for Caregiver Applicant for Re-
    questing the Driving Record Check, 144
  motor vehicle insurance check, 145
Driving under the influence of alcohol (DUI),
    and background check, 143

Ear infection, 6
Early child care study, of National Institute
    of Child Health and Human Develop-
    ment, 2–3
Early childhood education program, and pro-
    fessional child caregivers, 34
Earned income credit (EIC), 224–225
Education, of caregiver and quality of care,
    146
Emergencies, medical and household. *See also*
    Emergency information file
  and caregiver's repeated exposure to emer-
    gency information, 187–188
  emergency information to be posted at each
    phone, 193–196
  preparing caregiver for, 186
  proper procedures for handling, 185–205
  providing written reminders concerning,
    192
  requiring coursework in emergency infant
    and child resuscitation techniques,
    146–149, 187
  written instructions for medication, 193
Emergency information
  exposing caregiver repeatedly to, 187–188
  reviewed during caregiver orientation, 196
Emergency information file
  child-care agreement copy in, 188

Childhood Emergencies, Health, and Safety
    Resource List in, 188, 189–190
  consent form for emergency medical care in,
    188–192
  consent form sample in, 191
  Information About Our Child form in, 188
  preparing, 188–192
Emergency information sheet, 193–196
  sample, 195
Emergency medical care and procedures for
    children
  consent form for, 188–192
  Instructions for Providing Verification of
    Training in Emergency Medical Proce-
    dures for Children, 149
  requiring coursework in resuscitation tech-
    niques, 187
  sample consent form for, 191
  verifying coursework in, 146–149
Emotional bond
  establishing lasting, 5
  one-on-one care and promoting healthy, 4–5
Emotional health, and in-home child care,
    3–6
Emotional maturity, in student caregiver, 20
"Employee's Withholding Allowance" (Form
    W-4), 222–223
Employer identification number (EIN), 213
"Employer Information Bulletin 96-03: The I-
    9 Process in a Nutshell," 30
"Employer Information Bulletin 96-09: Infor-
    mation about the Form I-9," 30
Employers. *See also* Federal guidelines, for
    employer; Parents; State guidelines, for
    employer
  flexibility of, and lowering child care costs,
    54
  handling conflict with caregiver, 179–181
  household, and employment eligibility veri-
    fication requirements, 29, 30
  keeping copies of tax forms and tax records,
    226
  and positive working relationship with
    caregiver, 177–184
  and terminating employment of unsatisfac-
    tory caregiver, 181–183
"Employer's Checklist for Keeping Track of
    Caregiver's Schedule and Payment of
    Salary and Taxes," 208–212
Employment
  federal eligibility requirements for, 212
  unsatisfactory caregiver and termination
    of, 181–183
English language school, letter to, announc-
    ing child-care opening (sample), 45
Expenses, of in-home child care. *See* Costs, of
    in-home child care

Extended family. *See also* Family
as caregivers, 24–25

Family, letter to, announcing child-care opening (sample), 42
Fathers, and quality of nonmaternal care, 2,
53
Fax, usage with job announcement fliers, 40
Federal guidelines, for employer
determining if required to pay Social Security and Medicare taxes, 217
federal requirements for employment eligibility, 212
federal requirements for paying Social Security and Medicare taxes, 212–213
filing federal Form W-2 and Form W-3,
221–222
notifying employee about earned income
credit (EIC), 224–225
obtaining employer's identification number
(EIN), 213
options for paying Social Security/Medicare
taxes, 220–221
paying federal unemployment tax (FUTA),
223–224
for paying Social Security and Medicare
taxes, 219–221
taking federal income tax credit for child-
care expenses, 226–227
withholding federal income tax, 222–223
Federal income tax, withholding, 222–223
Federal income tax credit for child-care expenses, 226–227
Federal unemployment tax (FUTA), 223–224
Feedback
from caregiver and "A Report On Our
Child's Day" form, 202, 203
to caregivers, 199, 201
discussions and dissatisfaction with caregiver's performance, 182
Ferson, M. J., 7
Financial advantage, of in-home care, 10–12
Financial burden, lost time from work and
child illness, 7
Flexibility
and in-home child care, 8–9
showing toward caregiver, 61
Form 1040 ES, "Individual Quarterly Estimated Tax Form," 219
Form I-9, and employment eligibility verification, 29, 30
Forms. *See also* Advertising, child care position
Academic Transcript Request Form, 148
child-care agreement form, 91–109
Child-Care Agreement Form (sample),
95–109

Child Caregiver Qualities Questionnaire,
66–67
Child Care in the Home Job Interview
Form, 117, 120–126
Childhood Emergencies, Health, and Safety
Resource List, 188, 189–190
Consent Form for Emergency Medical Care,
191
Criminal Record Request Form for a Child
Caregiver Job Applicant, 135–136
emergency information sheet, 193–196
Emergency Information Sheet (sample),
195
Employer's Checklist for Keeping Track of
Caregiver's Schedule and Payment of
Salary and Taxes, 208–212
Form for Calling a Job Reference Provided
by the Child-Care Applicant, 159–161
for hiring child caregivers, xxix
Infectious and Communicable Diseases
Medical Examination Form for Child
Caregiver, 151
Information About Our Child Form,
172–175
Initial Phone Call Form for In-Home Child-
Care Applicants, 73–76
Instructions for Caregiver Applicant for Re-
questing Academic Transcript, 147
Instructions for Caregiver Applicant for Re-
questing the Driving Record Check, 144
Instructions for Caregiver Applicants on
How to Request a Child Abuse and Ne-
glect Record Check form, 138–139
Instructions for Caregiver Applicants on
How to Request Criminal Record Check
form, 133–134
Instructions for Providing Verification of
Training in Emergency Medical Proce-
dures for Children, 149
Instructions for Undergoing the Infectious
and Communicable Diseases Medical Ex-
amination, 151
job application form, 79–89
List of Important Phone Numbers, 193, 194
Orientation Checklist, 171
A Report On Our Child's Day form, 202,
203
Request Form for a Child Abuse and Ne-
glect Background Investigation on a
Child Caregiver Job Applicant, 141–142
Form SS-5 ("Application for a Social Security
Card"), 214
Form W-2, "Wage and Tax Statement,"
221–222
Form W-3, "Transmittal of Wage and Tax
Statements," 221–222

Form W-4, "Employee's Withholding Allowance," 222–223
Free room, in exchange for child care, 55
Friends
    considerations in choosing as caregivers, 24–25
    letter to, announcing child-care opening (sample), 42
Full-time caregivers, vs. part-time caregivers, xxviii–xxix
FUTA. *See* Federal unemployment tax (FUTA)

Giebink, G. S., 7
Graduate students. *See* Students
Grandparents, and quality of nonmaternal care, 2, 53
Greenspan, N. T., 4, 5
Greenspan, S., 4
Growing Child (monthly newsletter), and keeping caregiver informed of child's developmental stages, 204

Handbook for Employers: Instructions for Completing Form I-9, 212
Hays, C. L., 9
Henderson, F. W., 7
Hepatitis, 6
Home
    child care applicants and appeal of clean, organized, 60
    touring after job interview, 117
Home advantage, and benefits to child, 5–6
Hours, tracking. *See* System, for tracking hours and paying salary and taxes
Housecleaners, advantages as caregivers, 27
Household emergencies. *See* Emergencies, medical and household
Household Employer's Tax Guide (Publication 926), and compliance with federal tax laws, 212–213
Household Employment Taxes, Schedule H (Form 1040), 219

I-9 process, of employment eligibility verification, 29, 30
IBM-compatible (PC) Diskette, 232–233
Illness, child
    benefit of in-home child care and, 53
    lost time from work and, 7
Immigrant caregivers
    advantages of using, 27–29
    considerations in using, 29

and employment eligibility verification requirements, 30
    interviewing, 118
    phone contact and immigrant applicants, 77
    reaching immigrant caregiver applicants, 31
    screening process and job application forms, 112
Immigration and Naturalization Service (INS) Employment Authorization, and immigrant caregiver applicants, 27
Immigration Reform and Control Act of 1986, 29, 30, 212
Indemnification agreement on job application form, 85, 158
Individual Quarterly Estimated Tax Form (Form 1040 ES), 219
Infant. *See* Child
"Infant/Child CPR" course (American Red Cross), 146–149
Infectious and communicable disease medical examination for caregivers, 150
    employer's payment of, 150
    Infectious and Communicable Diseases Medical Examination Form for Child Caregiver (sample), 151
    Instructions for Undergoing the Infectious and Communicable Diseases Medical Examination (sample), 151
Infectious and Communicable Diseases Medical Examination Form for Child Caregiver (sample), 151
Information
    about applicants for in-home child care (*See* Job application form(s); Phone contact)
    concerning child's care (*See* Child-care agreement form; Report on Our Child's Day, A)
    Information About Our Child Form (sample), 172–175
    providing information about child, home, and job responsibilities, 169
    providing to caregiver, 164–165
Information About Our Child form, 172–175
    and administering child's medication, 193
    in emergency information file, 188
In-home caregiver(s). *See* Caregiver(s)
In-home child care. *See also* Child care
    advantages of, 2–13, xxvi
    affordability of, xxi
    availability of, xxi
    defined, xix
    emotionally healthy care secured with, 3–6
    high quality care ensured by, 2–3
    and organized/family-centered day care, xix
    parental control over as advantage of, 2

In-home child care *(Continued)*
  parental needs met by, 8–12
  physically healthy care provided by, 6–8
  regional cost variations of, 51
Initial job interview. *See* Job interview
Initial Phone Call Form for In-Home Child-Care Applicants, 73–76
INS Handbook for Employers (U.S. Department of Justice)
  and employment eligibility verification requirements, 29, 30
  ordering, 30
Instincts, parental, and caregiver relationship, 200
Institutions
  to contact using letters announcing child-care opening, 43
  and sample letters announcing child-care opening, 44–47
Instructions for Caregiver Applicant for Requesting Academic Transcript (sample), 147
Instructions for Caregiver Applicant for Requesting the Driving Record Check (sample), 144
Instructions for Caregiver Applicants on How to Request Criminal Record Check form (sample), 133–134
Instructions for Providing Verification of Training in Emergency Medical Procedures for Children (sample form), 149
Internal Revenue Service, *Household Employer's Tax Guide* (Publication 926) of, 212–213
Interview process. *See* Job interview
IRS Form SS-4 ("Application for Employer Identification Number"), 213
Istre, G. R., 6

Jaakkola, J. J. K., 6
Jaakkola, N., 6
Jereb, J., 7
Job announcement fliers, 36–40
  for live-in child caregiver (barter arrangement), 39
  for live-in child caregiver on salary (sample), 38
  for non-live-in child caregiver (sample), 37
Job application form(s), 79–89
  checklist for evaluating, 113–114
  and child-care agreement form, 92
  effect on job interview, 116
  and interview process, 80
  laws and regulations concerning, 80–81
  sample, 82–89
  screening completed, 111–114
  screening immigrants by, 112

Job description. *See* Child-care agreement form
Job interview
  arranging trial employment period during, 119
  atmosphere during, 117
  at will employment relationship, 119
  for child-care applicants, 60
  Child Care in the Home Job Interview Form (sample), 120–126
  and child's presence, 117
  conducting, 115–126
  conducting initial interview, 117–118
  conducting second interview, 118–119
  and immigrant caregivers, 118
  initial interview guidelines, 116–117
  job application form usage and, 80, 116
  notetaking during, 117–118
  time of initial interview, 118
Job offer, and infectious and communicable disease medical examination for caregivers, 150
Job Reference Provided by the Child-Care Applicant, Form for Calling, 159–161

Labor departments, state/federal, and laws regarding employment, 119n
Laws and regulations. *See also* Federal guidelines, for employer
  and *at will* employment, 119
  and child abuse and neglect record check, 137
  and criminal record background check, 131–132
  employment eligibility verification requirements, 29, 30
  and hiring caregivers, 16n, xxxi–xxxii
  indemnification agreement on job application form and, 158
  and job application form, 80–81
  and limitations on background searches, 130
  protecting former employers providing references from lawsuits, 158
  and requesting applicant's driving record, 143
Lawsuits
  and former employers providing references, 158
  preventing in termination process, 182
  wrongful discharge, 119
Learning and development, and child/caregiver relationship, 4–5
Legal document, using child-care agreement form as foundation for, 93

Letters, announcing child-care opening,
40–47
for church or synagogue (sample), 44
for department chairperson at university or
college (sample), 46
for family, friends, and work associates
(sample), 42
for organization or English language school
(sample), 45
personal contacts for, 40
for university/college/seminary office of student affairs, job placement, or career development (sample), 47
Lifestyle, downsizing, to decrease child-care
costs, 56
List of Important Phone Numbers, and emergencies, 193, 194
Live-in child caregiver
addendum to child-care agreement for,
106–109
sample job announcement for (barter arrangement), 39
sample job announcement on salary, 38
Louhiala, P. J., 6
Love, in child care, 12

Macintosh diskette, 233–234
Mailings, student orientation packets, using
to reach college applicants, 22
Makintube, S., 6
Male retirees, as caregiver applicants. *See*
Men; Retirees
Male students, as caregiver applicants. *See*
Men; Students
Meals, offering to caregiver, 55
Medical and household emergencies. *See*
Emergencies, medical and household
Medical care
consent form for emergency, 188–192
consent form sample, 191
Medical examination, infectious and commu-
nicable disease, for caregivers, 150
Medical procedures for children, verifying
coursework in emergency, 146–149
Medicare taxes
determining if required to pay, 217
federal requirements for, 212–213
options for paying, 220–221
paying, 212–213, 219–221
Medication, written instructions for, 193
Men. *See also* Fathers
as caregivers, 17–19
and child sexual abuse, 18
experience as child caregivers and, 18
Meningitis, 6

Mickey, P. F., Jr., 182
Minimum wage, and caregiver's pay, 51n
Monitoring child's care
caregiver and maintenance of child's schedule, 202
and daily conversation with caregiver,
200–201
general guidelines for, 199–200
informing caregiver of child's developmental stages, 204
with "A Report On Our Child's Day" form,
202, 203
specific tips for, 200–204
Motor vehicle insurance, listing caregiver on
employer's, 145–146
Motor vehicle insurance background check,
145
Murph, J. R., 6

Nannies, 34
salaries for live-in/non-live in, 51
term usage, xxiv
National Institute of Child Health and Human Development
data on higher quality caregiving of infants,
53
results of early child care study of, 2–3
Neighbors
considerations in choosing as caregivers,
24–25
swapping child care with, 56
Networking
and locating immigrant caregivers, 31
and locating stay-at-home parents for child
care, 26
and reaching retiree caregiver applicants,
23–24
and sample letters announcing child-care
opening, 40–43
Newsletters, sample job ads for caregiver in,
40, 41
Newspapers
sample job ads for caregiver in, 40, 41
student, using to reach college applicants,
21
Nonauthoritarian beliefs, about childrearing,
64
Non-live-in child caregiver, sample job announcement for, 37
Nonsmoker, advertising for, 36n
Nonverbal messages, from child care applicant, 72–77
Notetaking, during job interview, 117–118
Nurmi, T., 7, 53
Nutrition, in in-home care situation, 7–8

One-on-one care. *See also* Child care
for child under five, xxvii
and infants, 2
Open criminal records, 132
Ordering Form for Computer Diskette and
Additional Copies of This Book, 229–231
Organization, letter to, announcing child-care
opening (sample), 45
Organized/family-centered day care, and in-
home child care, xix
Orientation, of caregiver, 163–175
child and, 165–168
information about child, home, and job re-
sponsibilities, 169
Information About Our Child Form (sam-
ple), 172–175
information/instructions during, 164–165
Orientation Checklist (sample), 171
and review of emergency information, 196
Orientation Checklist (sample), 171
Osterholm, M. T., 6
Overtime pay, and caregiver's pay, 51n

Parents. *See also* Employers
and control of child's care, 2
convenience of in-home care for, 10
and extended family/friend caregiver relationship, 25
and financial advantage of in-home care,
10–12
instincts of, and caregiver relationship, 200
intuitive instincts of, 116
schedule of, and in-home care, 8–9
teaching and instructing caregivers, 18
Parents As Teachers program, and materials
on child development, 204
"Parent's day out program," 56
Partners of students, and employment as
caregivers, 22
Part-time caregivers. *See also* Caregiver(s)
and full-time caregivers, xxviii–xxix
housecleaners as, 27
retirees as, 23
students as, 19
Pay. *See* Salary
Personal computer, and letters announcing
child-care opening, 40
Personalized list of important caregiver qualities, 68
Phone contact
with applicants, as screening process,
71–77
with friends, to get names of potential applicants, 40–43
and immigrant applicants, 77

Initial Phone Call Form for Applicants for
In-Home Child Care, 73–76
Phone information (emergency)
emergency information sheet, 193–196
list of important phone numbers, 193, 194
sample information sheet, 195
Physical health, and in-home child care
good nutrition and, 7–8
reduction of exposure to infectious/commu-
nicable diseases, 6–7
sleep schedule and, 8
Physician, for caregiver's infectious and communicable disease medical examination,
150
Pickering, L. K., 6
Placement offices (university), using to reach
college applicants, 22
Pönkä, A., 7, 53
Pools, of potential in-home child care applicants, 15–34, xxii
Predictability, importance to child, 4
Preemployment drug screen, 152
Preschool
quality of care in, xxvii
for two years or older child, 56
Professional child caregivers
advantages of using, 32
considerations in selecting, 32–33
locating, 34

Qualities
Child Caregiver Qualities Questionnaire,
66–67
to look for in caregiver, 63–69
Personalized List of Important Caregiver
Qualities, 68
Required Qualifications for Child Care-
givers, 65
Quality Assurance Expert, parent as, 201
Quality of child care, ensuring, 2–3
Questions, open-ended, for job interview, 117

References. *See also* Background investigation
eliciting full responses from, 157–158
Form for Calling a Job Reference Provided
by the Child-Care Applicant, 159–161
and hiring caregivers, xxx–xxxi
knowledgeable, 155
and lawsuits against former employers who
provide references, 158
phoning applicant's, 153–161
from potential employer, 117
speaking directly to, 155–156
Reichler, M. R., 7

Relationships
  building positive, 178–181
  business, of employer and caregiver, 165
  child/caregiver, and child's learning and development, 4–5
  handling conflict and successful, 179–181
  maintaining positive working relationship with caregiver, 177–184
  parents and extended family/friend caregiver, 25
Relatives
  advantages of, as caregivers, 24
  considerations in choosing, 24–25
Reminders, written, concerning emergencies, 192
Repetition, of information/instructions in caregiver orientation, 164–165
Report on Our Child's Day, A, 202, 203
  emergency and medical reminders on, 192
  keeping track of child's medication on, 193
Request Form for a Child Abuse and Neglect Background Investigation on a Child Caregiver Job Applicant (sample), 141–142
Required Qualifications for Child Caregivers, 65
Resources, for medical emergencies, 188, 189–190
Resuscitation procedures, caregiver's training in, 146–149, 187
Retirees
  advantages of, as caregivers, 22–23
  considerations in choosing, 23
  locating, for child care, 23–24
Reves, R. R., 6
Routine, child and, 167–168
Routsalainen, R., 6

Salary. *See also* Barter arrangements, for child care; Cash arrangements, for child care; System, for tracking hours and paying salary and taxes
  and caregiver's value, 179
  child care applicants and appeal of high end, 61
  current pay range of child caregivers, 51
  for extended family caregivers, 24
  for in-home caregivers, 51
  sample job announcement for live-in child caregiver on, 38
Salminen, E., 7, 53
Schedule
  child's eating and sleeping, 8
  of parents, and in-home care, 8–9
Schedule H (Form 1040), "Household Employment Taxes," 219

Scheduling system, for child-care hours, 214–215
Schwartz, B., 7
Screening process. *See also* Background investigation
  for applicants through phone conservation, 72–77
  job application form as part of, 79–89
  for job applications, 111–114
Second job interview. *See* Job interview
Security, of home environment, 5
Seminarians, partners of, employing as caregivers, 22
Seminary, letter to, announcing child-care opening (sample), 47
Severance pay, in termination process, 182
Siblings
  and day care costs, 51
  in day care setting, 52
Sleep, and in-home care, 8
Social Security card
  applying for, 214
  of new employee, 214
Social Security taxes
  determining if required to pay, 217
  federal requirements for, 212–213
  options for paying, 220–221
  paying, 219–221
State employment/unemployment taxes, 225–226
State guidelines, for employer
  complying with state requirements, 225–226
  taking state income tax credits or deductions for child-care expenses, 227
State income tax credits/deductions for child-care expenses, 227
Stay-at-home parents
  advantages as caregivers, 25–26
  considerations in using as caregivers, 26
  locating, for child care, 26
Stereotypes, and child caregiver, xxiv
Stick-on notes, and written emergency reminders, 192
Stovsky, Renee, 6
Strategies, to lower child care costs, 54–56
Students
  advantages as caregivers, 19
  considerations when using, 19–20
  partners of and employment as caregivers, 22
  reaching applicants, 20–22
Synagogue, letter to, announcing child-care opening (sample), 44
System, for tracking hours and paying salary and taxes, 207–228
  and caregivers' time sheets, 215–217

System, for tracking hours and paying salary and taxes *(Continued)*
 complying with state requirements, 225–226
 determining if required to pay Social Security/Medicare taxes, 217
 and employer identification number (EIN), 213
 Employer's Checklist for Keeping Track of Caregiver's Schedule and Payment of Salary and Taxes, 208–212
 and federal income tax credit for child-care expenses, 226–227
 federal requirements for employment eligibility, 212
 federal requirements for paying Social Security and Medicare taxes, 212–213
 and federal unemployment tax (FUTA), 223–224
 filing federal Form W-2 and Form W-3, 221–222
 keeping copies of tax forms and tax records, 226
 notifying employee about earned income credit (EIC), 224–225
 paying Social Security and Medicare taxes, 219–221
 taking state income tax credits or deductions for child-care expenses, 227
 using organized scheduling system for caregiver, 214–215
 viewing employee's Social Security card, 214
 withholding federal income tax, 222–223

Taxes. *See also* System, for tracking hours and paying salary and taxes
 paying for caregiver, 212–213
Tax forms/records, 226
Taxpayer Identification Number (TIN). *See* Employer identification number (EIN)
Teens, for in-home child care, 55
Termination process, for unsatisfactory caregiver, 181–183
 termination meeting in, 183
 termination notice in, 182
 warnings in, 182
Time
 of job interview, 118
 saving, and in-home care, 10
Time sheets for caregivers
 for barter arrangements, 215–217
 for cash arrangements, 215
 and emergency information file, 188
 "Monthly Time Sheet and Pay Form," 216

"Weekly Hours for Child-Care Barter Arrangement," 218
Toddler. *See* Child
Tracking of hours. *See* System, for tracking hours and paying salary and taxes
Training in emergency medical procedures for children, verifying, 146–149
Transcripts, requesting. *See* Academic record check
"Transmittal of Wage and Tax Statements" (Form W-3), 221–222
Transportation, and child care, 10, 52–53
Trial period of employment, arranging during job interview, 119
Trust, child's development of, in significant relationship, 4
Turnover, of caregivers, securing low rate of, 4

Undergraduates. *See* Students
United States Department of Justice, *INS Handbook for Employers* of, and employment eligibility verification requirements, 29, 30
Universities and colleges
 letter for department chairpersons at, announcing child-care opening (sample), 46
 letter to, announcing child-care opening (sample), 47
University job placement officers, using to reach college applicants, 22

Vacations, and caregiver, 9

"Wage and Tax Statement" (Form W-2), 221–222
Waiving background investigation, considerations for, 129–130
Warnings, issuing in termination process, 182
Work associates, and letter announcing child-care opening (sample), 42
Work schedules (parental), and lowering child care costs, 54–55
Written documentation, in termination process, 182
Written instructions, during caregiver's orientation, 165
Wrongful discharge lawsuits, and *at will* employment relationship, 119

YMCA, courses in emergency resuscitation procedures for children, 149, 187

☎ Call Toll-Free Anytime to Order with Credit Card: 1-888-601-CARE (2273)
St. Louis, MO area residents call: 314-862-6636
(Please have credit card information on hand when you call.)

FAX Fax Credit Card Orders Anytime to: 1-314-725-6350
✉ Send orders with checks or money orders to Family CareWare, Inc.
(Please fax or mail both pages of this order form.)

Family CareWare, Inc., Order Form
Dept. B, P.O. Box 50257, St. Louis, MO 63105-5257

Name (please print) _____

Address _____
UPS is unable to deliver to a box number.

City _____ State _____ ZIP _____

Daytime Phone (___)_____ Evening Phone (___)_____
We will only call if we have a question about this order form.

Ship to: (if different)

Name (Please print) _____

Address _____
UPS is unable to deliver to a box number.

City _____ State _____ ZIP _____

Gift Message: _____

Method of Payment
(Please make check or money order payable to Family CareWare, Inc.)

☐ Check   ☐ Money Order
☐ VISA   ☐ MasterCard   ☐ AmEx   ☐ Discover

Card Number:

☐☐☐☐/☐☐☐☐/☐☐☐☐/☐☐☐☐

Expires ☐☐☐☐

Signature_____|_____
Required for all charges   Date

··

QTY. TOTAL

COMPUTER DISKETTE—*IN-HOME CHILD CARE:*
A Step-by-Step Guide to Quality, Affordable Care
@ $9.95 (U.S.), $13.95 (Canada)
**Please see the following page for important
information about this diskette.**
Specify: _____ PC version _____ MAC version   _____ _____

BOOK—*IN-HOME CHILD CARE:*
A Step-by-Step Guide to Quality, Affordable Care
@ $24.95 (U.S.), $34.95 (Canada)   _____ _____

BOOK-DISKETTE Discount Package Special—
save $5.00 (If purchased together) @ $29.90 (U.S.),
$43.90 (Canada)
Specify: _____ PC version _____ MAC version   _____ _____

SUBTOTAL   _____
MO Residents Add 6.475% **Sales Tax**   _____
Shipping and Handling (See costs below.)   _____
TOTAL   _____

Shipping and Handling Costs: $1.50 per diskette (First Class Mail); $5.00
per book or for Book-Diskette Package Special (UPS Ground Service)

THANK YOU FOR YOUR ORDER.

☐ (Check) I want to be included on Family CareWare, Inc.'s, mailing list.

☐ (Check) I give my permission for Family CareWare, Inc., to give my contact information to other trusted vendors of child-related items. My children are the following ages: _____

Return Policy
Defective computer diskettes, while extremely rare, will be exchanged at no
cost. Please return the damaged one and we will send you a new one. Family
CareWare, Inc., offers a full money-back guarantee (less shipping and handling and a re-stocking fee of 15% of the cost of the returned item, plus any tax,
which will be credited to your account or deducted from your refund) on *unopened* computer diskettes and *unblemished* books, if purchased directly from
Family CareWare, Inc., and returned within 30 days with a copy of the Family
CareWare, Inc., receipt or your canceled check.

Important Information About Computer Diskette

This book's computer diskette will allow you to copy and modify all of the over 40 forms contained in this book (see List of Boxes and Appendices A and B). *This diskette is not intended to be used without this book, which contains important information about the forms, as well as the diskette's instructions (see Appendix B).* If you use this diskette without this book, you do so at your own risk.

- The IBM-compatible (PC) version requires the following:
  Media: 3.5″ HD diskette
  Word Processing Programs: WordPerfect 5.1 or higher for DOS; WordPerfect 5.2 or higher for Windows 3.x or Windows 95; Microsoft Word 2.0 or higher for Windows 3.x or Windows 95; Microsoft Works 2.0 or higher for Windows 3.x or Windows 95; or Rich Text Format (RTF)
- The MAC version requires the following:
  Media: 3.5″ HD diskette
  Word Processing Programs: WordPerfect 3.0 or higher; Microsoft Word 4.0 or higher; ClarisWorks 1.0 or higher; or Rich Text Format (RTF)

Regretfully, we are *unable* to offer technical support. If you encounter difficulties, consult your word processing or operating system manual. Defective disks, while extremely rare, will be exchanged free of charge.